Praise for

Home and Native Land

This book compels readers to interrogate the regulatory forces of multiculturalism from various historical and contemporary, activist, disciplinary, and theoretical lenses. It invites and provokes readers to consider alternatives to current hegemonies, and should be read by both critics and supporters of multiculturalism.

— **Rita Kaur Dhamoon**, Department of Philosophy &
Political Science, University of the Fraser Valley, and author of
Identity/Difference Politics

A critical collection that makes a significant contribution to current discussions about multiculturalism as policy and discourse in Canada. This book develops the important idea that the organization of difference and belonging in Canada is an ongoing colonial project that requires the regulation of indigenous peoples, lands, and racialized others under a national narrative of white settler multiculturalism.

— **Eve Haque**, Department of Languages,
Literatures and Linguistics, York University

Home and Native Land
Unsettling Multiculturalism in Canada

edited by
May Chazan, Lisa Helps,
Anna Stanley, & Sonali Thakkar

Between the Lines
Toronto

Home and Native Land: Unsettling Multiculturalism in Canada

© 2011 May Chazan, Lisa Helps, Anna Stanley, and Sonali Thakkar

First published in Canada in 2011 by
Between the Lines
401 Richmond Street West
Studio 277
Toronto, Ontario M5V 3A8
Canada

1-800-718-7201

www.btlbooks.com

Library and Archives Canada Cataloguing in Publication

　　　Home and native land : unsettling multiculturalism in Canada / edited by May Chazan . . . [et al.].
Includes bibliographical references and index.
ISBN 978–1–897071–61–8

1. Multiculturalism–Canada.
FC105.M8H65 2011　　　　305.800971　　　　C2011-901530-7

Cover image: "Three Sisters," preparatory sketch for mural, pencil and digital media, Anders Swanson, 2006.
Cover design by Jennifer Tiberio
Text design and page preparation by Steve Izma
Printed in Canada

Between the Lines gratefully acknowledges assistance for its publishing activities from the Canada Council for the Arts, the Ontario Arts Council, the Government of Ontario through the Ontario Book Publishers Tax Credit program and through the Ontario Book Initiative, and the Government of Canada through the Canada Book Fund.

Contents

Part 4: Bodies

Acknowledgements

WE ARE GRATEFUL TO the Pierre Elliott Trudeau Foundation for generously sponsoring the 2007 conference, *From Multicultural Rhetoric to Anti-Racist Action*, where the idea for this volume took root. Particular thanks are due to Bettina Cenerelli, Josée St. Martin, and Maya Jegen. We also appreciate support for the conference from the Association for Canadian Studies, and thank all panellists and participants for engaging in provocative discussions that opened up a space for this volume to emerge.

Numerous fellow Trudeau Foundation community members have been important interlocutors throughout, especially James Tully, Constance Backhouse, Jillian Boyd, D. Memee Lavell-Harvard, Marie-Joie Brady, Lisa Freeman, Kate Hennessy, Rod MacDonald, and Kevin Chan. The staff at Between the Lines have been supportive at every stage of this book and we are especially grateful to BTL editor Amanda Crocker, who guided us through the process of turning an idea into a book, and to our copyeditor Andrea Kwan, whose efforts far exceeded what any of us imagined under the purview of copyediting, and whose thoughtful suggestions greatly improved the volume. This book would be greatly diminished without Anders Swanson's wonderfully evocative artwork on the cover. We thank him for his kind permission to use it, and for his interest in this project, and are grateful to contributor Laurie Bertram, who proposed the image in the first place. This volume owes its existence to the contributors and their dynamic critical interventions: what a pleasure it has been to work with each of them. Sonali, Lisa, and May thank their dissertation supervisors – Marianne Hirsch and Joseph Slaughter, Franca Iacovetta, and Mike Brklacich, respectively. May also thanks Ben and Zoe, and Anna expresses her gratitude to Phil.

Most importantly, we thank each other. This volume has been a truly collaborative process. During the time it took for this book to be born, one of us has had a baby, one got a job in Ireland, one moved between New York and various cities in Germany, and one was engaged in the creation of various social enterprises on the west coast of Canada. Yet despite our disparate lives, we have maintained a shared vision and a cohesive and *fun* working relationship.

Introduction: Labours, lands, bodies

May Chazan, Lisa Helps,
Anna Stanley, and Sonali Thakkar

THE ACT OF "UNSETTLING" HAS MANY IMPLICATIONS – not only for the aims of this book, but also for the very shape of multicultural discourse in Canada over the past thirty-plus years. Since the advent of official multiculturalism in 1971, under the Trudeau government's policy of multiculturalism within a bilingual framework, Canada has achieved what may appear to be a multicultural consensus. There is agreement among politicians and citizens that some version of multiculturalism – whatever its limitations – is here to stay, lodged deeply at the heart of Canada's national identity both at home and abroad. To unsettle multiculturalism would entail disrupting what seemed, at least for a while, downright commonsensical.[1]

However, like other scholars and activists before us, we are convinced that the meaning of multiculturalism is not, and never has been, fully settled. One of the oldest meanings of "unsettled," according to the *Oxford English Dictionary*, is that which is "not (yet) quietly or firmly established." The parenthetical "yet" is telling. It indicates both a desire to achieve consensus, thereby settling the debate and fixing meaning, as well the difficulty of doing so. At the same time, we note that in Canada, particularly, multiculturalism is itself a politics of settlement – a story tied closely to the appropriation and settlement of space and meaning, and to securing the material and symbolic contours of the state. One of our ambitions for this volume is that it should unsettle multiculturalism while simultaneously showing how multiculturalism is continuously being unsettled. As Rinaldo Walcott notes, official multiculturalism is not static; the state has regularly revised the policy and its rhetoric in accordance with "competing ideas" about the work multiculturalism should do.[2]

Such revisions are readily visible even in multiculturalism's earliest

1

incarnations. The initial impetus for a multiculturalism policy did not stem from an expansive understanding of Canada's manifold diversity. Rather it came from attempts to solve long-standing tensions between French and English Canada by way of a "bicultural" and "bilingual" framework."[3] In this context, members of some of Canada's other European ethnic groups, including Ukrainians and Italians, intervened with their objections to a French-English cultural power-sharing agreement that would potentially sideline their long-term contributions to Canada.[4] Multiculturalism was thus at first a way to mediate among these groups' claims, and to expand upon the narrow framework of Canada's "two founding nations." It was only later that multiculturalism became a master narrative with which to address all issues of Canadian diversity, including not only migration from the Global South and from the post-colonies, but also the status of Aboriginal peoples, who, in discussions in advance of the failed Meech Lake Accord, were posited as the "third founding nation."[5]

As even this mini-history suggests, multiculturalism has always been adaptable and changeable. In part, multiculturalism has remained unsettled because different groups and interests have taken advantage of its fluidity to make a variety of claims that aim to *settle* identities and arrangements. These include both arrangements about access to the state and its resources and, as several of the contributors to this volume argue – focusing in particular on the long-standing and ongoing appropriation of Aboriginal lands – arrangements about the very organization of landscape and physical space. Indeed, one of the priorities of this book is to try to understand current discussions and recent instrumentalizations of multiculturalism in light of Canada's status as a settler state that was founded on colonial relations with Aboriginal peoples that persist to this day.

Perspicacious critics have noted Canadian multiculturalism's generally blind and potentially cynical posture toward this colonial relation.[6] This collection attends closely to how multiculturalism sustains such a colonial relation and shapes the terms according to which it is continually renegotiated. As several of the contributors show, contests over land and resources are increasingly organized around the politics of recognition.[7] These developments suggest the continued utility of multiculturalism as a discursive field, and indicate the extent to which its terms of reference bear energetically on the organization and meaning of state space.

It is this discursive saturation – the quiet seepage of multiculturalism's logics and registers into a host of domains – that this book investigates, and it does so by displacing (or unsettling) "multiculturalism" as its primary object of study. A main aim of this book is to unsettle multiculturalism by tracking its manifestations in discourses that seemingly have little to say about diversity, integration, and the other explicit preoccupations of traditional understandings of multiculturalism. To this end, the book does not offer a thoroughgoing critique or analysis of Canadian multicultural policy. Rather, contributors examine multiculturalism obliquely, assessing how multiculturalism's wavering reflection appears in and inflects discussions about labour migration, the historical settlement of land, and the racialization of poverty, to name a few. Other contributors consider instances in which multicultural discourse is explicitly invoked but awkwardly so, as in the example of land claims debates that adopt and are assimilated to the ill-fitting language of recognition.

The myriad instances in which multiculturalism either brushes up against other policy discourses or tellingly flickers out of sight can be loosely grouped under the three rubrics of labours, lands, and bodies, and this book is thus organized around these terms, with the chapters clustered accordingly. Each term delineates a set of substantive, far-reaching policy debates on issues of significant import – debates that seem to have little to do with multiculturalism yet are either inflected by its assumptions or expose its contradictions and discontinuities. We have in mind these shifting and sometimes surprising correspondences when we note multiculturalism's discursive saturation, a saturation that might be better understood as sedimentation: that which settles and collects, even if out of sight. Multiculturalism's influence as a means of settling arrangements and legitimizing settlements suggests that despite the mythos of Canada as home to a multiplicity of peoples, multiculturalism might in fact render home uncanny, at least for some. In Freud's formulation of the uncanny, which he describes as a sensation that something is familiar yet foreign, he uses the term *unheimlich*: literally, unhomely. The powerful painting by Winnipeg-based artist Anders Swanson reproduced on the cover of this book shows three women sitting in a seemingly empty landscape. But this scene occupies merely the topmost quarter of the image; the rest shows the buried detritus of those who were there previously and still inhabit the space, albeit in an unexpected sense. The painting thus resonates with our title and with the volume's interest in the unhomely or uncanny, asking, ironically: *whose home and native land?*

The gradual sedimentation of multiculturalism, however, can only be understood through a consideration of the events of the past decade. These events have graphically illustrated that multiculturalism can also be unsettled, even upturned, from within when the centrist political institutions that helped enshrine the term in official discourse (thereby temporarily lending it the patina of consensual commonsense) begin themselves to question the multicultural consensus and its limits. After the September 11, 2001, attacks on New York City and Washington, D.C., multiculturalism became open to both contestation and revision. Certain racialized populations – most notably Muslims – came to represent the limits of multiculturalism, supposedly demonstrating that some communities were unassimilable and some values intolerable.[8] Such sentiments, coupled with the ready fetishization of national security above all else, culminated in a large-scale reassessment of the place of reasonable accommodation in North American society. In Canada, this reassessment was most visible in the form of the Bouchard-Taylor Consultation Commission on Accommodation Practices Related to Cultural Differences that took place in Quebec in late 2007 and early 2008, and in the press coverage that the Commission's hearings received. The reassessment also generated scenes of heightened intolerance, such as the infamous Hérouxville decree, an official code passed by that town's municipal council designed to advise new Quebecers of the province's cultural norms.

Thus, some critics declared that multiculturalism appeared to be "dead." Writing in the *Walrus*, Canadian pollster and pundit Allan Gregg sketched a global portrait of failure and exhaustion, moving from the bombed subways of London to the suburbs of Paris to Sydney's beaches, ultimately questioning what all of this meant for Canadians: "we" who had taken multiculturalism most deeply to our bosoms, "we" who believed that Canada was "immune to violence rooted in ethnic divisions."[9] This belief, he argued, was now shaken in the face of sociological data showing the failure of second-generation immigrants to assimilate. Yet importantly, as Uzma Shakir argues in her contribution to this volume, it is not that second-generation immigrants, and in particular people of colour, have "failed to assimilate"; rather, they still face racism and systemic discrimination, which keeps them economically and socially marginalized. In August 2006, in an oft-cited *Globe and Mail* article, "End of the multicultural myth," columnist Margaret Wente also pointed to multiculturalism's failure. She asserted "In Canada, we can afford to cling to our multicultural illusions – that differences are to be celebrated, and make our land a better place. . . . But, secretly, we don't really believe that differences are okay."[10] A worthy experiment, then, had run its course; to persist in pursuing it was to risk grave political and civic peril.

These post-9/11 panics were framed as an overdue re-examination of multiculturalism and what it had wrought, sociologically speaking. The mainstream critique seemed to turn on multiculturalism's inefficacy as a framework for promoting conviviality – as if its pragmatic championing and discursive pre-eminence over two decades had been, at best, benevolence and at worst naiveté. Even as multiculturalism appeared to be up for a wholesale renegotiation, there were also indications that it was still useful as an assimilative technique and a security measure that would facilitate community self-policing. At the conference *Muslims in Western Societies* hosted by the Trudeau Foundation in November 2006, for example, McGill political science professor Rex Brynen argued that multiculturalism could in fact be Canada's best security and counterterrorism technology: educate Canadian Security Intelligence Service (CSIS) personnel, make links with Muslim communities, show tolerance, gain "their" trust, and "they" will begin to police themselves.[11]

Some of these post-9/11 developments seemed to cynically push forward already nascent political agendas and retrenchments (e.g., heightened security measures, "tough on crime" provisions, increased power to deport non-citizens). Others, such as the Bouchard-Taylor hearings, appeared to spring from a rather anguished sense that it was time for a national self-examination. What was striking to us, as observers of these debates, was that whatever the tone, the re-examination of multiculturalism as a cornerstone of Canadian identity actually had relatively little to say about lingering and heightened forms of racialization and material inequality in Canadian society. Even as multiculturalism was being questioned (again), little attention was focused on one of the long-standing critiques of (Canadian) multicultural discourse: that is, the way it glosses over questions of racism. This volume is, in part, a reaction to this continued silence.

We are, by no means, the first to note these gaps and absences. Multiculturalism's perpetual state of unsettlement springs partly from sustained and trenchant accounts of its limitations, mostly advanced by critics on the Left. These critiques have developed along several lines. Rinaldo Walcott notes how multiculturalism functions as "a category of naming and administration" that focuses primarily on people of colour. At opportune moments, however, the category is expanded to include "white" ethnic groups such Poles, Italians, etc., in order "to demonstrate the economic promise Canada offers new immigrants."[12] Himani Bannerji, writing from a Marxist perspective, has emphasized the correspondence between multiculturalism's blind spots regarding racism and the absence of attention, within the policy, to material inequalities. For her, these inequalities cannot be addressed by a generalized language that makes appeals about cultural accommodation.[13] Moreover, such a lopsided focus on culture has not resulted in an increased politicization of culture. As Eva Mackey and Carol Tator et al. have suggested, multiculturalism's precepts resist such politicization, working instead to diminish and declaw cultural claims that are articulated in the service of radical politics.[14] This management and depoliticization of culture exists alongside its commodification, which renders certain forms and expressions mere celebrations of so-called ethnic heritage.[15] Thus, Bannerji has noted that multiculturalism becomes a managerial strategy, positing a collection of decontextualized cultural fragments that exist around a cultural core – a core comprised of white Canadian culture and the hegemonic population Mackey has termed "*Canadian*-Canadians."[16]

We were struck by the remarkable (but perhaps unsurprising) relevance of these "old" critiques, as well as by the vehemence with which multiculturalism had become the sacrificial object of post-9/11 politics, with little regard for its conflicted and contested histories. Multiculturalism as an official policy seemed to be up for renegotiation at the very moment when racism – a racism that critics argue multiculturalism had never really addressed – was manifesting itself with extraordinary virulence. In her introduction to *Casting Out: The Eviction of Muslims from Western Law and Politics*, Sherene Razack pointed to the media portrayal of the "terror sweeps" in June 2006 when seventeen Muslim men were arrested in Toronto for allegedly planning to blow up the CN tower and Canadian security headquarters. "Uncharacteristically naming race," she observed, "Canadian newspapers covering the June terror arrests openly referred to Muslims as 'brown-skinned' and were at pains to make the distinctions between those who were merely 'Canadian born,' as the seventeen accused are, and those who are truly Canadian by virtue of possession of Canadian values, if not Canadian skin."[17]

This re-emergence of old questions, with seemingly little acknowledgment of the ongoing struggles and critiques within multicultural discourse, provoked us to organize the conference *From Multicultural Rhetoric to Anti-Racist Action* at the University of Toronto in 2007, from whence this volume originates. Though we attended to 9/11 and its political and social repercussions as a discursive flashpoint, we were wary of focusing only on the spectacular and even lurid dimensions of the so-called crisis of multiculturalism and its corresponding responses, such as the Bouchard–Taylor hearings. In framing this volume, then, we acknowledge a number of very real dangers in placing too much emphasis on the role of 9/11 and its aftermath in reshaping and reorienting power relations and the discourses that legitimize and normalize them. The power to displace bodies, deport bodies, and read bodies in particular ways by no means began on September 12, 2001, even as such powers were given new impetus in the wake of the attacks. As Neil Smith has argued, the events of 9/11 "were coldly appropriated to the purpose of cementing a long desired, episodic but ultimately chimerical global hegemony."[18] Derek Gregory has further asserted that the "geopolitical configurations, economic alignments, and cultural formations mobilized during the months that followed September 11th have complex genealogies reaching far back into the colonial past."[19] To ignore these genealogies leaves us "blind," in Gregory's words, to "the banality of the colonial present and to our complicity in its horrors."[20]

This book takes up the challenge of thinking genealogically. It emphasizes the urgency of colonial histories in the present and suggests the limitations inherent in understanding them as problems of multicultural recognition. Contributors Brian Egan and Emilie Cameron demonstrate the pervasiveness of multiculturalism's language and logic of recognition in Aboriginal land claims. They not only question the appropriateness of recognition in this instance, but also demonstrate how the extension of recognition shores up the state. Reflecting on how recognition and reconciliation projects aim to render difference legible, Egan notes that "legibility refers to the task of organizing that which lies within the state's domain – peoples, natures, territories – so as to make possible a range of basic state functions." In their respective contributions, Grace-Edward Galabuzi and Nandita Sharma explore the implications of these insights about multicultural recognition. Both show in different ways how recognition works to ensure state functioning, and renders certain bodies strategically legible or indeed illegible – processes of the production of social difference that have been heightened in the imperial afterglow of 9/11.

Post-9/11 responses to multiculturalism have largely been vehicles to reproduce the sterile and misleading language of "tolerance" and "reasonable accommodation" and do not get to the root of the problem.[21] In the original framing of the 2007 conference, we felt that the term "multiculturalism" – even as its death was supposedly upon us – continued to be deployed as a way of silencing discussions about race and racism. We wanted to create a space for scholars and activists to speak critically and openly about what multiculturalism continues to conceal, and in so doing, to put race (and lingering systemic racism) squarely on the agenda and at the heart of our dialogue. We wanted to examine where in Canadian public policy (besides post-9/11 debates about multiculturalism) race and racism were discernable in subtle and not-so-subtle ways. How, we wondered, does racism silently inflect discussions about immigration policy and global labour migration, Aboriginal land claims and questions of recognition, and the continued and persistent racialization of bodies?

This volume examines the current historical moment in a way that shifts attention towards a more critical terrain. If one of our primary ambitions is to unsettle multiculturalism in Canada by foregrounding continued forms of racism and discrimination, equally important to us is the identification of where and how violent forms of "othering" continue to operate in Canadian society. The "labours" section of the book encapsulates our efforts to contextualize and unsettle multiculturalism within the realities of global labour migration. In chapter 5, Sharma maps the emergence of the official state policy of multiculturalism in the early 1970s to the beginnings of the globalization of capital. She explores the ways in which multicultural discourse was imbricated with class and race relations as capitalists and workers grappled with the changing global flows of capital and labour that accompanied the emergence of neo-liberal political economy. In chapter 6, Margaret Walton-Roberts, describing what she calls "unbounded multiculturalism," argues that, depending on Canadian economic interests, "the rights of multiculturalism are [either] projected onto the global landscape" or are "suddenly constrained and ruled out through the retraction of citizenship and the protection of privileged sections of the labour market." In this instance, multiculturalism appears selectively in official discourse, functioning as a legitimizing alibi at some moments and disappearing at others.

Echoing this theme of differential inclusion, other contributors foreground the cultural labour and discursive heavy-lifting performed by stories of immigration and the (often gendered) work of settlement and domestication. Within the discursive field of multiculturalism, Laurie Bertram argues in chapter 9 that these stories – which themselves showcase the labour involved in making home and establishing a cultural presence on the land – work to secure and normalize differential access to the state and its resources. They also reveal how the complicated logics of multiculturalism have contributed to the colonization of Aboriginal peoples and ongoing contests over land and resources. Early settler accounts of inhabiting and forming attachments to the land,

Bertram argues, are reworked in contemporary multicultural narratives about heritage, echoing and reinforcing what were in fact settler appropriations of Aboriginal land. Here, in the material and symbolic work of settlement, homemaking, and territorialization, the lands and labour rubrics that structure this book's analysis overlap in an articulation central to deciphering multiculturalism as a politics of settlement.

In chapter 7, Egan notes that multiculturalism is "grounded"; it is a story of the nation that settles not only identity and meaning, but also land and space. In situating their analyses of multiculturalism within questions about lands – questions about the ongoing appropriation and dispossession of lands, attachment to land, and habitation of lands – this volume's contributors situate the production and maintenance of colonial relations squarely in the foreground of multicultural practice. Perhaps one of the most important instances of multiculturalism's discursive saturation, then, is the manner in which its registers and tropes (of belonging, rootedness, arrival, recognition, and so on) breathe life into the colonial relations upon which Canadian identity and nation are settled. As Glen Coulthard, Egan, Cameron, and Bertram all demonstrate, this is a relation that is not only still "live" (in the sense that struggles over lands are still ongoing and still matter) but that must also be constantly maintained, managed, and nurtured.[22] In chapter 8, Cameron shows how discourses of multiculturalism and multicultural understandings of difference work to settle Aboriginal peoples and their claims to lands safely and securely in the interstitial (and ghostly) spaces of the past. "Just incorporation" of Aboriginal difference into the multicultural nation state, she argues, is framed as an exercise in reconciling the historical experience of immaterial, dead, and expired cultures – an exercise that works to reinscribe colonial relations, and reproduce settler claims to space. In chapters 2 and 7, Coulthard and Egan draw on the work of Charles Taylor to connect the politics and practices of recognition and reconciliation through which land claims politics are currently negotiated to the logics and ontological frameworks of liberal multiculturalism. Projects of recognition and reconciliation are the outcome of a multicultural fantasy, and, as Egan argues, neither attend to the nation's colonial history nor address its illegal expropriation of lands and resources. Rather, such projects mark attempts on behalf of the state to reconcile Aboriginal title "*to* crown sovereignty," and to "neatly confine . . . troubling questions about human and territorial diversity . . . within the contours of the Canadian state."

Both Egan and Coulthard remind us that Canada is not only a colonial and multicultural state, but a capitalist one too: the colonial relation maps easily onto a framework of political and economic superexploitation in which expropriation of land and resources feature prominently. Coulthard challenges the notion that the colonial relationship can be transformed via a politics of recognition, arguing instead that this politics fundamentally misunderstands colonial power and leaves untouched the economic and political structure of the colonial relation. Multiculturalism and its concomitant politics of recognition and reconciliation, in this instance, offer a political ontology and cultural imaginary instrumental to reproducing colonial-economic dynamics.

Bodies – the third section of this book – pervade questions of both lands and labours but also constitute a rubric of their own. Bodies are put to work, surveilled, racialized, marginalized, and read in particular ways within and against official multicultural policy. At the same time, as Natasha Bakht illuminates in her chapter on classical south Indian dance, bodies themselves can be unsettling to multiculturalism. Despite the fact that various bodies are read differently, striking correspondences between these readings emerge, revealing that bodies are central to the ways in which multiculturalism is both enacted and experienced. Both Cameron and Bertram examine the way that Aboriginal bodies and Aboriginal presences are rendered ghostly in settler mythologies. As Cameron explains, these tropes of Aboriginal haunting have become a mainstay of recent critical writing. Such "postcolonial ghost stories," she argues, "both register Indigeneity and undermine the specific claims of Indigenous peoples." As she suggests, to imagine Aboriginal peoples as ghosts – vanishing, spectral, only on occasional perceptible – involves a "politics of vision" that can engender Aboriginal invisibility while seeming to suggest a progressive willingness to grapple with the injustices of the past.

However, even as Aboriginal peoples are figured as ghostly and invisible, other racialized bodies are imbued with excessive visibility and a surplus of presence thanks to the colour of their skin. Yet as Galabuzi and Uzma Shakir suggest in chapters 4 and 11, respectively, marking some bodies as excessively present and aggressively visible is no less a technique of rendering them invisible. Shakir describes the efforts of the Toronto-based Colour of Poverty Campaign to address the persistent and crippling correspondence for immigrants in Canada of being racialized and poor. The soothing public perception is that immigrant poverty is a "newcomer phenomenon" – something that migrants graduate out of within half a generation. Yet Shakir argues that the lived reality of ethno-racial communities in Toronto and empirical research together suggest that racialization and the economic marginalization it engenders do not dissipate over time. For his part, Galabuzi argues that the state's designation of some people as "visible minorities" denotes "a hyper visibility" that "served to reinforce the fact that race was becoming more prominent as an organizing principle of life even as it was losing its critical edge in popular discourse because of its displacement by multiculturalism." This elaboration of visibility combined with the displacement of race as a category of critical analysis, he asserts, works to hide the experiences of these minorities "in plain sight." Chapter 3, George Elliott Clarke's "manifesto," puts forth a series of proposals to make Canada less ethnocentric and more truly multicultural; some of these are whimsical and many are provocative, but most are concerned with the significance of visibility, and with affirming the fact of visible difference by reflecting it in Canadian institutions and symbols. In making a case for expanding the "presence of visible minorities" in public life, he asserts that it is only when Canadian institutions "begin to look like Canada itself" that "racist marginalization of visible minorities" might be reduced.

If, as we have suggested, the post-9/11 panic around difference and diversity focused on the policy and ideology of liberal multiculturalism – treating it as if it were the only account of a differentiated and differential reality rather than just one of many possible explanatory modes – we felt it was crucial to stay focused on the persistent realities of racialized exclusion. To us this means recognizing that long-standing questions of racism and racialization by no means began with 9/11. There are numerous other policy discussions underway, and political and economic practices in place that have little to do with questions of reasonable accommodation, and thus do not overtly invoke the language of *multiculturalism*. Yet, at the same time, these critical issues, such as how labour is organized and mobility is restricted beyond and within national borders, land is perceived and allocated in this still-settler state, and bodies are read and put to work (or not), are most certainly inflected by assumptions about race as well as by systemic racism. One of the innovations of this volume is that it brings together and centralizes the three themes of labours, lands, and bodies in order to illustrate the continued power, limitations and, at times, destructiveness of multiculturalism, both as a policy and as a discourse. In short, this volume takes as its starting point the fact that debates about the death of multiculturalism eclipse the reality that racism persists.

Part 1

Unsettling Multiculturalism

1 Disgraceful: Intellectual dishonesty, white anxieties, and multicultural critique thirty-six years later

Rinaldo Walcott

Introduction: The legacy of Europe's global reign

THE EVENTS OF SEPTEMBER 11, 2001, appeared to have solidified a consensus on multiculturalism: that is, that until that moment, multi-culturalism in its state form had been settled policy. In this chapter, I argue that such claims are patently false and are more indicative of white anxieties post-9/11 than of any previous multicultural consensus. Not only has state multiculturalism always been a contested policy, but the very idea of multiculturalism itself has always been and will continue to be a contested idea. Western liberal democracies like Canada adopted various forms of state multiculturalism to manage and neutralize post-World-War-II struggles for social and economic justice by racial and cultural minorities, and to constrain the movement of mainly non-white migrants into national spaces which had formerly imagined, represented, and performed themselves as entirely white. State multiculturalism sought to contain such "uprisings" through policies centered on identity and culture while maintaining and retaining the power to authorize and legitimize the late-capitalist material relations of the nation-state. However, continual upheavals in state multicultural rhetoric have meant that even the state has often revised its idea of multiculturalism, and thus its policy, in response to compet-ing ideas of what multiculturalism is and what it should do.

I am therefore suggesting that one cannot fully make sense of post-9/11 multiculturalism debates without taking into account the context of Western global expansion over the last five hundred years, a period in which Europe reordered the globe under its own terms or ways of knowing as the only legitimate way of being. More specifically the making of the Americas, especially settler colonies like Canada, and the invention of the modern nation-state in its current liberal democratic form, are all clearly implicated in the conversation. The implication comes through the discourse and language of freedom, which has been contested for the last five hundred years by a range of different groups and peoples since freedom did not apply equally to all. The post-9/11 claim that multiculturalism is over represents a kind of intellectual dishonesty that refuses to take seriously both state reforms and compromises in the context of peoples' resistances to being managed – it is indeed an ahistorical claim.

In this post-9/11 world, pundits have attempted to enshrine liberal democracy as the only system that guarantees human freedom and emancipation.[1] Such a willfully impartial rewriting of liberal democratic ideals is interesting since it conceals the brutal forces of unfreedom that made freedom an ideal for others in the first instance. The pundits have thus refused to engage the history of human dreadfulness upon which liberal democracies of the West have been founded – all of them instituted through enormous acts of violence. As Toni Morrison reminds us in *Playing in the Dark*, "the slave population, it could be and was assumed, offered itself up as surrogate selves for meditation on problems of human freedom, its lure and its elusiveness."[2] She also adds, "we should not be surprised that the Enlightenment could accommodate slavery; we should be surprised if it had not. The concept of freedom did not emerge in a vacuum. Nothing highlighted freedom – if it did not in fact create it – like slavery."[3] Taking as evidence New World slavery and Aboriginal colonialism, which constitute the foundations of the Americas as we presently live them, Morrison's comments bring home the point that while five hundred years of European global hegemony has cemented one version of what freedom is, other ideas of freedom still remain among us.

In her discussion of Hegel and Haiti in the pages of *Critical Inquiry*, Susan Buck-Morss attempts to reanimate the debate concerning modernity and its discourse of freedom. She argues that Western political philosophy has failed to grapple with the implications of slave labour's spread in the colonies at the exact time that the Enlightenment discourse of freedom as "the highest and universal political value" was being produced by Enlightenment thinkers.[4] She further asks how we can, in our times, produce this same blind spot, if it is indeed a blind spot and not an intentional act in our scholarship. And, she cautions us not to place the counterevidence of what Paul Gilroy once brilliantly called "the counter-cultures of modernity" as simply the story of non-white peoples only.[5] Buck-Morss wants us to mix it up, so to speak.[6] What she documents and demonstrates is the centrality of unfreedom to Europe's now-realized global ambitions and aspirations, especially in the face of Europe's decline as a global colonizer and the U.S.A.'s rise as a new imperial power. Her challenge is to forms of intellectual dishonesty, as I call them, by some Western academics and pundits who refuse to acknowledge the troubled origins of European ideas of freedom, nation, and democracy.

Buck-Morss' argument makes clear that the afterlife of European colonization of the Americas has silenced the evidence that Indian genocide and near-genocide, as well as African enslavement, form the backbone of European modernity – both materially and intellectually. Both Sibylle Fischer and Michel-Rolph Trouillot build on Buck-Morss' position in their reading of the culmination of Haiti's 1791 revolution as central to the emergence of the key tenets of European political philosophy and liberal democratic states.[7] European philosophy had to ignore, write against, and collude with practices of unfreedom, which lay at the source of its very making. Thus, the epistemological violence inherent in European political philosophy is not new, but rather takes its imprimatur from a history of intellectual practice that has always sometimes looked the other way, as Buck-Morss excellently points out. This is especially so in the present moment when scholars in the social sciences and humanities are struggling to think through the current global situation. In this instance, the idea of multiculturalism has been negatively racialized and bears the brunt of liberal philosophy's disdain.

I suggest that in a post-9/11 world a re-engagement with European modernity's genres of the human is required. This re-engagement must negotiate a number of overlapping and contradictory flows and contexts, and must recognize that for politics to happen there must be a "symbolic drawing of the boundary; there has to be some symbolic divide," as Stuart Hall puts it.[8] In the "eventful moment" of 9/11, then, George W. Bush was right about one thing: the "us against them." The "with us or against us" of his rhetoric produced the necessary and important arbitrary closure to proceed to war and to further harden global capital in its neo-liberal guise with the aim of reordering the world. While Bush's early comments produced this arbitrary closure for certain conditions of neo-liberal ideologies to unfold globally in relation to a civilizational divide, the rhetoric found its legitimacy in public intellectual debates, popular culture, policy debates, and a range of other contexts under which post-Columbus European expansion ordered life globally and could thus proceed as if it was natural, normal, and the law. But such hegemony has always been challenged. The post-World-War-II uprisings by racial minorities in the West and by colonized peoples stand as examples of how states could be remade and even produced in the aftermath of those important contests.

The idea of multiculturalism and state multiculturalism

Multiculturalism as an idea is a central element of the post-civil-rights, new-social-movements, postcolonial "racial contract," as Mills terms it, of the second half of the twentieth century and the beginning of the twenty-first.[9] In this instance, it is a racial contract premised on European modernity's categorizations of people who have over time come to genuinely take those categories as both serious and meaningful to their lives. The multicultures of Europe's imaginary now play a role in defining and redefining what culture might mean; thus, the idea of multiple cultures coexisting is now a fixture of our times. This role has to be also understood in light of the massive movements of peoples across geopolitical spaces, as they constitute new modes of living and new forms of social life. In some abstract ways, these new modes of human life and sociality might also be conceived of as multiculturalism.

One of my central claims in this chapter is that state multiculturalism borrows from the idea of multiculturalism and redirects it as a tool of the state. State multiculturalism is invested with the power to manage a range of differences that might prove potentially troubling in a hegemonic state's bid to retain its exclusive authorizing powers. The idea of multiculturalism provides avenues for living with difference that do not always have to obey coercive state power. Thus, this idea allows for forms of social relations that take difference as central to human existence – not as a problem but as a set of creative and non-coercive ways to approach living life to its fullest potential. Indeed, the idea of multiculturalism shares with liberal democracy the ideal that human beings can reach beyond themselves to fashion a world of social good that is valuable to all. Yet post-9/11, the negative side of multiculturalism has been accentuated.

These days, everyone has something to say about the failures of multiculturalism as both an idea and as policy. We can find these comments in the unlikeliest of places. David Cronenberg, in discussing *Eastern Promises,* his film about the Russian mafia and the smuggling of young Eastern European girls as sex slaves, is quoted in the *New York Times:*

When you have a culture that's embedded in another, there's a constant tension between the two. . . . In the U.S. the melting pot was supposed to mean you come and you absorb American values. But in Canada and England the idea of multiculturalism was something else. At its worst it's you come and you live there, but you live in a little ghetto of your own culture that you brought with you. I suppose that's happening in the States with the Spanish language. Can multiculturalism really work? I don't know, but it's an interesting study.[10]

The article proceeds to tell us that Cronenberg recalls growing up in a mainly Jewish Toronto area that was repopulated by Italians as the Jews moved north. He recalls hearing Dean Martin through walls "and learning about Fellini from an Italian-Canadian boy. 'That's the good part of multiculturalism,' he said. 'That's the dream of it. The bad parts are the animosities brought from other countries.' "[11] Cronenberg's comments on multiculturalism are interesting not the least for the ways in which they demonstrate that the popular intellectual debate concerning multiculturalism has penetrated all kinds of realms.

While *Eastern Promises* dramatizes the trafficking of women across various borders, it is in no way about traveling/migrating antagonisms from Russia to England; rather, the antagonisms are internal to the migrants (and perhaps even generations of migrants). Cronenberg's reference to the ethnic, cultural, and linguistic ghettoization of Spanish language in the U.S. is equally interesting since he was speaking as a Canadian, who is presumably familiar with Canada's two official languages. What, then, was he trying to say? In statements such as Cronenberg's, a certain kind of symptom – the symptom' of the racialized other – becomes more easily visible. This spectre of the racialized other, invented in the moment of European expansion and solidified in its modernity, with its systemic categorizing of people, places, and things, continues to structure our contemporary world. Indeed, it is this categorization that drives state multiculturalism along with its management and containment strategies.

Thus, in 1971 when Pierre Elliott Trudeau introduced Canada's Multiculturalism Policy, the opposition leader Robert Stanfield rose in the House to emphasize that the policy in no way changed the character of the Canadian nation as constituted by two founding peoples. This understanding of Canadian nationhood has been reified in a range of state practices, such as the bilingual nature of the nation, certain measures of citizenship, and the continuing adherence to the idea of the Queen of England as the head of the nation. Similarly, when the

Mulroney government of the 1980s – a period and a government implicated in the unfolding of neo-liberal arrangements, such as the gradual dismantling of the welfare state in Canada – shifted multiculturalism from a policy to an Act of the Constitution, it was attempting to maintain state arrangements while benefiting from the new and ongoing migrations that are so central to Canada's capitalist economic health. What is important to recognize in both the announcement of the policy and the further creation of the Act is that the idea of multiculturalism remained contested even among the political and capitalist elites. Since 1971 multiculturalism as policy and practice in Canada has been contentious from a range of political ideologies and positions. Any suggestion otherwise is an ahistorical suggestion that is, quite frankly, disgraceful and intellectually dishonest.

And yet, in the last few years the Canadian public has been engaged in a debate concerning multiculturalism, citizenship, war, and terrorism, which fails to engage the history of either the policy or the idea of multiculturalism. Articles in the popular media by Allan Gregg (pollster), Michael Bliss (Canadian historian), Janice Gross Stein (political scientist), and Cecil Foster (sociologist) have all contributed to this debate in significant ways.[12] Importantly, Stein's essay "Living Better Multiculturally" sparked both kudos and criticism in both the *Globe and Mail* and the *Toronto Star*. *Globe and Mail* columnist John Ibbitson praised the essay, while *Toronto Star* columnist Haroon Siddiqui quarreled with it.[13] Stein's essay suggests that multiculturalism and, by extension, cultural rights run counter to the best practices of liberal democracies. She further argues that multicultural policies might in fact harm liberal democracies and render them relative states. The responses to Stein's article, both laudatory and critical, point out the need to engage more actively with both the interpretation of Canadian multicultural policy and the larger question of the idea of multiculturalism in a postcolonial world.

Gregg, Bliss, Stein, and Foster all assume that the idea of multiculturalism has been settled in Canada, yet all but Foster believe that the nation's comfort with multiculturalism requires either reassessment or renewed endorsement. Certainly the substantive changes we have witnessed globally require a renewed discussion of multicultural policies. However, I would argue that Canadian multiculturalism as policy, practice, and even as an idea has never been settled. Further, I believe that Canadian multiculturalism has been a useful instrument in the unfolding of neo-liberalism insofar as it has prompted various ethnic communities to support political parties that appeal to their ethnic interests.

Indeed, that the idea of multiculturalism continues to be unsettled can be seen in the varied responses to its circulation in the public sphere.

So, for example, Cecil Foster praises Canada for its multicultural accomplishments with tongue in cheek, suggesting that the queen of Canada is now black since Nova Scotia's Lieutenant Governor Mayann Francis and the former Governor General of Canada Michaëlle Jean are both black women. On the other hand, many anti-racist scholars and pundits on the political Left would argue that such appointments demonstrate a toothless practice of multiculturalism that does not adequately support the transfer of power to racialized Canadians; this is one of the earliest anti-racist critiques of state multiculturalism. Yet in another article, Foster argues that in Canada, multiculturalism has made race irrelevant and thus any discussion of Toronto Muslims plotting acts of terror ought not to be cast in terms of a critique of multiculturalism, but rather in terms of whether Canada desires to make race an essential element of its citizenship again.[14] However, anti-racist scholars and activists, as well as leftist critics, would argue that race always remains a salient element of Canadian citizenship.

In a different vein, Michael Bliss, Janice Stein, and Allan Gregg all contend quite earnestly that multiculturalism is at odds with Canadian social values due to its hijacking by various religious and cultural fundamentalists. In their view, most of these fundamentalists are a multicultural array of non-white Canadians. For Bliss, Stein, and Gregg, Canada is undermined as a nation by its unwavering support for the idea of multiculturalism and our collective faith in the policy and the Act to produce a common basis for the practice of citizenship. How might we make sense of these different positions by these public intellectuals? Is Foster correct that race no longer matters? Or are Bliss, Stein, and Gregg right in claiming that disunity and uneasy partnership characterizes the polity? Can partnership be assumed from our present social relations? And to whom are all those folks writing?

In fact, Foster's rhetorical and rather romantic claims can be traced to bureaucratic interpretations of the policy and Act. The Department of Canadian Heritage, which comprises the Multiculturalism Program, historicizes multiculturalism as having evolved over at least three different phases: cultural preservation and celebration (the Trudeau period); inclusion and anti-racism (the Mulroney period); and social cohesion (the post-Mulroney, pre-9/11 period). Thus, even at the level of governance, understandings of the policy and the idea are not settled. Engaging with the policy and the idea of multiculturalism carries important political imperatives, since a new multicultural logic is always possible. I am not of the school of thought that multiculturalism is an entirely useless idea; rather, I am conscious of it as producing what David Scott terms "a problem-space" from which new kinds of questions must emerge so that different kinds of answers and, more importantly, different kinds of desires might surface.[15]

In this regard, *Uneasy Partners: Multiculturalism and Rights in Canada*, a collection of essays by a group of public intellectual elites, claims to offer new questions about the multiculturalism debate.[16] However, this collection merely pursues old arguments that have been well worked over by scholars and intellectuals, many of whom I engage with below. What is particularly interesting, however, is that none of the numerous scholars who have spent significant time engaging with these issues are cited or discussed in the book. Such patent intellectual dishonesty is, in my view, part of the reason why the debate on multiculturalism in this country is one that has posed no new questions for the idea of multiculturalism. While at least three of the contributors to the collection count Canadian multiculturalism as a success, even those essayists fail to question the racial contract of which state multiculturalism is such a fundamental element.

The essays gathered in *Uneasy Partners* speak into an assumed void that does not and has never existed. Ignoring more than thirty years of scholarship and debate concerning Canadian multiculturalism, *Uneasy Partners* attempts to establish the legitimate spokespeople on the question of the future of Canadian multiculturalism. With its requisite contrarian (Haroon Siddiqui) and its cheerleader (John Meisel), the book is mainly concerned with either propping up the idea that multiculturalism in Canada runs counter to liberal democratic rights or that it implies the provision of those rights. I have argued elsewhere that this is hardly the case and that the idea of multiculturalism must be thought of as a part of rights discourses and, even further, as collective rights discourses, pushing the boundaries of what we think liberal democratic states and their citizens can be accountable and responsible for. *Uneasy Partners* is fundamentally concerned with a reassertion of white hegemonic pronouncements on the Euro-American "right" to determine the future of the state and thus of human life. To do so, it must both ignore more rigorous scholarship and invent itself *tout court*. It must also simultaneously co-opt what appears to be opposition to its claims by including the evidence of dissenters. In short, this book is an example of the racial contract *par excellence*.

Most recently, Cecil Foster has written two books on multiculturalism: *Where Race Does Not Matter* and *Blackness and Modernity*. While I have fundamental conceptual differences with many of Foster's claims, it is curious that he has not garnered more attention in the debate. As faulty as Foster's claims might be, he argues against a tribal view that would guarantee white and some racialized elites the intellectual and political apparatus to manage the nation-state. He recognizes them as a tribe when they would rather be unmarked as such and mark others instead. Foster writes,

> The last laugh of the jester would be heard in the 1960s, when Canadians decided that their country would be officially raceless. When they decided to make theirs the world's first officially multicultural country, Canadians were tapping into a view that had always been part of the Canadian body politic; they were harking back to the universalism and humanity that Lord Simcoe had epitomized.[17]

Foster then offers a further explanation in which Lord Simcoe's opposition to slavery is understood as recognition that "Canada was not exclusively European."[18] Further still, he sees evidence of this in the Toronto Caribana festival, held every year since 1967 on Simcoe Day, a date celebrated as Emancipation Day in the Caribbean. The main problem with Foster's claims is that he very clearly overreaches. Simcoe's opposition to slavery was progressive for its time, but it by no means signaled Canada as a non-white colonial nation-space; emigrationism was an important part of his anti-slavery stance. Similarly, contemporary multicultural policy, as I have stated above, is in no way a challenge to the national myth of Canada as a white nation-space or a raceless state. Rather, multicultural policy is arguably an acknowledgement of the racial state and is in essence a racial contract that binds the arrangement. My point here, however, is not to prove Foster incorrect, but to point to his interpretation of multicultural policy as one that must be ignored, lest it pose too many questions for Stein et al., who are hell-bent on whipping up hysteria about the multicultural threat. It does not take many difficult hermeneutic maneuvers to detect that race-talk is the foundation of this threat.

   In the last thirty years or so Peter Li, Singh Bolaria, Enid Lee, Barbara Thomas, Roxana Ng, Augie Fleras, Himani Bannerji, Richard Day, Eva Mackey, Sherene Razack, Marlene NourbeSe Philip, Dionne Brand, Neil Bissoondath, and a range of other scholars, activists, and public intellectuals have offered a breadth of political perspectives and positions on multiculturalism. None of these writers have been engaged in the most recent debates (despite the fact that Penguin

Canada brought Bissoondath's book back into print at around the same time that *Uneasy Partners* was published). Nonetheless, these perspectives have played a central role in how Canadian multiculturalism is understood in diverse circles. Thus it might be argued that the only consensus on Canadian multiculturalism in the last thirty-plus years is that it has become a fundamental Canadian entity, but a consensus on what it means and how it should work continues to elude us. Ideas and practices of multiculturalism remain contested sites and so they should be. If multiculturalism is at all an element of what might constitute new forms of social cohesion in an era that appears to be, at least rhetorically, balkanized, then thinking and struggling over what it might and could mean is a useful and productive endeavour. Stuart Hall's claim that migration is the question of the twenty-first century is crucial to this conversation. In my view, and as the chapter in this volume by Margaret Walton-Roberts illuminates, migration cannot be thought about outside of the ideas of multiculturalism and multicultures. Hall cautions that we must struggle with the conceptual and discursive meanings of multiculturalism to come up with a better term with which to think through these conditions – a challenge for those who would throw away or abandon the concept to corporate forces or the political Right.

Uneasy Partners is framed through the language of rights, especially with regard to the state management of its citizens. In Canada, that management takes place through the Charter of Rights and Freedoms. In his discussion of rights, Foster attempts to address the significance of the question of freedom. Discourses of freedom are in fact a significant question for liberal democracy, but he is so committed to his particular kind of liberalism that he never addresses the role of unfreedom in liberal democracy.[19] I argue that rights as organized by and governed through the state might be said to actually abort a more pure freedom.

The new questions confronting both the idea and the policy of multiculturalism are centered on notions of freedom and unfreedom. We need to better understand the nature of our contemporary unfreedoms. I assert this perspective in the context of the overwhelming managerialisms of neo-liberalism in various institutions and within global corporate capitalism. Neo-liberalism in its many and varied incarnations is a very specific assault on freedom; it manages our unfreedoms through what many have come to identify as an audit and surveillance culture. Contemporary debates about multiculturalism collude with these modes of unfreedom, as well as with attempts to manage both the planned and unplanned migrations of the twenty-first

century. In the context of multicultural encounters, th
course, and practices of surveillance and security now occ
place in managing the movement of people around the globe.

If we take Janice Stein's "Living Better Multiculturally" as a
tion, what kinds of answers or new questions might we provide
there a place for the question of unfreedom? And if migration is now a
de rigueur fact of human life, what would it mean to conceptualize multiculturalism as outside a narrative of arrival or, more broadly, of
progress? What would it mean to instead begin to think of encounters
with cultural difference as inevitable and therefore always the place
from which human engagement and thus negotiation proceed? It seems
to me that these sorts of questions pose different concerns for the ways
in which theorists are attempting to think about intensified cultural difference and movement. If we take seriously the importance of understanding that liberal democracy is founded not on freedoms, as the
intellectuals committed to the partial insights of European modernity
and its philosophy like to proclaim, but on unfreedoms, then the problem-space of multiculturalism as an idea begins to reveal itself. The rev-
elations take us down the road of having to consider how white
anxieties are framing this moment and its debates.

Disgraceful claims and white anxieties post-9/11

By "white anxieties" I mean to signal a state of aggression by Euro-
American intellectuals, policy analysts, and others who must now confront their ever-decreasing power to have their partial view of the
world appear as the only legitimate view. In this new context, a kind of
white anxiety has come into being in which previous compromises are
being rethought so as to preserve what can only crudely be called
"white power." White anxieties, in this case, are dressed up in terms of
debates on rights discourses, the future of the liberal democratic state,
tensions between the secular state and religion, and so on. In each case,
white anxieties betray themselves in their bearers' assumptions of the
role of stewards of the conversation, dialogue, and debate, thus posi-
tioning themselves as the protectors of the continually unfolding "freedoms" of secular liberal democratic societies. Consequently, all others,
usually racialized others, become the barbarians screaming at the doors.

Multiculturalism is both an outcome of European modernity (in its
initial moving of people around the globe in ways that disrupted previous settlements of those peoples) as well as a political compromise of
the post-World-War-II anti-colonial and civil rights resistances of

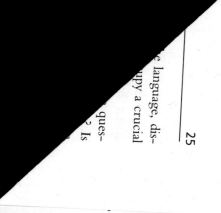

alized subjects. It is also a managerial
those who resist state-imposed policy-
e time, the idea of multiculturalism is
ibilities it offers for dealing with what
ery meaningful and real cultural differ-
iralism, as a condition of contemporary
lily overcome. Thus, Hall argues that we
ler "erasure" while we struggle over its
litical logic that might better address our
n.[20]

Any new multicultural political logic must recognize the importance of sustaining hope in a world that seems devoid of it. But even
more important than hope might be the politics of new and different
utopian futures that move beyond both the failed experiments of the
Left and what appears to be the unstoppable machine of capitalism.
Public discourse of utopian futures waned in the second half of the
twentieth century. Indeed, one of the triumphs of neo-liberal ideologies has been its very effective management of the imagination, alongside the management of the economy, institutions, populations, and so
on. I want to suggest that in this era of fundamentalisms of all kinds,
our inability to engage critically with new imaginative worlds, to think
critically and imaginatively about liberal democracies, or to imagine
worlds other than those we have experienced is one of the central
questions that intellectuals and activists engaging with the idea of multiculturalism must pursue. That ideas about multiculturalism were so
quickly marked as contentious in the post-9/11 world suggests that a
certain cultural order of modernity was profoundly disrupted by the
actions of that day. To paraphrase Sylvia Wynter, the rupture marked by
9/11 highlights the belief that the partial perspective of European
modernity can be the universally valid perspective.[21] It is this ideology
that has pushed the charge against multiculturalism, since one of the
possibilities of a hopeful multicultural logic is the unleashing of various
and competing conceptions of people, places, and things. In other
words, there have always been different conceptions of the human and
the world; multiculturalism could subversively recognize as much. Such
recognition, decidedly different from Charles Taylor's liberal philosophical use of the term, would require different human arrangements
across space and time around the globe and echoes Buck-Morss' critique of the discipline of philosophy with which I began.[22]

One might argue that the conclusive and substantive difference
between the post- and pre-9/11 world is that now the struggle over the

definition of European modernity has never been so visible. Drawing on Scott's conception of the problem-space, one could suggest that much anti-colonial struggle was premised on the flexibility of the terms of modernity to absorb all kinds of difference under its terrain of freedom and equality as ever-expanding qualities. Their expansion seemed to be halted in the unfolding of the neo-liberal global assault.

In my view, the rolling back of rights and freedoms reached its apogee in the post-1960s world with the election of Margaret Thatcher in Britain in the late 1970s, Ronald Reagan in the U.S. in 1980, and similar-minded chancellors in Germany and presidents in Japan. The international and domestic policies of these governments produced a narrative of demonization and practices of managerialism that still occupy a central place in neo-liberal practices today. The demonization of black youth in Thatcher's era continues to frame the experience of black youth in Britain even now. Reagan's double term built the framework for attacks on African American and Latino working classes and their communities. Through the rewriting of laws, so-called gang violence was targeted in U.S. urban centres, producing and reconfiguring what many scholars and activists have come to call either the new slave system of the U.S. or the prison industrial complex.[23] Most significant, however, are the forms of demonization, surveillance, and practices of otherization that accompanied this putatively non-economic side of the neo-liberal triumph. Attacks on multiculturalism as an idea first took root in public discourse and consciousness during this period.

What I am arguing here is that in various geopolitical spaces the formations that now seem to be boiling over into a robust conversation about multiculturalism were well underway prior to 9/11. However, it would be a mistake to look for a sure pattern across these different spaces. The Canadian context differs from that of Britain and the U.S. since in Canada multiculturalism was further entrenched as a national policy in the 1970s and 1980s. During this time, in Britain, Thatcher was dismantling the very interesting experiment of the Greater London Council. Such differences reveal the contradictions of neo-liberalism as a policy that should work similarly everywhere, yet does not; there is no global unanimity.

If we think of liberal democracy as a system of rules that confer various advantages upon those for whom the rules constitute a substantive portion of their cosmology, then liberal democracy becomes a system that does not de facto produce or provide a level playing field, as many of its intellectual defenders would have us believe. However, if one begins to place the development of liberal democracy within the context of other modes of knowing, one is forced to confront the unfreedom upon which liberal democracy's freedoms are articulated and canonized as normal. Once unfreedom is understood as an intimate and intricate element of liberal democracy, a different set of questions emerge for some of our contemporary discussions about multiculturalism.

. Debates such as the Danish cartoon controversy, the murder of Theo Van Gogh, and the wearing of the veil and other religious insignia in public places all point to the unfreedom that frames and underpins liberal democracy and is not an aberration to it. Liberal democracies are as much about structuring state-sanctioned unfreedoms as they are about providing reforms in relation to the constant evolution of the market and the population. Similarly, the controversies that have greeted Africans who have recently taken the treacherous trip across the strait to Spain, Italy, and Greece bring these ideas of modernity to the fore in terms of the global impact of unplanned migrations for the discourses and ideals of liberal democracies. The state policing of these migrants demonstrates quite clearly that liberal democracies are not fundamentally concerned with questions of freedom.

Let us take as an example the Dutch public intellectual, now based in the U.S., Ayaan Hirsi Ali. Hirsi Ali's work, including her collaborative film with Theo Van Gogh, *Submission*, and her two books, *The Caged Virgin* and the autobiography *Infidel,* provides us with a rich archive with which to think these problems through. The seductiveness of modernity's ideals is striking but at the same time it is clear that European modernity has only partially fulfilled its desire to realize all human potential. Ali's impact has more to do with progression, modernity's most easily recognizable trope, than with any specific insights she might offer on the threat that political Islam makes against the West. The narrative of progress is such a powerful and simultaneously commonsensical aspect of modernist discourse that it has become almost unmarked as a central tenet of the discourse. Ali inhabits it fully; it is indeed her *raison d'être.*

I am interested in Hirsi Ali because in Canada the same narrative of progress that animates her critique underpins the Canadian debate on the idea of multiculturalism. Hirsi Ali's critique mobilizes personal experience, as well as ideas of liberal democracy and its progressive narrative of freedoms through an engagement with questions of gender and religion, which translates well to the Canadian context. In fact, her argument on every count is that Islam is more fundamentalist than any other world religion. She writes in *The Caged Virgin* that "there are

Christians and Jews who raise their children in the belief that they are God's chosen people, but among Muslims the feeling that God has granted them special salvation goes further."[24] And she tells us that as she examined Islam she came to realize a number of elements:

> The first of these is that a Muslim's relationship with his God is one of fear. A Muslim's conception of God is absolute. Our God demands total submission. He rewards you if you follow His rules meticulously. He punishes you cruelly if you break His rules, both on earth, with illness and natural disasters, and in the hereafter, with hellfire.[25]

Hirsi Ali goes on to blame Islam's "backwardness" on tribal Arab history and values. Perhaps tellingly, the question of tribe and values also dominates the Canadian multiculturalism debate. Indeed, the question of tribe is central to my position. For what the postcolonial and the post-9/11 moments point to quite clearly is that the Euro-American tribe of whiteness is held together by an insistence that its view of the world is the only tenable view. That view has been instituted and perpetuated in coercive, violent, and non-coercive ways for over five hundred years. While many resistances have been mounted against its full institution, it has nonetheless triumphed in a fashion that exceeds its ongoing probability to maintain its hold and reach. Moreover, in moments of its potential demise, this tribal view has consistently been held together by all kinds of force. White anxiety works to bring into focus the networks necessary for holding the Euro-American tribal view of the world in place. The mounting articulation of different worldviews are mobilized as evidence that the Euro-American way is under siege. Thus, white anxiety also comes with a great deal of white paranoia.

Conclusion: We are all multicultural still

In her assessment of the Rodney King verdict in 1992, Judith Butler articulated the notion of white paranoia to make sense of why the jury would acquit in the case.[26] A similar condition is being expressed in the attacks on the idea of multiculturalism. These attacks reflect a desire to both hold on to the myth of Canada as a white nation-state and to simultaneously racially manage the necessary migrations for the perpetuation of late capitalism. Contrary to uncritical discourses that position rationality as fundamental to Euro-American political philosophy, white paranoia and anxiety operate in the fault lines of racial mythologies of "superior" and "inferior." They further impose an order on their own irrationality in terms of racial difference, while at the same time grappling with certain kinds of economic rationalities that complicate those ideational myths and practices. Stein et al.'s disgraceful and intellectually dishonest debate betrays the symptoms of white anxiety and paranoia not merely with "an empire that strikes back" – to use a phrase that helped to inaugurate the post-civil rights, postcolonial moment – but with an unruly empire that is everywhere and thus needs management.

If post-9/11 multiculturalism is now over, the problems of racism, colonialism, and Europe's global dominance remain firmly with us. On one hand, multiculturalism as state policy sought to put in place structures that would perpetuate various forms of dominance. On the other hand, the idea of multiculturalism sought to produce modes of being that might allow for a decolonial project of freedom. State multiculturalism was only meant to be a compromise on the way to producing different social relations and thus producing forms of humanity that might be radically different from those that European coloniality has bequeathed to us. Any debate that seeks to seriously engage the questions of multiculturalism must take seriously that the concept is deeply bound up in a European global domination that can only end if and when other ways of being are accorded the same conceptual and material expression as Europe's claims have been thus far.

2 Subjects of empire: Indigenous peoples and the "Politics of Recognition" in Canada

Glen S. Coulthard

OVER THE LAST THIRTY YEARS, the self-determination efforts and objectives of Indigenous peoples[1] in Canada have increasingly been cast in the language of "recognition." Consider, for example, the formative declaration issued by my community, the Dene Nation, in 1975:

> We the Dene of the NWT [Northwest Territories] insist on the right to be regarded by ourselves and the world as a nation.
>
> Our struggle is for the *recognition* of the Dene Nation by the Government and people of Canada and the peoples and governments of the world.[2]

Now fast-forward to the 2005 policy position on self-determination issued by Canada's largest Aboriginal organization, the Assembly of First Nations (AFN). According to the AFN, "a consensus has emerged . . . around a vision of the relationship between First Nations and Canada which would lead to strengthening recognition and implementation of First Nations' governments."[3] This "vision," the AFN goes on to state, expands on the core principles outlined in the 1996 *Report of the Royal Commission on Aboriginal Peoples* (RCAP): that is, recognition of the nation-to-nation relationship between First Nations and the Crown; recognition of the equal right of First Nations to self-determination; recognition of the Crown's fiduciary obligation to protect Aboriginal treaty rights; recognition of First Nations' inherent right to self-government; and recognition of the right of First Nations to economically benefit from the use of their lands and resources.[4] When considered from these perspectives, it would appear that recognition has emerged as the hegemonic expression of self-determination within the Indigenous rights movement in Canada.

The increase in recognition demands made by Indigenous and other marginalized minorities over the last three decades has prompted a surge of intellectual production which has sought to unpack the ethical, political, and legal significance of these types of claims. Influenced by Charles Taylor's catalytic 1992 essay, "The Politics of Recognition" much of this literature has focused on the relationship between the affirmative recognition of societal cultural differences on the one hand, and the freedom and well-being of marginalized individuals and groups living in ethnically diverse states on the other.[5] In Canada, it has been argued that this synthesis of theory and practice has forced the state to re-conceptualize the tenets of its relationship with Aboriginal peoples; whereas prior to 1969 federal Indian policy was unapologetically assimilationist, now it is couched in the vernacular of "mutual recognition."[6]

In this essay, I challenge the idea that the colonial relationship between Indigenous peoples and the Canadian state can be significantly transformed via a politics of recognition.[7] Following Richard Day, I take "politics of recognition" to refer to the now expansive range of recognition-based models of liberal pluralism that seek to reconcile Indigenous claims to nationhood with Crown sovereignty via the accommodation of Indigenous identities in some form of renewed relationship with the Canadian state.[8] Although these models vary in both theory and practice, most involve the delegation of land, capital, and political power from the state to Indigenous communities through land claims, economic development initiatives, and self-government processes. Against this position, I argue that, instead of ushering in an era of peaceful co-existence grounded on the Hegelian ideal of *reciprocity*, the politics of recognition in its contemporary form promises to reproduce the very configurations of colonial power that Indigenous peoples' demands for recognition have historically sought to transcend.

More specifically, through a sustained engagement with the work of anti-colonial theorist and psychiatrist Frantz Fanon, I hope to show that the reproduction of a colonial structure of dominance like Canada's rests on its ability to entice Indigenous peoples to come to *identify*, either implicitly or explicitly, with the profoundly *asymmetrical* and *non-reciprocal* forms of recognition either imposed on or granted to them by the colonial-state and society. Fanon first developed this insight in his 1952 text, *Black Skin, White Masks*, where he persuasively challenged the applicability of Hegel's dialectic of recognition, to colonial and racialized settings.[9] Against Hegel's abstraction, Fanon argued that, in *actual* contexts of domination (such as colonialism) not only are the terms of recognition usually determined by and in the interests of the master (the colonizer), but also that over time slave populations (the colonized) tend to develop what he called "psycho-affective" attachments to these master-sanctioned forms of recognition, and that this attachment is essential in maintaining the economic and political structure of master/slave (colonizer/colonized) relations themselves.[10] By the end of this essay it should be clear that the contemporary politics of recognition is ill-equipped to deal with the interrelated structural and psycho-affective dimensions of imperial power that Fanon implicated in the preservation of colonial hierarchies.

Recognition from Hegel's master-slave to Charles Taylor's "Politics of Recognition"

At its base, Hegel's master/slave narrative can be read in at least two ways that continue to inform contemporary recognition-based theories of liberal pluralism. In the first, Hegel's dialectic outlines a theory of identity-formation that cuts against the classical liberal view of the subject insofar as it situates social relations at the fore of human subjectivity. On this account, relations of recognition are deemed "constitutive of subjectivity: one becomes an individual subject only in virtue of recognizing, and being recognized by another subject."[11] This insight into the intersubjective nature of identity-formation underlies Hegel's often quoted assertion that "self-consciousness exists in and for itself when, and by the fact that, it so exists for another; that is, it exists only in being acknowledged."[12]

In the second reading, the dialectic moves beyond highlighting the relational nature of human subjectivity to elucidate what Hegel sees as the intersubjective conditions required for the *realization of human freedom*. From this perspective, the master/slave narrative can be read as a normative story in that it suggests that the realization of oneself as an essential, self-determining agent requires that one not only be recognized as self-determining, but that one be recognized by another self-consciousness that is also recognized as self-determining. It is through these reciprocal processes and exchanges of recognition that the condition of possibility for freedom emerges.[13] Hence Hegel's repeated insistence that relations of recognition be *mutual*. This point is driven home in the latter half of the Hegel's section on "Lordship and Bondage," in which he discusses the ironic fate of the master in a context of asymmetrical recognition. After the "life-and-death struggle" between the two self-consciousnesses temporarily cashes out in the hierarchical master-slave relationship, Hegel depicts a surprising turn of events in which the *master's* desire for recognition as an essential "being-for-itself" is thwarted by the fact that he or she is only recognized by the unessential and dependent consciousness of the slave – and, of course, recognition by a slave hardly constitutes recognition at all.[14] In this "onesided and unequal" relationship the master fails to gain certainty of "being-for-self as the truth of himself [or herself]. On the contrary, his [or her] truth is in reality the unessential consciousness and its unessential action."[15] Meanwhile, as the master continues to wallow in a lethargic state of increased dependency, the slave, through his or her transformative labour, "becomes conscious of what he [or she] truly is" and "*qua* worker" comes "to realize "his [or her] own independence."[16] Thus, the truth of one's independent consciousness and status as a self-determining actor is realized more through the praxis of the slave – through his or her transformative work in and on the world. However, for Hegel, "the revolution of the slave is not simply to replace the master while maintaining the unequal hierarchal recognition."[17] This, of course, would only temporarily invert the relation, and the slave would eventually meet the same fate as the master. Rather, as Robert Williams reminds us, Hegel's project was to move "*beyond* the patterns of domination [and] inequality" that typify asymmetrical relations of recognition. It is on this point that many contemporary theorists of recognition remain committed.[18]

Patchen Markell has recently suggested that one of the most significant differences between recognition in Hegel's master/slave narrative and the "politics of recognition" today is that state institutions play a fundamental role in mediating relations of recognition in the latter, but not the former.[19] For example, regarding policies aimed at preserving cultural diversity, Markell writes: "far from being simple face-to-face encounters between subjects, *à la* Hegel's stylized story in the *Phenomenology*," multiculturalism tends to "involve large-scale exchanges of recognition in which states typically play a crucial role."[20] Charles Taylor's "The Politics of Recognition" provides a case in point.[21] Drawing on the insights of Hegel, among others, Taylor mounts a sustained critique of what he claims to be the increasingly "impracticable" nature of "difference-blind" liberalism when applied to culturally diverse polities such as the United States and Canada.[22] Alternatively, Taylor defends a variant of liberal thought which posits that, under certain circumstances, culturally diverse states can indeed recognize and accommodate a range of group-specific claims without having to abandon their commitment to a core set of fundamental rights.[23] Furthermore, these types of claims can be defended on liberal grounds because it is within and against the horizon of one's cultural community that individuals come to develop their identities, and thus the capacity to make sense of their lives.[24] In short, for Taylor, our identities provide the "background against which our tastes and desires and opinions and aspirations make sense."[25] Without this orienting framework we would be unable to derive meaning from our lives – we would not know "who we are" or "where [we are] coming from."[26] We would be "at sea," as Taylor puts it elsewhere.[27]

Thus, much like Hegel before him, Taylor argues that human actors do not develop their identities in "isolation"; rather they are "formed" through "dialogue with others, in agreement or struggle with their recognition of us."[28] However, given that our identities are formed through these relations, it follows that they can also be significantly *de*formed when these processes run awry. This is what Taylor means when he asserts that identities are shaped not only by recognition, but also its *absence*:

> A person or a group of people can suffer real damage, real distortion, if the people or society around them mirror back to them a confining or demeaning or contemptible picture of themselves. Nonrecognition or misrecognition can inflict harm, can be a form of oppression, imprisoning one in a false, distorted, and reduced mode of being.[29]

This idea that asymmetrical relations of recognition can impede human freedom and flourishing by "imprisoning" someone in a distorted relation-to-self is asserted repeatedly in Taylor's essay. For instance, we are frequently told that disparaging forms of recognition can inflict "wounds" on their "victims," "saddling [them] with a crippling self-hatred";[30] or that withholding recognition can "inflict damage" on "those who are denied it."[31] And given that misrecognition has the capacity to "harm" others in this manner, it follows, according to Taylor, that it be considered "a form of oppression"[32] on par with "injustices" such as "inequality" and "exploitation."[33] For Taylor, recognition is elevated to the status of a "vital human need."[34]

The practical implications of Taylor's theory reveal themselves in his more prescriptive moments. For example, Taylor suggests that, in Canada, both Québécois and Indigenous peoples exemplify the types of threatened minorities that ought to be considered eligible for some form of recognition capable of accommodating their cultural distinctiveness. With respect to Indigenous peoples specifically, such recognition might require the delegation of political and cultural "autonomy"

to Native groups through the institutions of "self-government."[35] Elsewhere Taylor suggests that this delegation could entail "allowing for a
new form of jurisdiction in Canada, perhaps weaker than the provinces, but, unlike municipalities."[36] Accommodating the claims of First
Nations in this way would ideally allow Native communities to "preserve their cultural integrity," and thus help stave-off the psychological
disorientation and resultant unfreedom associated with exposure to
structured patterns of mis- or non-recognition.[37] Thus, in Taylor's construction, the institutionalization of a liberal regime of reciprocal recognition would better enable Indigenous peoples to realize their status as
distinct and self-determining actors.

While it is true that the normative dimension of Taylor's project
represents a marked improvement over Canada's "past tactics of exclusion, genocide, and assimilation," the logic undergirding this dimension
– where "recognition" is conceived as something that is ultimately
"granted" or "accorded" to a subaltern group or entity by a dominant
group or entity – prefigures its failure to significantly modify, let alone
transcend, the breadth of power at play in colonial relationships.[38]
Indeed, Fanon, on whose work Taylor relies to delineate the relationship between misrecognition and the forms of unfreedom and subjection discussed above, anticipated this failure over fifty years ago.

Frantz Fanon and the problem of recognition in colonial contexts

In the second half of "The Politics of Recognition," Taylor identifies
Fanon's classic 1961 treatise on decolonization, *The Wretched of the
Earth,* as one of the first texts to elicit the role that misrecognition plays
in propping up relations of domination.[39] Fanon's analysis in *The
Wretched* is also used to support one of the central political arguments
in Taylor's analysis, namely, his call for the cultural recognition of sub-
state groups that have suffered at the hands of a hegemonic political
power. Although Taylor acknowledges that Fanon advocated "violent"
struggle as the primary means of overcoming the "psycho-existential"
complexes instilled in colonial subjects by misrecognition, he nonetheless insists that Fanon's argument is applicable to contemporary debates
surrounding the "politics of difference" more generally.[40] Below I want
to challenge Taylor's use of Fanon in this context: not by disputing
Taylor's assertion that Fanon's work constitutes an important theoriza-
tion of the ways in which the subjectivities of the oppressed can be
deformed by mis- or non-recognition, but rather by contesting his

assumption that a more accommodating, liberal regime of mutual recognition might be capable of addressing the types of relations typical of those between Indigenous peoples and settler-states. Presciently, Fanon posed a similar challenge in his earlier work, *Black Skin, White Masks* (*BSWM*).

Fanon's concern with the relationship between human freedom and equality in relations of recognition is a central and reccurring theme in *BSWM* – the site of Fanon's convincing argument that the long-term stability of a colonial system of governance relies as much on the "internalization" of the forms of racist recognition imposed or bestowed on the Indigenous population by the colonial state and society as it does on brute force.[41] In this sense, the longevity of a colonial social formation also depends on its capacity to transform the colonized population into *subjects* of imperial rule. Here Fanon anticipates the well-known work of Louis Althusser, who would later argue that the recapitulation of capitalist relations of production rests on the "recognition function" of ideology, namely, the ability of a state's "ideological apparatus" to "interpellate" individuals as subjects of class rule.[42] Fanon's colonialism operates in a similarly dual-structured manner: it includes "not only the interrelations of *objective* historical conditions but also human *attitudes* to these conditions."[43] For Fanon, the interplay between the structural/objective and recognitive/subjective realms of colonialism was what ensured the hegemony over time.

On the subjective front, *BSWM* painstakingly outlines the myriad ways in which "attitudes" conducive to colonial rule are cultivated amongst the colonized through the unequal exchange of institutionalized and interpersonal patterns of recognition between the colonial society and the Indigenous population. Fanon reveals how, over time, colonized populations tend to internalize the derogatory images imposed on them by their colonial "masters," and how as a result, these images, along with the structural relations with which they are entwined, come to be recognized (or at least endured) as more or less natural. This last point is made agonizingly clear in arguably the most famous passage from *BSWM*, where Fanon shares an alienating encounter on the streets of Paris with a little white child. "Look, a Negro!" Fanon recalled the girl saying, "Moma, see the Negro! I'm frightened! frightened!"[44] At that moment, the imposition of the child's racist gaze "sealed" Fanon into a "crushing objecthood," fixing him like "a chemical solution is fixed by a dye."[45] He found himself temporarily *accepting* that he was indeed the subject of the child's call: "It was true, it amused me," thought Fanon.[46] But then "I subjected

myself to an objective examination, I discovered my blackness, my ethnic characteristics; and I was battered down by tom-toms, cannibalism,
intellectual deficiency, fetishism, racial defects."[47] Far from assuring
Fanon's humanity, the other's recognition imprisoned him in an exter-
nally determined and devalued conception of himself. Instead of being
acknowledged as a "man among men," he was reduced to "an object
[among] other objects."[48]

Without further consideration, Fanon's insights into the ultimately
subjectifying nature of colonial recognition appear to square nicely
with Taylor's work. For example, although Fanon never uses the term
himself, he seems to describe the debilitating effects associated with
*mis*recognition in the sense that Taylor uses the term. In fact, *BSWM* is
littered with passages that illustrate the innumerable ways in which the
imposition of the settler's gaze can inflict damage on the Indigenous
society at both the individual and collective levels. Even with this being
the case, however, a close reading of *BSWM* renders problematic Taylor's approach in several interrelated and crucial respects.

The first is Taylor's failure to adequately confront the structural
duality of colonialism itself. Fanon insisted, for example, that a colonial
configuration of power could be transformed only if attacked at both
levels of operation: the objective and the subjective.[49] This point is
made at the outset of *BSWM* and reverberates throughout Fanon's
work. In his introduction to *BSWM*, Fanon makes clear that although
he explores the "psychological" terrain of colonialism, he would not
decouple his discussion from a structural/material analysis of colonial
power. Indeed, Fanon claimed that there "will be an authentic disalienation" of the colonized subject "only to the degree to which things, in
the most materialistic meaning of the word, [are] restored to their
proper places."[50] Hence the term "sociodiagnostic" for Fanon's project:
"if there is an inferiority complex, it is the outcome of a double
process . . . primarily economic; [and] subsequently the internalization
. . . of his [or her] inferiority."[51] Fanon correctly situated colonial–capitalist exploitation and domination alongside misrecognition and alienation as foundational sources of colonial injustice. "The Negro
problem," wrote Fanon, "does not resolve itself into the problem of
Negroes living among white men [sic] but rather of Negroes being
exploited, enslaved, despised by a colonialist, capitalist society that is
only accidentally white."[52]

Fanon was enough of a Marxist to understand the role that the capitalist economy plays in overdetermining hierarchical relations of recognition. However, he was also much more perceptive than many Marxists

in his insistence that both the subjective realm of colonialism and the socio-economic structure be the targets of strategic transformation. The colonized person "must wage war on both levels," insisted Fanon. "Since historically they influence each other, any unilateral liberation is incomplete, and the gravest mistake would be to believe in their automatic interdependence."[53] Attacking colonial power on one front, in other words, would not guarantee the subversion of its effects on the other. "This is why a Marxist analysis should always be slightly stretched when it comes to addressing the colonial issue," Fanon would later write in *The Wretched*.[54] This "stretching" of the Marxist paradigm constitutes one of the most innovative contributions to classical Marxist debates on ideology. In Fanon's work, not only is the relationship between base and superstructure posited as both interdependent and semi-autonomous, but more significantly, those axes of domination historically relegated in Marxism to the superstructural realm – such as racism and the effects it has on those subject to it – are attributed a substantive capacity to structure the character of social relations.

Recently a number of scholars have taken aim at the contribution of recognition theorists like Taylor on analogous grounds: that their work offers little insight into how to address the more overtly structural and/or economic features of social oppression.[55] Moreover, this lack of insight has been charged with contributing to a shift in the terrain of contemporary political thought and practice more generally – from "redistribution to recognition," to use Nancy Fraser's formulation.[56] According to Fraser, whereas proponents of redistribution highlight and confront injustices in the economic sphere, advocates of the newer "politics of recognition" focus on and attack injustices in the cultural realm.[57] On the redistribution front, proposed remedies for injustice range between "affirmative" strategies, like the administration of welfare, to more "transformative" methods, like the transformation of the capitalist mode of production itself. In contrast, strategies aimed at injustices associated with misrecognition tend to focus on "cultural and symbolic change."[58] Again, this could involve "affirmative" approaches, such as the recognition and reaffirmation of previously disparaged identities, or these strategies could adopt a more "transformative" form, such as the "deconstruction" of dominant "patterns of representation" in ways that would "change everyone's social identities."[59]

Fanon's work, which anticipates the recognition/redistribution debate by half a century, highlights several key shortcomings in the approaches of both Taylor and Fraser. Taylor's approach is insufficient insofar as it tends to, at best, address the political economy of colonialism in a strictly "affirmative" manner, that is, through reformist state redistribution schemes such as granting certain cultural rights and concessions to Aboriginal communities via self-government and land claims processes. Although this approach may alter the intensity of some effects of colonial-capitalist exploitation and domination, it does little to address their generative structures – in this case, a racially stratified capitalist economy and the colonial state. At his weakest, Taylor focuses too much on the recognition end of the spectrum, and as a result leaves uninterrogated the deeply rooted economic structures of oppression. Richard Day has framed the problem this way: "although Taylor's recognition model allows for diversity of culture within a particular state by admitting the possibility of multiple national identifications," it is less "permissive with regard to polity and economy . . . in assuming that any subaltern group that is granted [recognition] will thereby acquire a *subordinate* articulation with a *capitalist state*."[60] From this angle, Taylor's theory leaves one of the two operative levels of colonial power identified by Fanon untouched.

This line of criticism is well worn and can be traced back to at least the early work of Marx. As such, it is not surprising that Taylor's variant of liberalism *as liberalism* fails to confront the structural/economic aspects of colonialism at its generative roots. This shortcoming in Taylor's approach is particularly surprising, however, given that, although many Indigenous leaders and communities today tend to instrumentally couch their claims in reformist terms, this has not always the case: historically, Indigenous demands for *cultural recognition* have often been expressed in ways that have explicitly called into question the dominating nature of capitalist social relations and the state-form.[61] The same can be said of a growing number of today's most prominent Indigenous scholars and activists.[62] Mohawk political scientist Taiaiake Alfred, for example, has repeatedly argued that the goal of any traditionally rooted self-determination struggle ought to be to protect that which constitutes the "heart and soul of [I]ndigenous nations: a set of values that challenge the homogenizing force of Western liberalism and free-market capitalism; that honour the autonomy of individual conscience, non-coercive authority, and the deep interconnection between human beings and other elements of creation."[63] For Alfred, this vision is not only embodied in the practical philosophies and ethical systems of many North American Indigenous societies, but also flows from a "realization that capitalist economics and liberal delusions of progress" have historically served as the "engines of colonial aggression and injustice" itself.[64] Taylor's approach, then, oriented as it is around dialogue and listening, ought to be more sensitive to the claims and challenges emanating from these dissenting Indigenous voices.

However, if Taylor pays insufficient attention to the structural/economic realm of domination, then Fraser does so from the opposite angle. In order to avoid what she sees as the pitfalls associated with the politics of recognition's latent essentialism and displacement of questions of distributive justice, Fraser proposes a means of integrating struggles for recognition with those of redistribution without subordinating one to the other. To this end, she suggests that instead of understanding recognition as the revaluation of cultural or group-specific identity, and misrecognition as the disparagement of such identity and its consequent effects on the subjectivities of minorities, recognition and misrecognition should be conceived of in terms of the "institutionalized patterns of value" that affect one's ability to participate *as a peer* in social life. "To view recognition" in this manner, writes Fraser, "is to treat it as an issue of *social status.*"[65]

Although Fraser's status model allows her to curtail some of the problems she attributes to identity politics, it does so at the expense of addressing one of the most pertinent features of injustices related to mis- or non-recognition. If many of today's most volatile political conflicts *do* include subjective/psychological dimensions to them in the way that Fraser admits (and Taylor and Fanon describe), then her approach, which attempts to eschew a direct engagement with this aspect of social oppression, risks leaving an important contributing dynamic to identity-related forms of domination unchecked. By avoiding this "psychologizing" tendency within the politics of recognition, Fraser locates what is wrong with misrecognition in "social relations" and not in "individual or interpersonal psychology."[66] This is preferable, we are told, because when misrecognition "is identified with internal distortions in the structure of the consciousness of the oppressed, it is but a short step to blaming the victim."[67] However, according to Fanon, this does not have to be the case. Fanon was unambiguous with respect to locating the cause of the "inferiority complex" of colonized subjects in the colonial social structure.[68] The problem, however, is that any psychological problems that ensue, although socially constituted, can take on a life of their own, and thus need to be dealt with independently and in accordance with their own specific logics. Fanon insisted that a change in the social structure would not guarantee a change in the subjectivities of the oppressed. Stated simply, if Fanon's insight into the interdependent yet semi-autonomous nature of the two facets of colonial power is correct, then dumping all our efforts into alleviating the institutional/ structural impediments to participatory parity (whether redistributive or recognitive) may not do anything to undercut the debilitating forms of unfreedom related to misrecognition in the traditional sense.

This brings us to the second key problem with Taylor's theory when applied to colonial contexts. I have already suggested that Taylor's liberal-recognition approach is incapable of curbing the damages wrought within and against Indigenous communities by the structures of state and capital, but what about his theory of recognition? Does it suffer the same fate vis-à-vis the forms of power that it seeks to undercut? As I have noted, underlying Taylor's theory is the assumption that the flourishing of Indigenous peoples as distinct and self-determining entities is dependent on their being afforded cultural recognition and institutional accommodation by the surrounding state. What makes this approach both so intriguing and so problematic, however, is that Fanon, who Taylor uses to make his case, argued specifically against a similar presumption in the penultimate chapter of *BSWM*. Moreover, like Taylor, Fanon did so with reference to Hegel's master/slave parable. In his work, Fanon argued that the dialectical progression to reciprocity in relations of recognition is frequently undermined in the colonial setting by the fact that, unlike the subjugated slave in Hegel's *Phenomenology*, many colonized societies no longer have to *struggle* for their freedom and independence. It is often negotiated, achieved through constitutional amendment, or simply "declared" by the settler–state and bestowed upon the Indigenous population in the form of political rights. Whatever the method, in these circumstances the colonized, "steeped in the inessentiality of servitude" are *"set free by [the] master."*[69] "One day the White Master, *without conflict*, recognize[s] the Negro slave."[70] As such the colonized subjects do not have to lay down their lives to *prove* their "certainty of being" in the way that Hegel insisted.[71] The "upheaval" of formal freedom and independence thus reaches the colonized "from without":

> The black man [sic] [is] acted upon. Values that [are] not . . . created by his actions, values that [are] not . . . born of the systolic tide of his blood, [dance] in a hued whirl around him. The upheaval [does] not make a difference in the Negro. He [goes] from one way of life to another, but not from one life to another.[72]

A number of important issues underlie Fanon's concern here. The first involves the relationship that he draws between struggle and the disalienation of the colonized subject. Simply stated, for Fanon struggle and conflict (and for the later Fanon, *violent* struggle and conflict) are the means through which imperial subjects come to rid themselves of the "arsenal of complexes" driven into the core of their being through the colonial process.[73] Thus, struggle – or *transformative praxis* – is the mediating force through which the colonized come to shed their colonial identities and are restored to their "proper place."[74] When recognition is conferred without struggle or conflict, this fundamental self-transformation – or as Lou Turner has put it, this "inner differentiation" at the level of the colonized's being – cannot occur, thus foreclosing the realization of authentic freedom.[75] Hence Fanon's claim that the colonized simply go from "one way of life to another, but not from one life to another"; the structure of domination changes, but the subjectivity of the colonized remains the same – they become "emancipated slaves."[76]

The second important point is that when Fanon speaks of a lack of struggle in the decolonization movements of his day, he does not mean to suggest that the colonized in these contexts were simply passive recipients of colonial practices. He readily admits that "from time to time" the colonized may indeed fight "for Liberty and Justice."[77] However, when this battle is carried out in a manner that does not pose a foundational challenge to the background structures of colonial power as such – which, for Fanon, will always invoke struggle and conflict – then the best the colonized can hope for is "white liberty and white justice; that is, values secreted by [their] masters."[78] Without conflict and struggle, the terms of recognition remain in the possession of the powerful to bestow on their "inferiors" in ways that they deem appropriate.[79] Note the double level of subjection here: without transformative struggle constituting an integral aspect of decolonization, the Indigenous population will not only remain subjects of imperial rule insofar as they have not gone through a process of purging the psycho-existential complexes battered into them by the colonial experience – a process of strategic *desubjectification* – but they will also remain so in that the Indigenous society will come to see the structurally limited and constrained recognition conferred on them by their colonial "masters" *as their own*. In effect they will begin to *identify* with "white liberty and white justice."[80] As Fanon puts it in *The Wretched*, these values eventually "seep" into the colonized and subtly structure and limit the realm of possibility of their freedom.[81] Either way, for Fanon, the colonized will have failed to reestablish themselves as truly self-determining: that is, as the creators of the terms and values by which they are to be recognized.[82]

This leads to my third and final problem with Taylor's politics of recognition: the misguided sociological assumption that undergirds his appropriation of Hegel's notion of mutual recognition. As I have noted, at the heart of Hegel's master/slave dialectic is the idea that both parties engaged in the struggle for recognition are dependent on the other's acknowledgment for their freedom and self-worth. Moreover, Hegel asserts that this dependency is even more crucial for the master in the relationship, for unlike the slave, he or she is unable to achieve independence and objective self-certainty through the object of his or her own labour. Mutual dependency is thus the background condition that ensures the dialectic progress towards reciprocity. This is why Taylor claims, with reference to Hegel, that "the struggle for recognition can only find *one satisfactory solution, and that is a regime of reciprocal recognition among equals.*"[83] However, as Fanon reminds us, the problem with this formulation is that when it is applied to actual struggles for recognition between hegemonic and subaltern communities, the mutual character of dependency rarely exists. In a lengthy footnote in *BSWM*, Fanon observes how the colonial master differs from the master depicted in Hegel's *Phenomenology*. "For Hegel there is reciprocity," but in the colonies "the master laughs at the consciousness of the slave. What he wants from the slave is *not recognition but work.*"[84] This is one of the most crucial passages in *BSWM* for it outlines in precise terms what is wrong with the recognition paradigm when abstracted from the face-to-face encounter in Hegel's dialectic and applied to the colonial environment. Although the issue is an obvious one, it has nonetheless been critically overlooked in the contemporary recognition literature: in relations of domination that exist between nation-states and the sub-state national groups that they "incorporate" into their territorial and jurisdictional boundaries, there is no mutual dependency in terms of a need or desire for recognition.[85] In these contexts, the "master" – that is, the colonial state and state society – does not require recognition from the previously self-determining communities upon which its territorial, economic, and social infrastructure is constituted. What it needs is land, labour, and resources.[86] Thus, rather than leading to a condition of reciprocity, the dialectic either breaks down with the explicit *non*-recognition of the equal status of the colonized population, or with the strategic "domestication" of the terms of recognition in such a way that the foundation of the colonial relationship remains relatively undisturbed.[87]

Anyone familiar with the power dynamics that structure the Aboriginal rights movement in Canada should immediately see the applicability of Fanon's insights here. Indeed, one need not expend much effort to elicit the countless ways in which the liberal discourse of recognition has been limited and constrained by the state, the courts, corporate interests, and policymakers so as to help preserve the colonial status quo. With respect to the law, for example, over the last thirty years the Supreme Court of Canada has consistently refused to recognize Aboriginal peoples' equal and self-determining status. This refusal has been based on the Court's adherence to legal precedent founded on the white supremacist myth that Indigenous societies were too primitive to bear political rights when they first encountered European powers.[88] Thus, even though the Court has secured an unprecedented degree of protection for certain "cultural" practices within the state, it has nonetheless repeatedly refused to challenge the racist origin of Canada's assumed sovereignty over Indigenous peoples and their territories.

The political and economic ramifications of the Court's actions have been clear-cut. *Delgamuukw v. British Columbia* declared that any residual Aboriginal rights that may have survived the unilateral assertion of Crown sovereignty could be infringed upon by the federal and provincial governments so long as this action could be shown to further "a compelling and substantial legislative objective" that is "consistent with the special fiduciary relationship between the Crown and the [A]boriginal peoples."[89] What "substantial objectives" might justify infringement? According to the Court, virtually any exploitative economic venture, including "the development of agriculture, forestry, mining, and hydroelectric power, the general economic development of the interior of British Columbia, protection of the environment or endangered species and the building of infrastructure and the settlement of foreign populations to support those aims."[90] So today it appears, much as it did in Fanon's day, that colonial powers will only recognize the collective rights and identities of Indigenous peoples insofar as this recognition does not throw into question the legal, political and economic framework of the colonial relationship itself.[91]

The above examples confirm only one aspect of Fanon's insight into the problem of recognition in colonial contexts: namely, the limitations that this approach encounters when pitted against these overt structural expressions of domination. Can the same be said about the subjective or psycho-affective features of colonial power?

With respect to the forms of racist recognition driven into the psyches of Indigenous peoples through the institutions of the state, church, schools, media, and by intolerant individuals within the dominant soci-

ety, the answer is clearly yes. Countless studies, novels, and autobio-
graphical narratives have outlined, in painful detail, how these
expressions have saddled individuals with low self-esteem, depression,
alcohol and drug abuse, and violent behaviors directed both inward
against the self and outwards toward others.[92]

Similarly convincing arguments have been made concerning the
limited forms of recognition and accommodation offered to Indigenous
communities through the law, self-government packages, land claims,
and economic development initiatives. The recent work of Isabel
Altamirano-Jimenez, Taiaiake Alfred, and Paul Nadasdy, for example,
have all demonstrated how the state-dominated institutional and discursive fields within and against which Indigenous demands for recognition are made and adjudicated can subtly shape the subjectivities of the
Indigenous claimants involved.[93] Significantly, these fields are by no
means neutral: they are profoundly hierarchical and power-laden, and
as such have the ability to asymmetrically determine how Indigenous
subjects think and act not only in relation to the topic at hand (the
recognition claim), but also to themselves and to others. Thus, Alfred,
echoing Fanon, suggests that the dominance of the legal approach to
self-determination has, over time, helped produce a class of Aboriginal
"citizens" whose rights and identities have become defined solely in
relation to the colonial state and its legal apparatus. Similarly, strategies
that have sought self-determination via mainstream economic development have facilitated the creation of new elite Aboriginal capitalists
whose thirst for profit has come to outweigh their ancestral obligations
to the land and to others. Moreover, land claims processes, which are
couched almost exclusively in the language of property, are now threatening to produce a new breed of Aboriginal property owner, whose
territories, and by extension very identity, risk becoming subject to
expropriation and alienation.[94] For Alfred, all of these approaches, even
when carried out by sincere and well-intentioned individuals, threaten
to erode the most traditionally egalitarian aspects of Indigenous ethical
systems, ways of life, and forms of social organization.

Self-recognition and anti-colonial empowerment

The argument that I have sketched to this point is bleak in its implications. Indeed, left as is, recognition appears to inevitably lead to subjection, and as such, much of what Indigenous peoples have sought over
the last thirty years to secure their freedom has, in practice, cunningly
assured its opposite. In this sense, my argument may seem to adhere to

an "outdated" conception of power, one that postcolonial critics, often reacting against Fanon and others, have worked so diligently to refute. The implication of this view is that Indigenous subjects are *always* being interpellated by recognition, being constructed by colonial discourse, or being assimilated by imperial power structures.[95] As a result, resistance to this totalizing power is often seen as an inherently reactionary, zero-sum project. To the charge that Fanon himself seems to have espoused this totalizing view of colonial power, scholars have suggested that he was unable to escape the Manichean logic so essential in propping up relations of colonial domination to begin with.[96]

I want to rescue Fanon, at least partially, from this indictment. However, to assess the degree to which Fanon anticipates and accounts for this general line of criticism, we must first unpack his theory of anti-colonial agency and empowerment.

As I have argued, Fanon did not attribute much emancipatory potential to Hegel's politics of recognition in the colonial arena. Yet this is not to say that he rejected the recognition paradigm entirely. Like Hegel and Taylor, Fanon subscribed to the notion that relations of recognition are constitutive of subjectivity and that, when unequal, they can foreclose the realization of human freedom. On the latter point, however, he was deeply skeptical as to whether the mutuality that Hegel envisioned was achievable under contemporary colonialism. But if Fanon did not see freedom as naturally emanating from the slave being granted recognition from his or her master, where, if at all, did it originate?

In effect, Fanon believed that the road to self-determination instead lay in a quasi-Nietzschean form of personal and collective *self*-affirmation.[97] Rather than remaining dependent on their oppressors for their freedom and self-worth, Fanon argued that the colonized must struggle to critically reclaim and revaluate the worth of *their own* histories, traditions, and cultures against the subjectifying gaze and assimilative lure of colonial recognition. According to Fanon, this self-initiated process is what "triggers a change of fundamental importance in the colonized's psycho-affective equilibrium."[98] The colonized must initiate the process of decolonization by recognizing *themselves* as free, dignified, and distinct contributors to humanity.[99] Interestingly, Fanon equated this self-affirming process with the praxis of the slave in Hegel's *Phenomenology*, which he saw as illustrative of the necessity for the oppressed to "turn away" from their master-dependency, and to instead strive for freedom on their own terms and in accordance with their own values.[100] This is also why Fanon, although critical of the latent essentialism undergirding the work of the négritude poets, nonetheless saw their project as necessary.[101] Fanon understood that the individual and collective revaluation of black identity at the heart of projects such as the négritude movement served as a source of pride and empowerment, and helped jolt the colonized into an "actional" existence, as opposed to the "reactional" one characterized by *ressentiment*.[102] As Robert Young has argued, this process of critical self-affirmation led to the development of a "distinctive postcolonial epistemology and ontology" which enabled the colonized to begin to conceive of and construct radical alternatives to the colonial project itself.[103]

Thus, Fanon's call in *BSWM* for a simultaneous turn inward and away from the master, far from espousing a rigidly binaristic, Manichean view of power relations, instead reflects a profound understanding of the complexity involved in contests over recognition in colonial and racialized environments. Where Hegel's life-and-death struggle occurred between only two opposing forces, Fanon's colonial encounter was multidimensional, adding a racial/cultural aspect to the dialectic. He thereby underscored the multifarious web of recognition relations at work in constructing identities and establishing (or undermining) the conditions necessary for human freedom and flourishing. Fanon showed that the power dynamics in which identities are formed and deformed were nothing like the simplistic hegemon/subaltern binary depicted by Hegel. In an anticipatory way, then, Fanon challenged the negative and all-subjectifying view of interpellation that would plague Althusser's recognitive theory of ideology more than a decade later. For Althusser, the process of interpellation always took the form of "a fundamental misrecognition"[104] that served to produce within individuals the "specific characteristics and desires that commit them to the very actions that are required of them by their [subordinate] class position."[105] Fanon's innovation was that he showed how similar recognitive processes worked to "call forth" and empower individuals within communities of resistance.[106]

This is not to say that Fanon completely escaped the "Manicheism delerium" that he himself was so astute at diagnosing.[107] Those familiar with the legacy of Fanon's later work, for example, know that the "actional" existence that he saw self-recognition initiating ·in *BSWM* would in *The Wretched* take the form of a direct and violent engagement with the colonial society and its institutional structure. "At the very moment [the colonized come to] discover their humanity," he wrote, "they must "begin to sharpen their weapons *to secure its victory*."[108] In Fanon's later work, violence would come to serve as a

"kind of psychotherapy of the oppressed," offering "a primary form of
agency through which the subject moves from non-being to being,
from object to subject."[109] In this sense, the act of revolutionary violence, rather than the affirmative recognition of the other, offered the
most effective means to transform the subjectivities of the colonized, as
well as to topple the social structure that produced colonized subjects
to begin with. Violence provided "the means and the end" of decolonization.[110]

Conclusion

In the end, Fanon appears to have overstated the "cleansing" value he
attributed to anti-colonial violence.[111] Indeed, many Algerians have yet
to fully recover from the legacy of the eight years of carnage that constituted Algeria's war of independence with France. Nor was the Front
de Libération Nationale's (FLN) revolutionary seizure of the Algerian
state apparatus enough to stave off what Fanon would call "the curse of
[national] independence": namely, the subjection of the newly "liber-
ated" people and territories to the tyranny of the market and a post-
independence class of bourgeois national elites.[112] But if Fanon was
ultimately mistaken regarding violence being the "perfect mediation"
through which the colonized come to liberate themselves from both
the structural and psycho-affective features of colonial domination that
he identified so masterfully, then what is the relevance of his work
today?[113] To quote Homi Bhabha, is Fanon's contribution to anti-colonial thought and practice "lost in a time warp"?

I hope I have shown here that it is not. Fanon's insights into the
subjectifying nature of colonial recognition are as applicable today to
the liberal "politics of recognition" as they were when he first formulated his critique of Hegel's master-slave relation. Moreover, his dual-
structured conception of colonial power still captures the subtle (and
not so subtle) ways in which a system of imperial domination that does
not sustain itself exclusively by force is reproduced over time. Taiaiake
Alfred has recently asserted that under these "post-modern" imperial
conditions "opression has become increasingly invisible; [it is] no
longer constituted in conventional terms of military occupation, oner-
ous taxation burdens, blatant land thefts, etc.," but rather through a
"fluid confluence of politics, economics, psychology and culture."[114] If
the dispersal and effects of colonial and state power are now so diffuse,
how is one to transform or resist them? Here, Fanon's earlier work
remains key. In that all-important footnote in *BSWM* where Fanon

showed how the condition of the slave in the *Phenomenology* differed
from those in the colonies, he suggested that Hegel provided a partial
answer: that those struggling against colonialism must "turn away"
from the colonial state and society and find in their own *transformative
praxis* the source of their liberation.[115] In today's context, this process
will and must continue to involve some form of critical individual and
collective *self*-recognition on the part of Indigenous societies, not only
in an instrumental sense as Fanon seemed to have envisioned, but with
the understanding that our cultures have much to teach the Western
world about the establishment of profoundly non-imperialist relationships within and between peoples and the natural. Also, the empowerment that is derived from this critically self-affirmative and self-
transformative process of desubjectification must be cautiously directed
away from the assimilative lure of statist politics of recognition, and
instead be fashioned toward our own on-the-ground practices of freedom. As the feminist, anti-racist theorist bell hooks explains, such a
project would minimally require that we stop being so preoccupied
with looking "to that Other for recognition"; instead we should be
"recognizing ourselves and [then seeking to] make contact with all
who would engage us in a constructive manner."[116] In Canada, the
strategies and tactics adopted by a growing number of today's Indigenous activists – in reserve settings such as Grassy Narrows and Six
Nations, or in the urban centres of Vancouver, Winnipeg, and Toronto
– have begun to explore the emancipatory potential of this type of politics: a politics that is less oriented around attaining an affirmative form
of recognition from the settler-state and society, and more about critically revaluating, reconstructing, and redeploying culture and tradition
in ways that seek to prefigure a radical alternative to the structural and
psycho-affective facets of colonial domination.[117]

3   For a multicultural, multi-faith, multiracial Canada: A manifesto

George Elliott Clarke

THIS IS NOT A THEORETICAL ARGUMENT, for so many other scholars are better equipped than I to diagnose the failures of federal and provincial multiculturalism policies, and to dissect these racialist and exclusivist and mainstream-enhancing proclivities. I know that I cannot survey all the recherché philosophical and socio-political discourses on multiculturalism, which are increasing exponentially because Canada (due to its continued obeisance to our largest trading partner and its military reaction to the Islamicist guerilla attacks on New York City, N.Y., and Washington, D.C., of September 11, 2001), has increased scrutiny of Arab Canadians, Muslims, and all brown-skinned and dark-skinned Canadians, and, simultaneously, has wondered, openly, about the value of tolerance and the worth of diversity.

Yes, I have written in defence of multiculturalism in recent years. Indeed, despite the welter of books and Royal Commissions and op-ed pieces opposing multiculturalism, I feel that my admittedly simplistic affirmations still hold: 1) the promulgation of official multiculturalism in 1971 marked the first occasion that the Government of Canada recognized – *positively* – that peoples not primarily Anglo-Saxon, Celtic, Gallic, "Caucasian" (i.e., white), or Aboriginal or Métis were also Canadian; 2) this recognition implied, again for the first time, that the Government of Canada had a relationship, not just to regions and provinces, but to actually existing (Canadian) ethnicities; 3) whatever the electoral possibilities that political parties sought to exploit by doling out grants and favours, it is still true that the first anthologies of literature by racialized and so-called ethnic minorities (and several of the first books) were assembled by intellectuals who took the state's money – which was also their community's money – and used it to commence a conversation that has immeasurably enriched Canadian literature; and

4) the appearance of art and intellectual work by racialized and ethnic minorities has also permitted, from time to time, here and there, the construction of potent coalitions, either in fact, or in terms of influence, allowing for dramatic instances of cross-fertilization and new ways of articulating identity and being.

True, I am impatient with both leftist and rightist critiques of multiculturalism. For the Left, the policy just whitewashes racism and upholds the status quo (white supremacy with a smile); for the Right, it dyes *pure laine* Canadian values – British or French – in the too-bright colours of too many (violent and vicious) "foreigners," untutored in the humanitarian virtues and intellectual excellence that is Western civilization, especially as represented by Anglophones. I think leftist critics are right in their anti-state condemnation of multiculturalism, but wrong to not see how popular groups – everyday Canadians – make multiculturalism work for them in their neighbourhoods, schools, and other public spaces (as well as in intercultural marriages and homes). I think rightist critics are simply wrong, particularly when they blather about "Canadian values" everyone is supposed to uphold: what, pray tell, are these values, beyond those articulated in the Charter of Rights and Freedoms?

But I am verging on becoming theoretical. Thus, I will turn to the first example of multicultural politics – the Constitution of Canada – and propose several practical amendments that, I hope, will bring us closer to realizing the worthwhile dream of establishing a veritable multiracial, multicultural, and multi-faith Canada.

I. Indigenize the monarchy

The Constitution Act, 1867, Section 3, Clause 9, reads: "The Executive Government and Authority of and over Canada is hereby declared to continue and be vested in the Queen." I am no constitutional expert, but it would appear that the "Queen" referenced here would be the reigning monarch at the time, namely, Queen Victoria. Presumably however, via the force of this declaration, her heirs and descendants have continued to exercise sovereign authority over Canada, down to Queen Elizabeth II today, and to do so legitimately. But there is an inconsistency here, in that the Charter of Rights and Freedoms, in Section 27, holds that "this Charter shall be interpreted in a manner consistent with the preservation and enhancement of the multicultural heritage of Canadians." If what is good for the Charter is good for the entire Constitution Act, then I fail to see how the maintenance of an overseas-based monarchy, connected to one ethnic group and to one religion, preserves and enhances the "multicultural heritage of Canada." Rather, should we choose to retain the monarchy, it should be made Canadian and absolutely not ethnocentric. Indeed, the current system, in effect a monopoly on sovereign power for one ethnicity, must end. I personally believe that the monarchy should be restructured to allow for a selection, by public lottery, of our Head of State, to serve ceremonially for ten years. He and/or she and his or her immediate family would be replaced every ten years. (I trust that the fundamental democracy of a lottery system would allow for people of various ethnicities to serve as our "Royal Family" over time.)

II. Enforce civil (human) rights and affirmative action programs

Under Section 92, Clause 13, of the Constitution Act, 1867, provincial legislatures in Canada are primarily responsible for "Property and Civil Rights" as well as for, under Clause 16, "generally all matters of a merely local or private nature in the province." I interpret the interrelationship of these two clauses as providing for, or rather, demanding, that provincial governments must establish and, where they already exist, enforce human rights codes, including egalitarian access to employment. This point is supported by the Charter of Rights and Freedoms which expressly protects, in Section 15, Clause 2.1, "any law, program or activity that has as its object the amelioration in a province of conditions of individuals or groups including those that are disadvantaged because of race, national or ethnic origin, colour, religion, sex, age or mental or physical disability." In recent years, "affirmative action" has been replaced by the phrase, "employment equity," and, worse, reactionary governments have bid the public to consider such programs as "unfair." (I name here the Mike Harris-led Government of Ontario between 1995 and 2003.) Yet, in federally regulated businesses such as banking, air travel, and telecommunications, employment equity or affirmative action programs have vastly expanded the presence of visible minorities in these industries, partly because these employers must provide an annual report to Parliament on the numbers of women, persons with disabilities, and visible minority group persons hired and promoted.

All levels of government must become just as pro-active about every sector of economic activity, oversee professional accreditation bodies, and, pitilessly enforce anti-racism and affirmative action programs, with the provision of annual reports detailing the results achieved. Enforcement must also require, as provided by Section 24, Clause 1, of the Charter of Rights and Freedoms, public, financial support of "anyone whose rights or freedoms, as guaranteed by [the] Charter, have been infringed or [who have been] denied [to be able to] apply to a court of competent jurisdiction to obtain such remedy as the court considers appropriate and just in the circumstances." Aye, governments must support the ability of those who have been victims of discrimination to sue for redress. In addition, the ability of provinces to legislate "generally all matters of a merely local or private nature" suggests they may – or must – promote multiculturalism and anti-racism, including the provision of redress programs for communities adversely affected by previous, racist regulations. One such program could include the dedication of 1 per cent of provincial sales taxes to affirmative action, skills retraining, professional accreditation, and public awareness mandates.

III. Secularize public schools

Section 93 of the Constitution Act, 1867, establishes the provision of Christian ("Denominational") schools and, specifically, Protestant and Roman Catholic schools, in several provinces, including Ontario. In Ontario, as in other jurisdictions, the Protestant Christian schools have become, for practical effect, public, non-denominational, and secular schools, while Roman Catholic schools continue properly to offer Christian instruction, supported by taxpayers. In a multicultural, multifaith, and multiracial society, this anomaly is patently unfair, and it has been declared so by no less an authority than the United Nations. As painful as it is to ask that a long-standing privilege and right be rescinded, fairness demands that no religiously oriented schools receive public funding. In other words, all religious schools should be private schools, with all public schools becoming secular. This change need not frustrate the tutelage of students in spiritual and moral discipline, particularly if a mandatory course is developed that would educate all students in the principles of sound citizenship and fundamental charity, as derived from major world religions.

IV. Diversify the judiciary, boards, agencies, and commissions

Although visible minority groups continue to progress in winning nominations and elections to municipal chambers, provincial legislatures, and the House of Commons, especially in areas where our numbers are decisive, this instrument of public participation and representation is not the only one available to us. Just as governors have been pro-active in appointing "Caucasian" francophones and women to the Supreme Court of Canada as well as to other bodies, so now must governors use their powers to appoint visible-minority-group francophones, women, and others to the Supreme Court of Canada, provincial courts, and other boards, agencies, and commissions. True, this procedure is cosmetic, but appearances matter. When the Supreme Court of Canada, the Senate, and official boards, agencies, and commissions begin to look like Canada itself, the possibility for racist marginalization of visible minorities should be reduced. Indeed, apart from elected persons, the next level of power in Canada resides with appointees to various regulatory and service institutions. These bodies must be diversified. I propose that at least two members of every appointed body be an Aboriginal person and a visible-minority-group person. Let us imagine the day when the Head of the Supreme Court of Canada is an Aboriginal person, the Director of the Royal Canadian Mounted Police is a black woman, the Canadian Ambassador to the United States is of Chinese heritage, and the Governor of the Bank of Canada is a South Asian francophone. The fact is, that day could be tomorrow. With the appropriate government action, this vision is achievable now.

V. Recognize métissage

Section 35, Clause 2, of the Charter of Rights and Freedoms defines "Aboriginal Peoples of Canada" as including "the Indian, Inuit, and Métis peoples of Canada." With this declaration, Canada became the first nation on earth to constitutionally recognize people of mixed "racial" heritage, albeit within the category of Aboriginal peoples. I think it would be healthy for Canada to declare itself to be, not only multicultural, but a nation respecting hybridity, I mean, métissage – the intermingling and intermarrying of peoples of many different cultures and backgrounds. Such a public declaration would help free citizens from the tyranny of coerced, or forced, identification with any particular "race," culture, or ethnicity. It would emphasize that we are, in every way, a "rainbow" people, further dethroning the current ethnocentric leadership.

VI. Affirm African and Aboriginal Canadian uplift

In March 2004, Doudou Diène, Special Rapporteur on racism, racial discrimination, and xenophobia to the United Nations Commission on Human Rights, delivered a report to the United Nations declaring that Canada practices racism in particular against people of African–Negro heritage and Aboriginal peoples. Given this finding, which was rejected by the Government of Canada and all but ignored by the mass media, I believe that the Canadian government must make amends. Certainly, the federal government must apologize for the slavery practiced in Canada during the colonial era, and some form of reparations or redress should be instituted, specifically for African Canadians of whatever background. A memorial for slavery abolitionism should also be erected in Ottawa. As for Aboriginal Canadians, I propose that 1 per cent of every property tax collected in Canada be assigned to First Nations peoples' governments, as a kind of permanent rent for the land that was primordially theirs and then coerced, stolen, and wrested from their stewardship by colonial and settler governments.

VII. Champion a tax on imperialism

In terms of foreign policy, I think Canada should use its international leverage to push for the levying of a tax on all governments whose antecedents (or present administrations) participated in (or still play a part in) the conquest, seizure, and annexation of foreign territories, with the purpose of exploiting their peoples and resources for their overseers' advantage. If such a tax were instituted, it would transfer some wealth from Western Europe to Africa, Asia, the Caribbean, South America, and the South Pacific; and from the United States to the Philippines, Cuba, Africa, and South America; from Japan and Germany to the sites of their former conquests; and from Russia (once the Soviet Union) to its once-subject areas. I admit that the imposition of such a tax will be difficult – and difficult to calculate. If successful, however, it should make imperialist powers (and wannabes) think twice before conquering "new" territories.

★ ★ ★

To conclude, if the above measures, especially the first six are adopted, Canada will begin to look visibly more inclusive (egalitarian in opportunity and power-sharing), from the monarch on down. We will finally have achieved a truly multicultural, multi-faith, and multiracial Canada.

First, however, radicals must drop their suspicion of the State; instead, they must seize it – democratically – to begin to utilize its awesome power to democratize Canadian society. Because the default of the state is always rightist (or status quo conservative), the right-wing need do nothing but complain about progress and run afoul of anti-hate speech laws. True, constitutional reform cannot deliver heaven, but unless we attempt the initiatives I outlined above, Canada will be indistinguishable from an ethnocentric hell.

4   Hegemonies, continuities, and discontinuities of multiculturalism and the Anglo-Franco conformity order

Grace-Edward Galabuzi

> Any organization of power not only generates institutions and policy mechanisms but also sustains ideas that legitimate it. Such a dominant ideology justifies the existing order of power relations by indicating the benefits accruing (or accruable) to all the principal parties, including in particular the subordinate or less favoured. So long as these latter acquiesce in the dominant mode of thought, their demands are likely to be reconciled within the existing system of power.   – Robert Cox

ROBERT COX'S EXAMINATION OF IDEOLOGY PROVIDES an appropriate starting point for my discussion of the purposes of Canadian official multiculturalism policy as a mechanism of hegemony maintenance. These purposes, I argue, are central to the complex role that official multiculturalism and its related discourses and practices play in mediating the relationship between Canada's racialized peoples and its majority white population in the early twenty-first century. While it may seem inconsistent with conventional wisdom, I will show that official multiculturalism serves as a mode of legitimation for an otherwise monocultural Eurocentric Anglo-Franco order. Through it, subaltern ethnicized and racialized "others" are reconciled to this order via a systematic process of hegemony maintenance. Using processes of consent and coercion, official multiculturalism assumes the dual task of mediating material relations between white settler communities and populations of ethnicized "others" by validating "difference" even as it consolidates the cultural, social, political, and economic advantages for Canadians of European descent. But this project, born of a strategic compromise in response to the vulnerability of Anglo-Franco conformity to postwar dialectical possibilities of subaltern insurgency, now stands prone to rupture because of the deteriorating material and sociocultural conditions of racialized groups as manifest in the racialization of poverty.

A crisis long in the making: Continuities of multicultural regimes and subaltern challenges

A crisis is underway that will unsettle the now-familiar terrain of Canadian multiculturalism. In significant ways, multiculturalism has come to represent the commonsense understanding of how to organize and manage relations between the dominant white settler population and the various ethnicized and racialized populations in the country. From the vantage point of the early twenty-first century, three events signal the descent into crisis for the multiculturalism regime: the reassertion of white-supremacist forms of Anglo-Franco conformity under the guise of a "clash-of-civilizations" approach to national security that has arisen under the "war on terror"; the Canadian elitist reconsideration of key elements of the multiculturalism regime, such as reasonable accommodation and cultural and religious tolerance, due to increasing anxiety about the loss of European distinctiveness among communities of European descent as patterns of global immigration change; and the deteriorating material conditions of an expanding population of racialized groups who are increasingly subject to poverty and other forms of social exclusion in Canadian society.[1] Under these circumstances, the multiculturalism regime has begun to lose legitimacy as a means of managing difference and diversity in a liberal democratic society that has otherwise imagined itself as cosmopolitan and tolerant of difference.

Canadian multiculturalism's postwar emergence can be partly attributed to a similar array of destabilizing factors that precipitated the crisis of legitimacy in the then-dominant Anglo-Franco conformity model of managing relations between dominant and subordinate populations. Multiculturalism represented a strategic compromise between Anglo-Franco populations and the "others" for managing relations between them, later becoming institutionalized as Canada's official multiculturalism policy. A Gramscian analysis of the Canadian official multiculturalism policy helps tie the conditions of emergence with the impending crisis neatly together.[2] In the post-World-War-II period, when multiculturalism emerged and acquired political, intellectual, and moral authority as a framework for organizing ethno-racial relations with the dominant

Anglo-Franco population, it helped to secure an otherwise vulnerable Eurocentric Canadian national project. It was so successful that it became incorporated into the Canadian hegemonic order and became routinely referred to as a Canadian value.[3] However, today, official multicultural-ism faces real threats from both above and below, which will likely spell its demise. It confronts a moment of crisis that we can only better understand if we reach back to the period of its emergence and draw some insights for crafting a response that may provide some advantages in what is likely to be a Gramscian war of position.[4]

The need to historicize: Recovering the future by reaching back in time

An important aspect of Gramscian analysis is the need to historicize – to locate the process under review in its proper historical context. Mul-ticultural discourses and practices emerged in response to post-war human-rights critiques of an explicitly white supremacist concept of Canadian society, which dominated until the 1950s. These critiques had the effect of exposing the inconsistency between Canadian state and elite championing of universal human rights abroad and the adher-ence to patently racist and colonial state policies imposed on ethnic and cultural minorities at home. State Aboriginal policies, as well as immi-gration and human-rights policies, began to undermine Canada's growing international reputation as a leader in the post-war new world order based on universal principles of a common humanity. In this context the critiques – which later evolved into multicultural discourses and potential practices – constituted a strategic compromise between the dominant Anglo-Franco elites and the insurgent ethnocultural and racialized populations in the 1950s and 1960s. These populations made common cause with the Canadian labour movement, drawing inspira-tion from the decolonization processes taking place in Asia and Africa, and from the civil rights struggles in the United States. This strategic compromise paved the way for multiculturalism to become a dominant Canadian discourse for managing intercultural and interracial relations in the 1970s and 1980s. In Gramscian terms, multicultural policy brought "the interests of the dominant group into harmony with those of the subordinate groups and incorporated them into an ideology expressed in universal terms."[5] Multiculturalism became a powerful myth, maintaining both discursive and material dimensions that deployed the socially constructed categories of ethnics and "visible minorities"[6] in order to regulate the everyday lives of racialized and ethnicized minorities in Canada. Its emergence served the purpose of "order maintenance" at a time when the dominant Anglo-Franco myths had lost their salience in the face of the challenges from subaltern social forces. Suddenly, the insistence on Britishness or Frenchness as the passport to Canadian identity was no longer explicitly defensible and the marginalization and isolation of those of non-British or non-French heritage could not be sustained. Indeed, in this context, America's assimilation policies seemed more humane than Canada's obstinate attachment to Anglo-Franco conformity.[7]

Interestingly, the Canadian multicultural imagination overlooks Indigenous realities in its management of cultural difference. Indigenous resistance against internal (Anglo-Franco) colonial rule remains largely undocumented in multicultural discourse and off the radar, even among anti-racist critics of multiculturalism.[8] The Canadian multicultural project largely ignored Canadian-Indigenous relations. This is consistent with colonial assumptions that Canada was uninhabited land – *terra nullia*. So despite the brutal dispossession of territory and resources, and the political and cultural oppression of Indigenous peoples, Canada understood itself as a culturally pluralistic society, in which the Anglo-Saxon "majority" had accommodated the cultural demands of the French "minority" – and was now ready to embrace the tolerance of "others," with multiculturalism as the next logical step in its liberal democratic development. Such a conception of multiculturalism, with its silences, is highly problematic and must be engaged by anti-racism discourse. Importantly, the erasure of the Canadian state's relationship to Aboriginal peoples ultimately afforded prominent political theorists, such as Charles Taylor and Will Kymlicka, room to proclaim a discursive transcendency over social inequality in Canada through a multicultural mode of governmentality that ensured group-differentiated rights and procedures for redress when grievances arose.[9]

It is in this context of multiculturalism that I situate the post-World-War-II challenge by human rights activists, and by labour, anti-racist, and cultural autonomy movements that forced a reconsideration of the dominant order. Two other international developments at this time were also highly significant. First, anti-colonial struggles in the global South had forced the retreat of the British Empire, which, struggling to survive, sought to mobilize Canadian resources, thus exposing Anglo-Canada's complicity in the British colonial project. Second, the Cold War, which was playing out as an international ideological conflict between communism and capitalism, East and West, helped generate pressure in the West for human rights action as part of a broader response to the communist challenge. These developments helped promote the integration of the "other" European immigrants – Eastern and Southern Europeans particularly – into the Canadian body-politic as part of a broader set of anti-communist practices. These events were critical in inducing dialectical processes that led to a new order for managing cultural and racial difference – an order that would ultimately lead to the Canadian state's passage of the Multiculturalism Act in 1988 and the regime it instituted.

Even as these events unfolded, many of the subjects of the multiculturalism policy – the ethnicized and racialized others – remained largely consigned to the periphery of a Eurocentric monocultural colonial order. The strategic deployment of multicultural discourses as a hegemony-making process of consent and coercion, invoked at key moments of disjuncture in the late twentieth century, became an essential element of Canadian management of difference. Such hegemonic appropriation of multiculturalism in effect regulated the lived experiences of racialized peoples in Canada, reconciling them to the Anglo-Franco conformity standard of the Canadian socio-political and cultural order. At the same time, it channeled the material struggles of racialized peoples away from a focus on the structural processes responsible for their oppression towards merely symbolic gains with only marginal cultural and material value. In reflecting on that twentieth-century moment of transition, I suggest that the early twenty-first century represents a similar moment of crisis in the legitimacy of the multicultural order.

The capacity of the Anglo-Franco conformity order to dialectically deploy multicultural discourses and practices even as it consolidates itself is under threat in the twenty-first century. This threat is generated by new tensions arising from socio-economic pressures from below as articulated by anti-racist critics of multiculturalism,[10] and loss of confidence from above, manifested by the elite challenges to notions of reasonable cultural and religious accommodation and the debates about the limits of tolerance.[11] A Gramscian analytical perspective offers a framework within which we can understand both Canadian multiculturalism's contribution to hegemony-making and the potential emergence of counter-hegemonic agencies. Such agencies would be responsible for generating anti-racist discourses and practices that would recapture vital political momentum and work to undo the structural racism embodied in the Canadian multiculturalism order.

The emergence of Canadian multiculturalism: A Gramscian analysis

An analysis of official multiculturalism as ideology is not new. Kogila Moodley and Laverne Lewycky, among others, have pointed to the ideological uses of the Canadian multicultural project.[12] Moodley suggests that official multiculturalism was superficial and had the effect of depoliticizing multiculturalism as an idea. She asserts that the policy "trivializes, neutralizes and absorbs social and economic inequalities."[13] This analysis provides significant insight into the uses and abuses of multiculturalism by the Canadian state. What is missing, however, is a social relational dimension to the analysis. Here is where Gramsci's historical materialist approach is particularly useful.

One way to understand the juxtaposition of Canada's international reputation as a multicultural mecca of intercultural relations and its persistent infliction of social economic inequality and social distance on racialized peoples is to expose the multicultural project as part of the hegemony-making processes of consent and coercion that Gramsci so ably articulated.[14]

Himani Bannerji has invited us to think through what she calls "the different discursive articulations and uses of multiculturalism."[15] Such an invitation requires that multiculturalism be engaged in a number of ways: as a process of hegemony-making or maintenance that involves the generation and dissemination of particular legitimating knowledge; as representing the creation of institutions and norms within both the state and civil society; as leading to the generation of social forces that implicate both state and civil societal elites within both dominant and minoritized communities; and as defined by contradictions upon which dialectical outcomes are based, including both current right-wing and left-wing challenges to multiculturalism.

A Gramscian analysis makes possible such a deepening of the ideological critiques. It transcends the negative representation of the concept of ideology, and goes beyond what Karl Peter has referred to as the "myth of multiculturalism."[16] It allows for an exploration of the "recognitional" value of multiculturalism for "ethnicized others," despite the fact that the process requires their official construction as "ethnicized entities" – ethnics, visible minorities, immigrants – by the state and that the related policy impact on their lives remains highly tenuous. Gramsci's concept of hegemony provides analytical possibilities because it transcends the use of ideology as simply a "regime of truth" and speaks to the social relational implications of hegemony-making.[17]

Hegemony here is understood as a direct or indirect form of domination whose key constitutive elements, consent and coercion, become the accepted and commonsense operating principles of society and the social order.[18] Such an understanding allows the analysis to move beyond the process and conditions of knowledge production to consider the structures of domination that obscure key aspects of social, political, and economic life such that dominant society is able to avoid challenges from subaltern groups. In essence, a Gramscian analysis raises central questions of social relations and power. As Barry Smart has suggested, such an approach transforms "the terms of the debate from a preoccupation with the ambiguous concept of ideology and its effects to a consideration of the relations of 'truth' and 'power' which are constitutive of hegemony."[19] In suggesting that hegemonic processes generate what he refers to as historic blocs, Gramsci provides an understanding of hegemony as encompassing complex social processes in which "material forces are the content and ideologies the form."[20]

According to Barnor Hesse, "multiculturalism refers to particular discourses or social forms which incorporate marked cultural differences and diverse ethnicities . . . [it] can be named, valued, celebrated, and repudiated from various political perspectives."[21] It is arguable that, from its inception, Canadian multiculturalism represented both a way of conceptualizing cultural difference and a practical imperative for its incorporation into the Anglo-Franco framework that defined the Canadian national project. By the 1970s, official multiculturalism had emerged not only as a dominant Canadian discourse, but also as a practice for intercultural relationships at home that was celebrated around the world. In the Canadian imagination, multiculturalism was a promising means of managing relations among diverse cultural populations. However, little or no mention was made of the subordinate position of the diverse, racialized realities of immigrants largely from the global South – some of whose families had been in Canada for generations – in relation to those whose European character and aspirations defined the Canadian nation. Few noted the core, monocultural realities of the colonial order around which ethnicized and racialized "others" orbited, even as they endured processes of social exclusion that remain largely unaffected and disaffected by it.

Dominant multiculturalism proceeds by essentializing race, ethnicity, and culture in ways that decouple them from the agency of their subjects, thereby neutralizing their capacity to challenge the imposed order. Yet, essentializing race or ethnicity is a dialectical process deployed by various social forces that, for various purposes, engage in a "clash of essentialisms." This dialectical process, involving the privileging of some essentialized bodies and modes of social organization over others, plays out as part of the multicultural project. Nonetheless, counter-hegemonic agencies can be located within the interstices opened up by the contradictions within this clash of essentialisms.

Indeed, such contradictions can and often do create space for progressive policy measures, such as the Employment Equity Act of 1986, aimed at addressing discriminatory employment practices and barriers to the labour market faced by racialized workers, the (now defunct) Court Challenges Program, and the funding for advocacy groups under the auspices of Multiculturalism Canada, to name but a few. But they can also give rise to right-wing, reactionary forces that increasingly inhabit the debate about official multiculturalism today. In this regard, official multiculturalism constitutes a site of struggle within which contending social forces give way to a historic bloc. It emerged to successfully mobilize the ideological and material resources needed to address the strategic dilemma thrown up by the crises in the institutional arrangements that structure access to society's resources. With race and class as key organizing principles of social life in Canada, a crucial part of the hegemony-making process involved the creation and propagation of appropriate *myths* that legitimized a hegemonic ideological project that had severe material implications for subaltern communities vis-à-vis access to economic, social, and cultural resources. To this end, official multiculturalism deployed the socially constructed categories of "ethnics" and "visible minorities" to regulate the everyday lives of racialized and ethnicized minorities in Canada.

The period preceding the emergence of official multiculturalism in Canada represented what Gramsci would have characterized as a passive revolutionary moment, in which contestation of commonsense understandings of the social order, in this case, ethnic and racial orders, proliferated. Some were challenges to the continuity of racism as an organizing principle of social, cultural, economic, and political life. These struggles involved racially and ethnically based organizing as well as class-based formations such as the labour movement.[22] Such anti-racist struggles successfully challenged the enforcement of immigration exclusion legislation, such as the 1923 Chinese Exclusion Act and other forms of immigration control that were important elements in maintaining the neo-European character of Canadian society.[23] Other struggles focused on the "cultural dualism" of the Anglo-Franco conformity order, as more and more Central, Eastern, and Southern Europeans settled in numerically significant numbers in various regions of

Canada.[24] Thus was Anglo–Franco conformity confronted with a strategic dilemma, which ultimately led to a post–war elite strategic compromise.

This post–war strategic compromise emerged from the unsettling of the Anglo–Franco conformity order, and included bilingualism and the point system in immigration – products of state choices that privileged certain struggles and claims over others. In this case, the struggles for cultural autonomy among ethnicized minorities were privileged over struggles against structural racism. Symbolic multiculturalism involving cultural expressions that did not threaten the organization of the economy and access to resources was preferred to the anti–racist aim of addressing the socio–economic and political subordinate position of racialized groups. Moreover, anti–racist claims also exposed the dominant order as colonial, white supremacist, and rooted in the differential exploitation of racialized labour and Indigenous resources. Official multiculturalism, then, provided a language and mode for regulating social relations that allowed Eurocentric monocultural dominance to be maintained. This strategic compromise also involved the creation of state and civil society institutions, such as human rights commissions, and publicly funded ethnocultural advocacy organizations and institutional arrangements, such as the "global concept" skills–based immigration policy, that further regulated relations between dominant and subordinate groups. Such arrangements established a stable order with compatible dominant ideas, material capacities, and a new common sense that informed dominant social relations.[25] While official multiculturalism admittedly made some headway in creating procedural and institutional processes to redress the grievances of ethnicized and minoritized groups, it did not threaten to undo the Anglo–Franco capitalist order, and thus, structural inequalities endured. More importantly, official multiculturalism failed to address the intersection of race and class as organizing principles of Canadian society. Rather, it was a myth that obscured the interlocking nature of class exploitation and racial domination.

Hegemony maintenance: Multiculturalism as a strategic compromise

> There cannot be one cultural policy for Canadians of British or French origins, another for the Aboriginals, and yet a third for all others. For although there are two official languages, there is no official culture. Nor does any cultural group take precedence over

another. . . . We are free to be ourselves. But this cannot be left to
chance. . . . It is the policy of this government to eliminate any
such danger and to safeguard this freedom.
            — Prime Minister Pierre Elliot Trudeau, 8 October 1971

The notion of a strategic compromise around managing the relations
between the dominant Anglo-Franco population and "cultural others"
is implicit in the various narratives of the emergence of multiculturalism. These narratives implicate ethnocultural elites, Canadian state
elites, responses to Quebec nationalism, electoral opportunism, and the
emergence of human rights and anti-racism movements. Intellectuals
from the various elites exercised moral leadership in the contestations
for state action but also in the struggles for the hearts and minds of the
subject populations.

One way to distinguish these narratives is to assess whether they are
top-down or bottom-up; that is, to investigate whether they are initiated by the state and by the dominant elite class, or by the subject populations. In the top-down approach, or multiculturalism from above,
multiculturalism is presented as the product of an enlightened state by
the likes of Prime Ministers John Diefenbaker (Conservative) and
Pierre Elliot Trudeau (Liberal), who responded to the challenges of the
liberal moment by enacting progressive legislation and policy (for
example, a Bill of Rights) and who anticipated the challenges of building a new nationalism that transcended the bicultural model by initiating visionary policy (official multiculturalism).[26] Seen in this way,
official multiculturalism represented a vision of a more cosmopolitan
Canada, one that did away with the central monopoly of the conquering monocultures and emphasized the equal co-existence of groups
with historical cultural differences (or at least one that did not call for
cultural genocide, nor demand that one culture be subordinated to a
dominant one). Multiculturalism policy as popularized in the 1970s
and 1980s was thus consistent with the ideas of modern liberalism.

Two instrumental aspects of the top-down narrative were the need
to reconcile Canada's international position as a middle power engaged
in the global humanitarian project and its legal regimes with respect to
immigration and its treatment of its non-Anglo-Franco populations.[27]
Canada's high-profile participation in global affairs through the United
Nations, where many Canadians acted as bureaucrats responsible for
putting flesh on the new organization and articulating its post-war
principles, also involved its advocacy for peaceful mediation of ethnic

conflicts around the world. That advocacy had to be reconciled with the place of non-Europeans in the Canadian population. The United Nations' high-minded liberalism had to be practiced at home as well, in order for Canada to maintain its credibility abroad. Second, there was the desire to undercut the Quebec nationalist movement whose claim to sovereignty rested largely on the idea of a two-founding-nation compromise.[28] There is also a version of the top-down narrative that suggests an even more instrumental motive on the part of the Liberal and Conservative governments: the need both to manage the risks associated with a shift in immigrant source areas from Northern Europe to Southern Europe to the Third World and to reap the electoral gains of this shift.[29]

The bottom-up narrative of the emergence of official multiculturalism suggests that popular demands forced the hand of the political elite and the Canadian state by demanding recognition of the diverse ethnic makeup of the population.[30] This narrative includes the emergence of a vibrant human rights movement that mobilized both ethnic elites and the labour movement to demand changes in immigration policy and recognition of the diversity of Canada's working classes. As the 1969 Royal Commission on Bilingualism and Biculturalism indicated, 26 per cent of people who were neither French nor English asserted their Canadianness (by the 1950s, over 70 per cent of this group were Canadian-born). Ukrainians, Polish, and Montreal Jews were particularly well represented in this number.[31] Several ethnic and racialized minority groups debated the "fact" of British and French ethnicity as representing Canadian identity. And this identity exclusion was matched by social and economic exclusion, as John Porter's work on the vertical mosaic meticulously documented.[32] Indeed, socio-economic marginalization would prove as important a catalyst for mobilization as was the cultural marginalization imposed by the Anglo-Franco conformity order. For the bottom-up narrative, the class-culture axis of exclusion was key in defining the subaltern insurgency against Anglo-Franco conformity.

One remarkable aspect of both of these narratives – elite co-optation and subaltern insurgency – is their silence with regard to Indigenous realities and the history of conquest, plunder, dispossession, and cultural genocide that constituted Canada's foundation as a European colonial society into which multicultural groups were either invited or were demanding to be recognized as part of. In some ways, this silence can be interpreted as ethnocultural complicity in the colonial project, where multicultural groups become the "privileged" other in a society where

Aboriginal people have been struggling for redress for over 400 years.[33] Alongside the top-down and bottom-up narratives, then, it is important to acknowledge the Aboriginal rights movement as another dimension of the insurgency that I described above. This movement was centred on land claims and Aboriginal self-governance, and has been documented by such authors as Eva Mackey, Taiaiake Alfred, Boldt and Long, and Frideres, among others.[34]

Because these processes are complex and dialectical, it is not always useful to privilege one narrative over the other. Rather, it is more helpful to recognize how these narratives were deployed in constituting a new alliance of social forces that implicated elites from both the dominant and subordinate groups. Beyond the abstract discourse of multiculturalism, a specific political project emerged that tasked multiculturalism with helping to reconstruct Canada's image as a tolerant liberal democratic society and respectable middle power, and to manage migration flows from Southern Europe and the Global South, where today 75 per cent of immigration — made up of predominantly racialized people — flows from. Once this project was accomplished, multiculturalism then acted to ensure social cohesion by enabling symbolic celebration of difference. Moreover, it was expected to eliminate racism and social exclusion, while encouraging social inclusion, all on very limited budgets and on even less political capital.[35]

Operationalizing official multiculturalism in Canada

Ironically, official multicultural policy arose out of the recommendations of the 1969 Royal Commission on Bilingualism and Biculturalism and, while Book IV of the report was titled "The Cultural Contributions of Other Ethnic Groups," its adherence to biculturalism provided a platform for challenging the dual cultural conception of Canada through a vibrant systematic policy debate on cultural pluralism in the country. The Report of the Royal Commission on Bilingualism and Biculturalism spoke to the growing multicultural nature of Canadian society and provided a basis for an official policy that recognized the multicultural reality and promoted cultural retention and ethnic diversity as part of the policy shift from assimilation to integration in dealing with the "other" Canadians: immigrants and refugees. In a time of widespread minority grievances in the United States that led to urban riots, it provided a means by which minority grievances in the Canadian context could be channeled and addressed through the strategic compromise. Moreover, new "South-North" immigration patterns that led to a substantial shift in the racial profile of the population in urban centres also spurred a shift in the management of racial relations to address the "immigrant" problem. In response to these issues, Canada moderated its Anglo–Franco conception of national culture in favour of a multicultural one as a fundamental characteristic of the society but retained its bilingual status.

In 1971, the federal Liberal government of Pierre Trudeau announced its official multiculturalism policy whose four key elements included: a) a commitment to remove cultural barriers to full participation in Canadian Society; b) state funding to ethnocultural groups for cultural maintenance; c) the encouragement of cultural interchange; and d) language training for immigrants to acquire one of the country's two official languages. A Multiculturalism Directorate was set up in the Department of the Secretary of State to administer the policy and to give the policy institutional force, although its level of funding did not reflect its mandate. The establishment of the Directorate represented a new "clientelist" relationship between the state and many ethnicized elites. Canada thus became the first country in the world to adopt an official multiculturalism policy through which growing state concerns about the integration of large numbers of ethnically and racially diverse newcomers could be addressed. However, the policy's privileging of cultural symbolism over social justice really just presented a façade of diversity without engaging the structural impediments to the full participation of immigrants.

Making the Canadian state truly multicultural would require a number of changes to the way it had always functioned. To this end, the state initiated a period of bureaucratic and legislative consolidation that saw the establishment of a Standing Committee of the House of Commons to review the implementation of multicultural policy across the government, and the creation of a Citizenship Branch in the Department of Immigration and Citizenship to support immigrant and refugee integration projects in communities, which continued to fund and support these projects when it was moved to the Department of Secretary of State in the mid-1980s. However, as immigration from the Global South escalated, the resources proved limited and the budgets were slow to grow to meet the need. In 1988, Canada's multicultural commitment was enshrined by the federal Conservative government in the *Canadian Multiculturalism Act: An Act for the preservation and enhancement of multiculturalism in Canada,* demonstrating that multiculturalism was a key policy objective across the political spectrum. The legislation aimed to foster mutual respect among Canadians, to encourage equitable participation in society of citizens of all ethnic and racial backgrounds, and to promote a sense of attachment and belonging to Canada among Canadians. It further required the government to submit an annual report to Parliament regarding its implementation. In 1991, the government also created a new Department of Multiculturalism and Citizenship to assume that purpose. However, the department did not last in the face of Euro-chauvinist critiques of the policy, particularly from Western Canada. In 1993, before leaving office, the Conservative government disbanded the Department of Multiculturalism. When the Liberals took over, they created a Department of Canadian Heritage that subsumed a diminished multiculturalism portfolio.

During the period of multiculturalism policy consolidation, other Liberal initiatives came to the fore that had implications for ethnicized and racialized minorities. In 1977, Canada passed the Canadian Human Rights Act, and in 1982, the Constitutional Act of Canada's Charter of Rights further enhanced legal protection for minorities and provided recourse for individual and group discrimination. Significantly, the "multicultural" character of Canada was addressed in Section 27 of the Canadian Charter of Rights and Freedoms in the Constitution Act of 1982. This section has largely been used as an interpretive clause in matters relating to individual rights and such collective rights as religious rights.[36] In the 1980s, two key reports dealing with discrimination in employment and its impact on racialized groups were released: a 1984 parliamentary taskforce report on the status of visible minorities titled *Equality Now!* and the Abella Report on Employment Equity in 1985, which ultimately led to the passing of the *Employment Equity Act* of 1986. This act introduced a voluntary employment equity regime for employers under federal jurisdiction.

The Canadian state strengthened its clientelist relationship with ethnicized and racialized communities in other ways that demonstrate the complex, dialectical relations with these communities under official multiculturalism. These largely focused on ways of popularizing the concept of multiculturalism as a character-defining Canadian value among both the minority and majority populations. Through the various iterations of the Department of Multiculturalism, for instance, the state began funding advocacy initiatives and giving some voice to communities. Needless to say, these resources were always subject to political and budgetary constraints; indeed, in the mid-1990s, during a deficit-fighting era, most were withdrawn. More recently, the federal government has developed Canada's Action Plan Against Racism, the aims of which are to strengthen social cohesion, implement Canada's human rights framework, and demonstrate federal leadership in the fight against racism and hate-motivated crimes.[37]

Official multiculturalism and the management of difference

Canada's official approach to ethnic and racial diversity has evolved over the years and while it is currently embedded within a broad policy and legislative framework, it continues to change to respond to shifting demands and reconceptualizations of the idea of multiculturalism.[38] Today, the policy recognizes and celebrates cultural diversity in its pronouncement that the Canadian government is committed to "making Canada the most inclusive country in the world, where opportunity is shared among all Canadians."[39] Today, the three fundamental goals of multiculturalism policy under the program are:

> Identity: fostering a society that recognizes, respects and reflects a diversity of cultures such that people of all backgrounds feel a sense of belonging and attachment to Canada.
>
> Civic Participation: developing, among Canada's diverse people, active citizens with both the opportunity and the capacity to participate in shaping the future of their communities and their country.
>
> Social Justice: building a society that ensures fair and equitable treatment and that respects the dignity of and accommodates people of all origins.[40]

In an important way, Canadian multiculturalism was inconsistent with the idea of assimilation, and more consonant with a more liberal integration approach that allowed ethnicized Canadians to express aspects of their cultures and celebrate their ethnicity. In immigration policy, official multiculturalism represented a shift from the paternalistic policy of "assimilation" for "preferred" immigrants that required strenuous efforts to impose exclusions on the immigration of the "non" preferred category – largely racialized immigrants. Official multicultural policy would allow members of non-dominant groups to symbolically retain their cultures and celebrate their ethnicity – through such cultural tropes as song, dance, food, and to some extent language. It represented an acknowledgement that Canada was a "cultural mosaic."[41] Official multicultural policy crystalized the contested idea of recognizing "difference" and validating diverse identities. Multiculturalism, then, provided an ideological framework that appeared to promote tolerance, equality, and pluralism. Through it, the state aimed to diminish potential social tensions that might arise out of the changing patterns of immigration, and thus made multiculturalism an important part of Canadian nation-building.[42]

Over time, however, official multiculturalism began to condition the expectations and actions of a whole set of state and non-state actors. But it also uncritically presented Canada as a "cultural mosaic" – a potpourri of cultures with equal access to state and society resources. Official multiculturalism (unintentionally) sanctioned the insertion of otherwise radical voices into liberal formalisms that had the goal of securing the existing social relations against the insurgencies that were arising. Perhaps not so ironically, it has been under the multicultural regime that the starkest manifestations of the social exclusion of racialized groups have become prominent.[43]

A growing body of literature analyzing the socio-economic performance and the political status of racialized groups has concluded that they are consistently subject to structural racism that confines them to the bottom of the vertical mosaic that Porter identified.[44] Processes of social exclusion coupled with the growth in the size of the racialized population reinforce the structural tendencies in a neo-liberal economy towards maintaining and reproducing the existing order. Racialized immigrants are brought into the "mosaic" often with total disregard for the very skills and qualifications that are the basis for their selection in an immigration system that patently commodifies their labour as opposed to incorporating them as potential citizens. These conditions have generated new strains in the multicultural compromise and point to a new crisis for the regime of diversity management in Canada.

The multicultural regime in crisis: Contradictions and dialectics

Because hegemony-maintenance deploys both consent-making and coercive processes, the multicultural regime has engendered praise as well as criticism in public opinion, and among academics, policymakers, and community activists. On the praise side, a recent book by Michael Adams gives a charitable assessment of the value of Canadian multiculturalism – especially its putative impact as a signifier of the value that society places on cross-cultural tolerance and cultural pluralism. Adams argues that this is an important political gain in a society whose founding and adherence to monoculturalism were a given until less than forty years ago.[45] According to the Economic Council of Canada's report, *New Faces in the Crowd,* as of 1992, multiculturalism had "already registered some modest success in reducing the amount of intolerance in

Canadian society."[46] Greg Gauld has suggested that "tough" issues relating to building a truly multicultural society like "hate propaganda, visible minority voices in Canadian literature, constitutional recognition of the Multicultural character of Canada, domestic effects of foreign policy . . . [signal] an entrenchment of the philosophy of multiculturalism in the Canadian political culture."[47] John Berry has used a cost-benefit analysis to suggest that Canada comes out ahead with its multicultural policy and its emphasis on intergroup relations, attention to human rights, equity, social participation, and balancing of individual and collective rights.[48]

On the other hand, critics on both the Left and Right have described the state approach to multiculturalism as largely symbolic. And both suggest that the way in which the policy is articulated and its programs are funded focuses mostly on symbolic cultural retention and celebration at the expense of true equality of access to full participation in Canadian life for ethnic minorities, immigrants, and refugees.[49] Others have pointed to the failure of the policy to address the class structure of Canadian society and therefore the real reality of the racialized and immigrant experience.[50] Bissoondath, for example, has accused the policy of engendering division and endangering Canadian unity.[51] Still others have zeroed in on the perceived inadequacy of the policy framework and resources, with Mazurek suggesting that the failure of the policy implies less the bankruptcy of the idea and more the institutional forces whose defence of the status quo overwhelmed a policy they were charged with implementing.[52] Bannerji and Walcott's critical anti-racist examination of official multiculturalism focused on how the state's emphasis on ethnic celebration undermines efforts by racialized communities to mobilize politically, and thus to advocate for state action to deal with structural barriers faced by immigrants, such as racism.[53]

Multiculturalism and racialization

Canadian multicultural policy acknowledged the demands of a more inclusive society and the reality of cultural difference, but did not fully break with the monocultural concept of Canadian society. The contradictions and limits inherent in the policy simply overwhelmed it. The dominant liberal ideology presented it as neutral, equating the experiences of all cultural groups and privileged cultural celebration as a positive expression of difference. Moreover, it attempted to resolve questions of racial difference within a liberal frame that would also secure capitalist relations. Its impact was thus to obscure race, class, and gender as key determinants of the marginalization, structural oppression, exploitation, and exclusion faced by racialized people in Canada. The privileging of symbolic celebration of cultural difference, then, had the effect of displacing claims and contestations of exclusion by subaltern racialized populations.

But the shallowness of official multiculturalism was a double-edged sword. On one hand, it provided long-sought-after recognition of difference as a means of validation under the guise of cultural democracy. On the other hand, it reinforced historical racial hierarchies and processes of colonialism, capital accumulation, and exploitation. There was little opportunity to discuss these oppressions in the context of the cultural celebrations that appealed to many of the racialized elite, since such celebrations attracted key political leaders seeking to bask in the glow of multiculturalism as diversity management. In essence, even as multiculturalism reinforced social closure by essentializing the identities of racialized peoples, hegemonic processes of consent were being deployed to legitimize it.

State policy further imposed a paternalistic relationship on minority cultures from which they could not escape to assert any real autonomy. Their voices became subordinated to a paternalistic funding relationship that muzzled their ability to articulate the experience of racialization as central to their existence. Bannerji has suggested that this subordination has had the effect of rearranging questions of social justice and unemployment into a neutral form of a culturally diverse life experience.[54] Concurrent with these developments was the growing devaluation of racialized labour through the state's failure to recognize international credentials. Official multiculturalism also served to intensify the ethnicization of political processes by emphasizing the cultural rather than class axis for political participation.[55]

While multicultural public policy acknowledged the demands for a more inclusive society and the reality of cultural difference, it did not actually break society's "white" monoculture but rather extended it to whole segments of previously ethnicized subjects. By redefining and expanding the concept of "whiteness," a majority of non-charter-class European groups were granted "white status," even as the process of racialization relating to people of colour deepened. The Canadian state asserted the fixed nature of racial difference by designating certain racialized groups as "visible minorities," denoting a hyper-visibility that masked not just the experience of racism, but also the fact that the vertical mosaic was becoming more racialized, and the victims more marginalized as the boundaries of "us" and the "other" became more defined. This reinforced the fact that race was becoming more prominent as an organizing principle of life even as it was losing its critical edge in popular discourse due to its displacement by multiculturalism. As Colin Mooers has suggested, even as racialized group members were becoming identified as visible minorities, their experiences were being hidden "in plain sight."[56]

These developments have emerged within existing racialized social structures that have not been undone by multiculturalism, but have rather morphed into new determinants of racialized life experiences. Some scholars, such as Balibar, have suggested that this represents a form of *neo-racism* – a form of racism whose dominant theme is the insurmountability of cultural differences. Neo-racism concentrates on the harmfulness of open borders and the incompatibility of traditions and lifestyles. In an ironic twist, it uses the very defence of difference to justify its cultural segregationist position.[57]

Through increased racialized immigration, Canadian society is becoming more "bottom heavy" with economically marginalized racialized peoples conjuring up images of a form of persistent separate existence even as racialized and non-racialized people share common urban space.[58] New boundaries have been drawn along historical, racial, and religious lines in order to secure the safety of the Canadian population against the perceived violence of others.[59]

Such illiberal practices raise questions about the equal application of the citizenship and civil rights of racialized peoples in a time when state elites use policies like racial profiling as part of global-local security regimes. Such policies are predicated on assumed complicity in criminal activities based on stereotypes of fixed racialized identities across space and time.[60] While racial profiling has a long history that dates back to Aboriginal cultural genocides, Chinese exclusions, and the internment of the Japanese in World War II, the current profiling of Arabs and Muslims in public places, in work places, and at border crossings, along with the persistent disproportionate stopping of African Canadians in Toronto streets by police, raises questions as to whether racialized people can make the same assumptions about their Canadianness as the non-racialized population. Whether the threat to national security trumps Charter of Rights protections and makes racial profiling an acceptable or necessary tool of law enforcement is a question that is often answered differently by and about different groups in Canada. Regardless of how it is answered, the question points to a significant challenge to the benign notion of Canada as a multicultural society. Similar concerns are raised by changing popular understandings of such concepts as "reasonable accommodation" and by the proliferation of debates on "the limits to tolerance."[61]

The crises of multiculturalism: Threats from the limits of tolerance, the war on terror, and economic apartheid

There are three dimensions of the current crisis of multiculturalism: elite reconsideration of key elements of multiculturalism, such as reasonable accommodation and tolerance; the reassertion of white-supremacist notions of Anglo-Franco conformity under the guise of various security regimes; and the deteriorating material conditions of an expanding population of racialized groups who are increasingly subject to poverty and other forms of social exclusion in Canadian society.

First, the reassertion of Anglo-Franco conformity is ironically rationalized by a critique of what some have claimed is a form of "strategic essentialism" on the part of cultural, racial, and religious minorities. But in truth, it is less about a new post-multicultural Canadian imaginary than it is about addressing white anxiety in a time of massive South-North immigration. Its deployment in the current war on terror also represents Orientalist conceptions of national security and community safety.[62] Recent right-wing critiques have singled out multiculturalism's incipient challenges to the neo-European character of Canadian society, which has been especially significant given the moral panic arising from the war on terror, related national security concerns, and the changing cultural composition of the country. Indeed, this panic has prompted proposals from security analysts, such as Martin Collacot of the Fraser Institute, that advocate oaths of allegiance to nebulously defined Canadian values.[63] A broader example of the reassertion of Franco-Anglo conformity lies in attempts to draw boundaries within the body politic and advocate a Eurocentric, Christian concept of Canada. This action is driven by elites but enjoys significant popular support. One way this is manifested is through new challenges to otherwise settled notions of reasonable accommodation.

The reinscription of white supremacy is also revealed in the suggestions by right-wing critics of multiculturalism that the autonomous agency of racialized groups seeking to segregate themselves into ethnic ghettos threatens social cohesion and national security. These critics have found new allies from both the centre and left of the political spectrum, who agree that the failure to "manage" cultural diversity is at the root of many of the problems facing Canadian society. This has fuelled a new debate about the limits of tolerance and the need for honest discussion about the terms of "integration." Muslims, Arabs, and South Asians are routinely singled out for their "dangerous" cultural or religious practices, the fear of which prompts calls for state limitation on cultural expression in order to protect those cultures' women and children, and the rest of society, from political Islam. These groups are asked to reconcile their cultural heritage to a Canadian standard based on values of liberty, equality, democracy, gender rights, as though these constitute the Canadian social order. In actual fact, what these elite demands represent is an important reconsideration of the top-down constructed liberal consensus on tolerance for cultural diversity in favour of an age-old mode of the Anglo-Franco conformity order.

The intellectual foundation for this reconsideration may well be Kymlicka's notion of "internal restrictions," which suggests that oppressive or illiberal acts can be imposed on members of a minority group by its leaders in order to protect cultural distinctiveness.[64] Such a reconsideration suggests that "multiculturalism taken to its logical extreme" can become detrimental to individuals within the cultural group. But beyond that, it implies that the practice of a particular form of cultural expression represents a threat to Canadian values. According to a recent Institute for Research in Public Policy survey, Canadians expressed overwhelming support for the notion of "limits to reasonable accommodation" however ill-defined. In a September 2007 survey, only 18 per cent agreed with the position that it is reasonable to accommodate religious and cultural minorities, while 53 per cent said such minorities should adapt to Canadian culture. In Quebec, only 5.4 per cent agreed with the proposition that it was reasonable to accommodate minorities while a staggering 76.9 per cent said immigrants should fully adapt to Quebec culture. In Quebec, 80.7 per cent were fully opposed or somewhat opposed to provision of prayer space in public space (with 57.6 per cent fully opposed) while only 12.6 per cent supported it. In Canada, 58.6 per cent were fully or somewhat opposed (with 38.1 per cent fully opposed), while 31.4 per cent supported or somewhat supported it.[65]

These sentiments were on display in 2007 as Quebec public opinion became the subject of intense debate about the limits of tolerance and reasonable accommodation and the distinctiveness of French Canadian culture. The results of the Quebec government's Bouchard-Taylor Commission, which was convened specifically to investigate accommodation for cultural differences, suggest a heightened attention to this issue.[66] According to the 2008 report, only thirteen cases relating to reasonable accommodation were documented between December 1985 and April 2002, compared to forty cases between March 2006 and June 2007. While the former group mostly dealt with concerned minorities and were addressed through formal and informal arrangements, the most recent ones were largely filed by dominant group members seeking either annulment of reasonable accommodation arrangements or demanding limits to accommodation. In terms of media coverage, of the seventy-three cases or incidents covered over the last twenty-two years, forty were covered between March 2006 and June 2007.[67]

These new understandings of such key concepts as reasonable accommodation suggest that the culture requiring state protection is the dominant one rather than those in the minority. The practical effect of this shift has been the eclipsing of claims for tolerance by cultural, religious, ethnic, and racial minorities, in favour of charges of intolerance of dominant practices and values against those same minorities. Whether framed as the limits of tolerance or as limits to reasonable accommodation, the proliferation of this discourse has coincided with elite and popular doubts about multiculturalism as a framework for managing and negotiating relations between and among diverse cultural, racial, and ethnic groups within Canada. At the same time, debates about integration as assimilation have become mainstream.

Second, key to the increasingly racial turn in contemporary discourses of citizenship and belonging are the issues of national security and community safety, which have been fueled by the war on terror as well as the growing numerical significance of multi-racial populations. While the rhetoric of multiculturalism has become increasingly detached from the material and institutional conditions that underlie the lived experiences of racialized peoples, it has remained effective in giving cover to the state and its elites, as they normalize security regimes at the international, national, and local levels. The result has been a proliferation of illiberal practices, ranging from widespread racial profiling in domestic spheres and border control processes – signified by such references as Driving While Black (DWB), or Flying While Arab (FWA) – to the security certificate detentions of Muslim men, and pervasive media references to young Canadian Muslims as home-grown terrorists. These practices also include escalations in the deportations of racialized failed-asylum claimants and non-documented residents, and the development of coercive community safety regimes that legitimate military-like assaults on largely racialized low-income communities to supposedly extract gang members. To this, we can add the routine criminalization of racialized youth in overpoliced neighbourhoods, and surveillance in malls, public places, and public and private housing complexes. Many of these illiberal practices are informed by moral panic over pathologized populations of racialized and religious minorities – a panic that is sustained by claims of a "dangerous cultural exceptionalism" of religious and racialized minorities within a framework of liberal multiculturalism.

Such practices derive from the persistent legacy of colonialism, suggesting that this early twenty-first century return of the racialized security threat – race as colour, place of origin, and associated religious identity – is a recovery of memory, or an acknowledgement of the limits of liberal multiculturalism in the service of Anglo-capitalist hegemony. Indeed, the colonial legacy allows for the reassertion of white supremacy through illiberal but increasingly popular discourses that essentialize cultural differences as fundamentally insurmountable and incompatible with normalized and universal modern "Western" values.

Third, within the context of globalization, economic restructuring has imposed precarious forms of work on the economy – contract, temporary forms of work with low wages, limited job security, and no benefits. These forms of work are the disproportionate refuge of racialized populations whose access to the labour market is subject to employment discrimination and barriers to access to professions and trades. Such conditions have intensified the vulnerability of racialized groups and recent immigrants, and compromised their life chances. The material implications of these developments are that these racialized groups experience differential social economic status, evident in such experiences as:

• a double-digit racialized income gap;
• chronic higher-than-average levels of unemployment;
• segregated labour market participation;
• deepening levels of poverty;
• differential access to housing and segregated neighbourhood selection;
• disproportionate contact with the criminal justice system;
• higher health risks;
• post-9/11 legislative and administrative measures that limit the free movement of racialized groups, especially members of Muslim, Arab, and Asian communities; and
• lack of representation in political institutions.[68]

These experiences are increasingly crystallized in what we have come to know as the racialization of poverty.

The racialization of poverty refers to a process by which poverty becomes disproportionately concentrated and reproduced among racialized group members, in some cases inter-generationally. What seems to explain these trends are structural changes in the Canadian economy that are occurring under the neo-liberal regime. The compound impact of these forces accentuates historical forms of racial discrimination in the Canadian labour market and creates a process of social and economic marginalization, the end result of which is the disproportionate vulnerability to poverty among racialized communities. The emergence of precarious labour conditions in Canadian labour markets is an important explanation for the racialization of poverty, which can also be linked to the entrenchment of privileged access to economic resources for a minority, but powerful, segment of the majority population. While this differential access explains polarizations in income and wealth in society as a whole, the concentration of economic, social, and political power along racial lines explains the growing gap between rich and poor as well as the racialization of that gap.[69]

Increasingly, research has shown that there are significant and enduring disproportionalities in the experience of poverty in Canada, particularly in urban centres. National and Census Metropolitan Area data show that racialized people are two or three times more likely to be poor than other Canadians.[70] The rates are even higher among recent immigrants and select groups, such as youth, women, and seniors of Arab, Latin American, Somali, Haitian, Iranian, Tamil, East Indian, and Vietnamese origin. While the Canadian low-income rate was 14.7 per cent in 2001, low-income rates for specific racialized groups ranged from 16 per cent to as high as 43 per cent.[71] Indeed, racialized community members and Aboriginal peoples are twice as likely to be poor as other Canadians due to the intensified economic and social exploitation of these communities that has been the legacy of historical racial and gender inequalities.

In the midst of this socio-economic crisis, different levels of government have responded by abandoning anti-racism programs and policies aimed at removing the barriers to economic equity. The resulting powerlessness, socio-economic marginalization, and loss of voice compound the minority population's inability to put issues of social inequality and, particularly the racialization of poverty, on the political agenda. They are unable to seek remedy effectively through political representation. This situation in turn reinforces school non-achievement, alienation, and higher drop-out rates, ensuring that children growing up in poor, often racialized, families are more likely to repeat the cycle of poverty.[72]

Unequal patterns of labour-market participation and vulnerability to racial discrimination faced by racialized group members and recent immigrants not only lead to disproportionately higher levels of low income, but they also determine poor neighbourhood selection, contact with the criminal justice system, and high health risks. They structure a racialized experience of poverty that creates social alienation, powerlessness, marginalization, voicelessness, vulnerability, and insecurity both in the workplace and in the community. This is particularly prevalent among racialized women, racialized youth, and racialized immigrants. These material conditions have the effect of disadvantaging the racialized population but also undermining the legitimacy of multiculturalism as a regime of diversity management that has the power to ensure equal access to opportunities for all Canadians. What it brings into relief instead is the reassertion of the vertical mosaic, but in this case, a colour-coded one.[73]

Conclusion

The emergence of internal contradictions within official multiculturalism has created dialectical openings for challenges to its hegemonic position from both above and below. This has led to the unsettling of dominant relations and the possibility of a reconstitution of a new hegemonic order that will require a new strategic compromise that potentially better reflects the demands of racialized peoples. These current circumstances provide a space for counter-hegemonic action that can take advantage of the loss of elite legitimacy for the multiculturalism regime, with the potential to make substantive claims against the Canadian state based on the material realities of racialized peoples.

Part 2

Labours

5 Canadian multiculturalism and its nationalisms

Nandita Sharma

IN CANADA, WE TEND TO THINK OF THE DISCOURSE of multiculturalism as uniquely ours, particularly since the Canadian state was the first to proclaim a policy of multiculturalism in 1971. However, it is important to note the roots of at least some aspects of multicultural discursive practice in the United States. So far, federal state officials there have chosen not to implement a policy concerning the matter, however, the discourse, and even the everyday practice, of multiculturalism is quite commonplace and in some important ways has influenced the trope of multiculturalism north of the border. In particular, the hegemonic association between immigration and multiculturalism and the related discourse that posits that all non-Natives are immigrants has spurred at least two developments that are evident in Canada.

First, in the period following the removal of legal exclusions against the immigration of various negatively racialized groups to Canada in 1967, multiculturalism borrowed from the American discourse of "we are all immigrants." This ideologically levelled the very real disparities between those mostly non-white persons who were constituted as "new" immigrants and the still-dominant white majority. By articulating the notion of a new, post-racist Canada, the discourse of multiculturalism sidestepped non-white persons' ongoing experience of racism. Secondly, the discourse of "we are all immigrants," by more-or-less writing those constituted as Native out of the dominant discourse of the contemporary Canadian nation, reconstituted prior colonial state identities in which distinctions were made among colonizers (those in charge), Natives, and immigrants. Ironically, the uncritical acceptance of the official discourse of "we are all immigrants" by some who had been constituted as Natives helped unleash a neo-racist reaction. Within Native nationalisms, the trope of "we are (almost) all immi-

85

grants" was transformed to "all non-Natives are colonizers" so that even those who came to Canada as a result of colonial activities elsewhere and who were/are placed in subordinated positions within the new Canadian national society, have come to be portrayed as *colonizers* simply because they are non-Natives. Not only has the discourse of multiculturalism produced a revamped "Canadian" identity, then, it has also given greater life to an "indigenous" identity, particularly in its binary manifestation of Native/non-Native.

By mobilizing both of these discursive shifts, multiculturalism constitutes a double ideological move. First, it legitimates a discourse that obliterates any distinction between colonizers and immigrants, thereby depoliticizing the process of constructing a racialized Canadian nation state through colonial practices. Secondly, the shifts that official multicultural discourse precipitated have paved the way for the conflation of processes of colonization with those of migration. Multiculturalism, then, has changed our understanding of Canadian nation-state building from an activity embedded within various imperialist projects (i.e., British and French) to a state-centric discourse in which colonizers become immigrants, immigrants become colonizers, and only Natives belong. This chapter questions these discursive practices, which are deeply embedded not only within previous colonial state practices of differential belonging but also within contemporary neo-liberal forms of capitalist globalization. It calls for a rejection of racialized, nationalized, and capitalist understandings of land and people and the relationships among them and challenges the sovereignty story with the naturalization of xenophobia that comprises Canadian multiculturalism.

Are we all immigrants?

Let us begin with the discursive origins of the hegemonic notion that, in Canada, "we are all immigrants," a notion that is most closely associated with the 1951 publication of Oscar Handlin's *The Uprooted*, which claimed that the United States was an "immigrant nation."[1] John F. Kennedy's posthumously published *A Nation of Immigrants* (1964) cemented this notion as part of the dominant American ideology of nationhood during key moments in the anti-racist civil-rights struggles, particularly in demands for change in the "racial contract," which privileged whites.[2] The idea that every non-Native was an immigrant, along with claims that the civil rights victories of the mid- to late-1960s eliminated racism from the operation of state and market, set the tone for how national multiculturalism policies have come to be represented around the world.

However, it is important to note that an even earlier example of multiculturalist discourse can be seen in Walt Whitman's 1855 portrayal of the United States as a "teeming nation of nations."[3] This shows that white settler societies, such as the United States or Canada, have long used the liberal discourse of multiculturalism as a practical measure to bridge the ideological gap between the racialization of national membership and the labour demands of employers for ways to cheapen labour, including the use of state racism. In Whitman's case, the strategy of incorporating negatively racialized groups into the nation was a response to criticisms that the U.S. was failing to live up to the qualities of democracy, equality, and individual liberty through which it defined itself (and was defined by other imperialists).[4]

Whitman's representation of the United States as a "teeming nation of nations" acknowledged the reality of America's multiple racialized groups in a way that neutralized the power relations underlying their forced relationships of inequality.[5] By pushing aside the historical conditions that allowed for the emergence of the United States (and the co-optation of the truly revolutionary intent of many fighting against the British Empire), Whitman's representation flattened the divisions and inequalities that characterized racist social relations in the United States.[6] Later, Oscar Handlin's consideration of everyone (other than those constituted as Native) as a "stranger in the land," along with Kennedy's depiction of the United States as "a nation of immigrants" (again, except Natives), moved away from Whitman's narrative of a multi-*national* United States to one that portrayed Europeans as the *original* immigrants. This too worked to deny the racist hierarchy established by elite Europeans in the United States. However, it also insidiously denied the violent colonization of the territories claimed by the United States by rendering colonialism as just another instance of human migration. By discursively placing immigration, rather than colonization, at the centre of the United States' nation-making project – indeed, by turning colonialism into a form of migration – such ideological representations helped to both disavow the violence of colonialism and to produce the liberal myth of an America that welcomes immigrants instead of a spatial, legal formation that recruited successive groups of migrants in order to exploit their labour in the service of expanding the power of the state and the profits of capitalists.

The shift from seeing elite Europeans as colonizers to seeing all non-Natives as immigrants was crucially important in that it obfuscated the very different ways in which various groups of people came to land in the United States. An astonishing example of this amnesiac relationship with the history of migration is displayed in President Kennedy's recasting of enslaved Blacks as "immigrants from Africa."[7] The discursive shift to "we are (almost) all immigrants" also helped to ideologically conceal how variously racialized groups were accorded very different economic, political, and social standings in the American body politic.

In particular, the differential access to, at first, United States citizenship, and later, legal entry to the United States after the establishment of border controls is wholly disavowed. No mention is made of the fact that the first United States Act pertaining to citizenship, the 1790 Naturalization Act, restricted citizenship to those "Aliens" who were "free white persons of good character," or that the first federal law establishing immigration controls worked to bar the entry of negatively racialized migrants from China. The discursive shift to "we are (almost) all immigrants" also steered discussion away from the reliance that elites (and later non-elites who were constituted as "white") had on the economic and cultural consequences of the United States' racialized politics of differentiating groups of "immigrants" and of homogenizing the colonially defined "Natives."

The trope that Europeans were simply the original immigrants prefigured in interesting ways the current discourse on model minorities. This representation of Europeans as the first immigrants dehistoricized and depoliticized the relative material success of various migrants from Europe. By failing to account for how "whites" were granted relatively privileged access to citizenship, migration, free land, the polity, and racialized ideas of societal belonging, this new discourse helped to consolidate the ideology of meritocracy (i.e., the American Dream) in the relationship between migration and class mobility in the United States.

Most importantly, the shift from an unabashed celebration of colonization to the discourse of "the colonizers too are immigrants" mobilized the ideology of an original American plurality, the touchstone of the contemporary rhetoric of multiculturalism. The discursive shift from legitimated ideas of stratified national belonging to a portrayal of the United States as having always been a liberal plurality was a disavowal of the violence of expropriation, genocide, and exploitation. It was also a disavowal of the many-layered discriminatory practices against "Natives" and "inassimilable" migrants. Moreover, multiculturalism became a way to maintain the ongoing power of racism in organizing the polity by minimizing claims of continued racism by non-whites. Kennedy's mobilization of the discourse of a multicultural plurality where everyone was on the same footing (a "nation of immigrants") was important therefore not only for how it reframed social relations but also for how it helped to neutralize both the United States' brutally racist past as well as the racism that continued in his day.

This depiction of the United States as "a nation of immigrants" is also part of a broader shift in racist discourses since the 1980s and 1990s that has ushered in new racisms. Central to these new racisms was the deployment of the ethnicity paradigm, a paradigm that, as Michael Omi and Howard Winant have pointed out, ignores continuing processes of racial formation and racism in the United States, and discounts the relationship of these processes to neo-liberal restructuring of the global capitalist system.[8] The ethnicity paradigm marries an essentialized, static, and separationist view of culture with the cultural attributes of racialized discourses, such as language, "ethnic" dress, "ethnic" customs, and "ethnic" traditions.

Such culturalist views complement the discourse of multiculturalism, as each portrays ethnicities/cultures as existing (unchangingly) in utter isolation from all others while deflecting attention from the process of racialization that is embedded within racial formations. Thus, the refusal to recognize the diasporic spaces and transnational cultures that were created through centuries of encounters, not only in the United States but around the world, was transported wholesale into the discourse of multiculturalism.[9] Multiculturalism, with its focus on ethnicity and its impoverished notion of "culture," was productive of neo-racist notions of highly racialized relationships between people and place. Indeed it can be said that a discourse of multiculturalism is a neo-racist discourse *par excellence*.

The shift from valorizing "whites" as colonizers to privileging "whites" in the process of immigration, and the shift from a discourse of "race" to one of ethnicity/culture were ideologically useful in concealing the economic and political basis for the United States' immigration reforms of 1965.[10] Even as the United States co-opted the most militant of anti-racist demands, reconfigured its geopolitical strategy towards the nominally decolonized and independent national states of the Third World, and recognized the need to expand its criteria for immigration in order to compete with other "Western" societies for much-needed (im)migrant labour, its 1965 changes were ideologically represented as a repudiation of a racist past and, with no hint of irony, contradictorily as a continuation of the long history of American hospitality towards newcomers. Canadian reform of racialized immigration policies and its racialized polity took place within this broader discursive/material frame and borrowed much from it. The absence of an official federal state policy of multiculturalism in the United States should not, therefore, blind us to the influence of the U.S. on Canadian debates about immigration and the emergence of Canada's discourse on multiculturalism.

Multiculturalism as a neo-liberal mode of belonging

As in the United States, it was, in part, the activities of anti-racist movements in Canada and nationalist independence movements against imperialism in the Third World that created pressure for the Canadian state to eliminate overt statements about preferring certain races and nationalities in its admittance criteria for immigrants (i.e., in the selection of those admitted to Canada as permanent residents). This resulted in the extension of the right for professional non-whites and their nuclear families to apply for permanent residency in Canada and a greater recognition of non-whites within Canada. Both of these are significant developments in the history of non-white migration to Canada.[11]

Yet, the fact that these developments also took place when capitalist enterprises, in general, were grappling with falling profits has been widely ignored. As technological advances in communication and transportation made it easier to shift more sites of production away from sites of consumption, many capitalists, aiming to lower operating costs, relocated their investments to territories where labour costs, as well as the other costs of doing business, such as environmental and labour laws or taxes, were much lower. This led Canadian state officials to try to make Canada more competitive as a site for capital investment. Acknowledging the context of these simultaneous and significantly overlapping social, economic, and political developments helps make sense of the move to represent the Canadian polity as multicultural. At the same time, we must pay attention to the refashioning of nationalist discursive practices. The expression of nationalism at this time became better attuned to the increasingly global processes of capitalist expansion, often named as rootlessness. This idea of rootlessness posed significant problems, however, for much of the proletariat, which saw itself as being very much rooted in the nation. The discourse of multiculturalism, then, enabled a re-imagining of the Canadian people for new times and, as discussed above, for new racisms.

Using Marx's insight that social organization is implicit in the organization of production, the simultaneous formation of new nationalized subjectivities for workers who understood themselves as operating within a Canadian society and new transnational subjectivities for those competing within a global capital market can be seen as part of the cultural effects of the global expansion of capitalism. Indeed, this is one of the conclusions that Ghassan Hage reaches in his study of Australian-style multiculturalism.[12] He theorizes that white elites have mobilized multicultural discourses not only as a means of co-opting more transformative demands but also as part of their own self-identity as cosmopolitan whites with distinctively global tastes, outlooks, and, importantly, investments.[13] In this sense, and especially when analyzed within the context of an expanding globalization of capitalist social relations, multiculturalism is best seen as both strategically useful and enriching to white elites as they come to imagine the space in which they – and their capital – operate as "global." In this sense, the representation of the polity as "multicultural" provides elites with a form of cultural capital that gives them an advantage in a world defined by increasing flows of capital, goods, and people. Elite whites' use of multiculturalist discourse that tolerates non-whites and includes them as members of the now supposedly non-racist nation is necessary in a world where support from non-white state leaders and officials is crucial.

The response against multiculturalism by those whites who were or are not in a material position to benefit from the further globalization of capital should be understood within this classed relationship. Since they have no capital to invest and, in fact, live an increasingly precarious existence due to global shifts in production, white workers often respond with hostility to any efforts to embrace capitalist cosmopolitism.[14] Of course, what non-elite whites also feel is a challenge to their superiority in relation to non-whites of all classes. The threat, however, comes not only from the usual non-white suspects but also from an emerging elite of cosmopolitan whites who revel in the transnational world of business opportunities by refashioning themselves as cosmopolites enjoying the increased variety of songs, dances, and food that the presence of non-whites is best known for within the framework of multiculturalism. The sense of white, working class betrayal, then, is aimed at what is often seen as elite whites' collusion with non-whites to alter the "racial contract" that explicitly and concretely privileged the white working class in previous eras. Interestingly, this same discourse has also helped to create the sense that only white workers have been negatively affected by neo-liberal changes in investment and state practices. Non-whites are thus rendered invisible and are even perversely seen as neo-liberalism's main beneficiaries.

Indeed, the class-based support for multiculturalism has been obfuscated by the portrayal of multiculturalism as a response to racism and as a means of protecting non-whites primarily from the white working class. The problem of legitimizing the Canadian state's facilitation of neo-liberal reforms, reforms that privatized formerly public assets and services, deregulated environmental and labour regulations, and further liberalized world trade, was ideologically resolved by focusing on the supposed new racial/cultural openness of post-1967 Canadian society. Opening up sites for new capitalist investments was accompanied by the multiculturalist rhetoric of an opening up of whites to the presence of non-whites in their (national) midst.

Since multiculturalism represented a deflection of more radical anti-racist demands, the economic success of some non-whites in Canadian society was displayed as evidence for the state's claim to anti-racism. Non-whites were put forth as living proof of Canada's diversity, thus bolstering the image of Canada that state officials were presenting to the international arena of investors and potential migrants with professional qualifications. This opportunistic aspect of multiculturalism supports the prevalent sense among multiculturalism's critics that non-whites have simply been set on a national and international stage to perform an elaborate phantasm of an anti-racist society that has never materialized.

Yet, however much globalization was on state officials' minds in the 1960s and 1970s, society was (and is) still imagined as national; it is therefore important to recognize multiculturalism as an attempt by the Canadian state to avert a crisis of legitimation – a crisis brought about, in part, by the expansion of state activities to include the management of the cyclical crises of capitalism. In the 1960s and 1970s, as the state increasingly took responsibility for ameliorating the effects of economic crises, it simultaneously expanded the social criteria for national membership while restricting legal avenues to joining the nationalized polity, particularly to those most devastated by neo-liberal state policies elsewhere and the related global scramble for new investment opportunities. The crisis of state legitimation was ultimately resolved through the mobilization of nationalist ideology and, most especially, the reconfiguring of Canadian immigration policy.

With the extension of permanent resident rights to non-whites in 1967 and the proclamation of multiculturalism policies in 1971, the promise of social equality and belonging for certain non-whites grew. Government acts at this time perpetuated the myth of Canada as a "just society" but did so precisely at a time when a major policy shift on immigration was being established. The new category of non-Canadian Others, also known as "non-immigrants" or "temporary foreign workers," comprised those excluded from the national citizenship that official "immigrants" (or "permanent residents") could now lay claim to. The categorization of the new Others as *non*-immigrants accomplished two things: their *de jure* exclusion from the civil rights of Canadian citizenship and, hence, the cheapening and weakening of their labour power, and their exclusion from the social meaning of being Canadian. In this way, not only was official multiculturalism a response to changing immigration policies, it also paved the way for new exclusions to be organized through immigration law.

Restricting the Canadian polity

Discussions of the 1967 reforms usually analyze the changes as an opening up of immigration to non-whites and, in a way, this is true. However, it is just as important to see these changes as resulting in other kinds of restrictions. Aside from the relatively small refugee admittance program, immigration (or permanent residence status) was restricted to a professional class of disproportionately male-gendered immigrants and, through their sponsorship, members of their nuclear families. This excluded – by law – those who didn't fit the *new* preferred immigrant characteristics. A wealth of literature has pointed out that even after the 1967 changes, racism continued to play a part in the state's process of immigration selection. However, middle-class cultural capital (or one's familial relationship to it), rather than how one had been racialized or which nationality one held, came to be a key determining category for permanent residency and hence a path to formal Canadian citizenship.

A far greater restriction was also imposed during this period. Along with the removal of the pre-1967 "preferred races and nations" immigration criteria, came another less-studied seismic shift in Canadian immigration policy. A mere six years following the 1967 reforms, the 1973 Non-Immigrant Employment Authorization Program (NIEAP) was launched. The NIEAP, which continues today, is a regulatory aspect of Canadian immigration policy that both consolidates and expands many of the previous labour recruitment programs that positioned migrants as a temporary, unfree, labour force.

People recruited to work through the NIEAP are legally tied to a particular employer, a particular occupation, and therefore to a particular geographical location in Canada. They are unable to change any of the conditions of their temporary employment authorization without the consent of immigration officials and without a new employer to whom they would also be tied. To varying degrees, they are denied access to social assistance programs, even those they directly pay into, such as old-age pensions and unemployment insurance, thereby subsidizing such programs for the citizenry. Significantly, my past research has shown that since the mid-1970s, the majority of people entering Canada to work were admitted as non-immigrant unfree workers while only a minority come with the rights of permanent residency. In 2004, the proportion of workers granted permanent residency was 35 per cent while 65 per cent were admitted as "temporary foreign workers."[15]

For those classified as non-immigrant workers, the lack of labour market freedom, the inability to decommodify themselves through access to the social wage, and the restriction of their labour market choices has ensured that they are amongst the cheapest workers and most vulnerable persons in the country. Not surprisingly, the NIEAP was – and continues to be – very much driven by employers' demands for a "flexible" and "competitive" workforce. This flexibility and competitiveness, however, is predicated on a legal denial of mobility and, therefore, a legal denial to actually compete in the labour market.[16]

Such state practices of this managed migration approach highlight the inherent contradiction between the demands of capitalism and notions of plurality. The right of Canada (and every other national state) to discriminate against those deemed to be *de jure* non-members is integral to the very architecture of the contemporary global system of national states. National states, through the institutionalization (and considerable expansion) of the idea of "national sovereignty," have claimed and gained the right in international law to determine national membership and therefore to determine who can and cannot cross into their claimed territories and to impose any number of restrictions against people who are admitted.

Consequently, in the making of immigration policy, national sovereignty rules. Within the realm of international law, people do not have the right to come to or live and work in Canada if they so choose (other than through the increasingly restricted right to seek asylum if a person fears persecution). In all cases, the state has the right to determine their status. Migration thus is seen to be a contract that the state has the power to more or less unilaterally revoke.[17] Significantly, as Radhika Mongia shows, the Canadian state first claimed this right as a means of opposing the entry of early twentieth-century South Asian migrants as British subjects, despite the fact that these migrants had been assured by the British Crown that they were as British as anyone else in the British Empire.[18] In claiming that Canadian national sovereignty was a more important determinant of Canadian state policies than the nation's privileged membership in the British Empire, the sovereignty of the Canadian state to determine its national membership came into being against the mobility rights of non-whites.

This aspect of sovereignty has allowed the Canadian state to discriminate against various racialized and nationalized groups of migrants in the past and presently. In the so-called post-civil rights era, the national sovereignty claim made it possible, in part, for states to reorganize nationalized labour markets along neo-liberal lines. By recruiting workers through managed-migration schemes, such as the NIEAP, or by severely restricting legal avenues to migration so that more and more people come as "illegals," the state has ensured that the majority of migrants working in Canada lack most, if not all, of the rights associated with membership in the Canadian polity. Canadian immigration policies therefore need to be seen as an ideological device with enormous material consequences. Thus, as I have argued elsewhere, the border is not just the physical boundary separating nationalized spaces but is a line of difference that authorizes the state to carry out practices against non-nationals that are unconstitutional and that are deemed unacceptable, undemocratic, and even manifestly unjust if carried out against citizens or permanent residents.[19] Restrictive immigration policies, therefore, are less about restricting access to Canadian territory than about differentiating amongst those within it – all the while obfuscating the source of the differential inclusion of those workers legally classified as "foreigners."

It is in such practices that we find one of the most important aspects of Canadianness – the continual construction of a negative duality between national subjects and foreigners that nationalist practices work to organize, and that immigration and citizenship policies operationalize. The experiences of those who live as foreigners in Canada are shaped by a constant denial of the social, political, and economic rights of citizenship, as well as a denial of their right to make themselves at home. The flip side of this nationalist scenario is that for those who are accorded the social and legal status of being Canadian, these denials often seem perfectly acceptable. Ideological practices of nationalism, which are never far from those of racism, as Étienne Balibar points out, need to be foregrounded in discussions of how subordination and exploitation have been reproduced through – not in opposition to – the more "inclusive" Canadian national polity and national imaginary of the late 1960s and early 1970s.[20] For this reason, it is important to go against both ideas of "race" and ideas of "nation," and oppose the power of national states to enact such a "nation."[21]

Are all immigrants colonizers?

While there are several ways that national belonging is shaped by neo-liberal practices, one is the racialization of culture. Culture, however, has arrived as a cadaver to the feast of Canadian multiculturalism. There are, of course, multiple cultures within Canada. What the idea of multiculturalism does, ironically, is to disavow the notion that we all share a single geopolitical space known as Canada, as well as a long past and present of countless encounters, interactions, and interdependencies. The idea of multiculturalism was and is an idea that presents each racialized community as having been born in splendid isolation from all others and each having a largely separate existence. The culture of multiculturalism imagines racialized cultures whose key epistemological frames are tradition and timelessness, and which are thus shorn of their dynamism and their socially constructed and relational characteristics.

Multiculturalism, in short, has helped to produce a culture of neo-racism whereby the idea of ethnic culture has replaced the much discredited idea of race. Like past racisms, neo-racist culture also demands racial separation but organizes this through the supposedly tolerant view that each different culture or ethnic group is best valued when left on its own, with its own supposedly unique basis for social organization.[22] In celebrating the tolerance of white Canadians for these so-called different people who, until recently, had been legal targets for discrimination, a new kind of racist understanding of Canada has been cemented. This is the neo-racist view that, along with continuing vertical hierarchies organized around the racialized duality of superior/ inferior, there exist horizontally organized cultural differences. Neo-racist culture, especially after the maturation of neo-liberal politics in the late 1980s, has insisted that these different cultures are best kept apart in fundamental ways. This view has done little to dislodge the centrality of whiteness. Rather, it has insulated whiteness further by representing it as just another culture amongst many, instead of as an emblem of power and a form of dominance over Others.

At first blush, the argument that official multiculturalism as practiced in Canada is a form of neo-racism might seem contradictory. The common-sense understanding of multiculturalism is that differences amongst the polity are to be celebrated instead of condemned. However, the emphasis on *cultural* differences embedded within the discursive practices of multiculturalism need to be juxtaposed with the creation of *material* differences amongst people in Canada, particularly those that arose due to immigration status or ideas of national belonging. Remembering that, in no small part, multiculturalism has come to be a proxy for "dealing with immigrants," the fact that the period of multiculturalism state policies in Canada is the same one that ushered in the Non-Immigrant Employment Authorization Program needs to be taken into account.

That Canada became more open to some non-whites as citizens at the same time that its immigration policies became more restrictive is not a coincidence. Multiculturalism needs to be understood not only as the co-optation of anti-racist demands that it was, but also as a co-optation of some of the targets of racism into the nationalist logics of the Canadian state. As the discursive frame of "we are (almost) all immigrants" came to replace the more politically charged duality of "some of us are Canadian: Others are immigrants," those who had been relegated to the category of immigrant could come to feel a greater sense of national belonging once (almost) everyone was recognized as such. Simultaneously, by re-identifying themselves as immigrants, white Canadians were able to understand colonialism as simply another wave of migration and the violence of colonialism as simply the byproduct of cultural encounters.

These double discursive shifts – the first being the shift in neoracist discourses from race to ethnicity; the second being the existential shift of whites from colonizers to immigrants – allowed for the formation of a citizenship contract that by no means voided what Charles Mills has termed the "racial contract." By embracing non-whites who held citizenship through their birth in Canada, or who had been admitted as permanent residents and therefore had legal access to citizenship, multiculturalism expanded the numbers of those who believed the Canadian state ruled on their behalf. This, in turn, helped to produce not only a changing body of national subjects but also a changing body of so-called foreigners whose subordination within the polity could be legitimated. Becoming legally and socially Canadian, particularly when the ability to do so was often class-based, produced a compact of citizens whereby those so classified could disregard the concerns of those who were classified not only as non-citizens but even as non-immigrants. While some within anti-racist movements clearly saw the subordination of non-immigrants as part of their struggle (the fight for the rights of domestic workers from the Caribbean and Asia is an important example of this),[23] most assumed that their battle against the denial of citizenship was mostly over and therefore focused their energies on the needs of citizens and permanent residents, often in opposition to "foreigners."

Hence, the much-discussed shift in Canadian immigration policy in 1967 and the other, much less-discussed shift of 1973 that led to a program designed to expand the numbers of temporary, migrant workers, need to be seen as intimately tied to one another.[24] Trudeau's 1971 proclamation of a policy of multiculturalism spread the 1967 changes throughout Canadian society while simultaneously making way for the 1973 intensification of unfreedom for a growing population of new migrants, many of whom were non-whites from the Third World. Such intensification was driven both by employers, who advocated for the NIEAP, and the Canadian state, which was eager to meet their demands.

However, this is not the end of the story. The NIEAP has not caused much of a stir in Canadian society largely because those who are being subjugated through it are classified as "foreign workers" who supposedly bear no relationship to the Canadian polity. An anti-racist agenda worthy of its name must take into account how racism is often institutionalized through nationalist practices that differentiate amongst those who are within Canada on the basis of their immigration and citizenship status. This line of thought is significant not only for our ability to challenge the exploitation of non-citizens and non-immigrants, but also for the much-heralded (and in some quarters, celebrated) claims of the "end of multiculturalism" some thirty years after its implementation, a discourse that further obfuscates both the history and current manifestations of racism in Canada.

Indeed, the "end of multiculturalism" rhetoric demonstrates the political maturation of neo-racist arguments. The racism that has come to be more prevalent than ever in the aftermath of 9/11 is a racism that insists that certain non-whites, particularly those who are, or who are perceived to be, Muslim, have a different culture. It is a racism that insists that these different cultures are incompatible with Canadian culture, and suggests that the mixing of cultures (or civilizations) is undesirable, leads to clashes, and, as such, is dangerous. This kind of racism, which is directed by the state especially against non-whites who are also non-citizens, is arguably even more virulent than in previous eras, when assimilation was seen as the cure for difference. Now that many people across the political spectrum view (ethnic) culture as an essential characteristic of self, the re-energized political project of nationalism demands not only that ethnic culture be recognized, but also that each ethnic culture have its own place in the world in the form of its own land base and political community. This is certainly the case in Canada where some white Canadians are reasserting the end of tolerance for Others and their different, supposedly incompatible, and incommunicable cultures. Importantly, the discourse of the end of multiculturalism signals a reinvigoration of anti-immigrant discourses, since "true" Canadians are once again being constituted as "not immigrants."

These neo-racist arguments are not limited to whites who imagine Canada as exclusively theirs, however. It is also evident in some claims of Indigenous sovereignty whereby only those constituted as "Natives" are seen to belong in the plethora of Native nations that are said to comprise Canada. Indeed, there are an increasing number of scholars and activists who argue that all non-Natives, including those who came to Canada because of their own experiences of colonialism or who were brought here as slaves, indentured labourers, refugees, or contemporary migrant workers, are settler-colonizers.[25] This trope confuses and wholly conflates processes of migration with those of colonialism, such that the only decolonization possible is one where everyone lives in their own "Native land" or where all non-Natives are subordinated members of newly sovereign Native polities.

This argument is heavily indebted to the racialization and nationalization of place. In particular, it reproduces colonial state practices of differentiating between Natives and non-Natives. Arguments for the sovereignty of Native national subjects transform the claim that "we are (almost) all immigrants," which conflates colonization with migration, to "all immigrants are colonizers," which conflates all migration to a mode of colonization. By this logic, the migrations of those constituted as Native are wholly denied (indeed the discussion of Natives having migrated is sometimes seen as a colonizing narrative as well) while the colonization of migrants is roundly rejected as a basis for a shared sense of "we-ness."

Thus, thirty years after the start of official multiculturalism, we see a proliferation of discourses that rely on the distinction between national subjects and foreigners. In the aftermath of 9/11, citizenship (or rather the absence of it) has been used to target specific groups of people. Indeed, the main way that the Canadian state has shown its support for the U.S.-led "war on terror" has been to target non-citizens for coercive actions in the name of securing the national space. Whether in the form of Canada's participation in U.S. practices of "extraordinary rendition" to torture, or in the issuance of national security certificates that allow the indefinite incarceration of non-citizens (and only non-citizens) without *habeas corpus* and other common rights of due process, or in the targeting of non-citizens in immigration raids in schools, homes, and workplaces for minor infractions of immigration law, the punishment of non-citizens has become the main way that the state performs its concern for citizens.[26] At the same time, those classified as (im)migrants to Canada are now seen as colonizers for their act of crossing national borders. Their mobility has thus come to be a central problem for both white Canadian and Native nationalists.

Hence, to more completely understand the legitimization of exploitation in Canada, we must not only take into account how antiracism struggles in Canada have tried to incorporate various subordinated groups into the Canadian polity, we also need to challenge sovereignty stories of all sorts – stories that insist upon there being a coincidence of identity, territory, and authority. This claim to sovereignty by the Canadian state forms the basis for legalized discrimination against those deemed to be foreigners, a category that has, throughout modern history, been used to differently include the Other, rather than simply exclude her or him. This claim to sovereignty also legitimates a racialized and ethnicized claim to land and to power.

Our struggles for decolonization must take great care to not merely mimic these sovereignty arguments or simply turn the binary identities imposed upon us on their head to agitate for a nation and a national state of our own. The liberatory (as opposed to nationalist) call, therefore, is a call for a "line of flight"[27] away from ruling ideas and ruling processes of national identifications and towards the ethical-political reconstruction of what has been called the "multitude" or the "motley crew."[28] The multitude is, as Sergio Fiedler puts it, "the trauma of bourgeois society."[29] Its basis of solidarity is fluid. "Fluid solidarities," according to Mohammed A. Bamyeh, are "perspectively fragmented" and subject to self-reflective revision.[30] Consequently, the multitude was in the past, and is still, capable of forming new forms of social relationships based on cooperation through and against existing national borders and racialized communities.[31] The power of the multitude thus lies in its democratic potential – its ability, if exercised, to refuse to succumb to the homogenizing dimensions of the state's transcendent, sovereign power that relies on nefarious projects of identification.

What is at stake is the creation of other forms of identities in which it is not possible to depict some people as foreign. As Chantal Mouffe argues, this will "involve constructing other forms of identity which are going to make people change their perceptions" towards those whose exploitation is legitimated through ideas of national Otherness.[32] Without opposing hegemonic understandings of society as national, we will not be able to make much of a difference in the lives of the so-called foreigners – the Others of modernity – who, in the neo-liberal era of neo-racism, are seen as the quintessential menace to national subjects everywhere.

One step towards challenging the almost-universal political legitimacy of national states and their sovereign right to determine national membership is being taken by No Borders movements and their call for two interconnected, contemporary common rights for every human being: the power to stay, or to prevent one's displacement and dispossession, and the power to move. In working for a world where people are neither defined by their historical relationship to particular places nor are expected to have a static sense of home, No Border movements are redefining the terrain of society itself, and taking a necessary first step in the re-imagining of political community that goes beyond the difference-creating violence of nationalisms of the colonizers or the colonized.

6 Multiculturalism already unbound

Margaret Walton-Roberts

MANY OF THE INTELLECTUAL DEBATES circulating today regarding Canadian multiculturalism tend to focus on how multiculturalism operates at the local or national scale. In this chapter, I consider how forms of citizenship participation practiced by Indian immigrants within the multicultural framework of Canada simultaneously configure local *and* transnational community development. I explore how Canada's official policy of multiculturalism informs the country's position in a landscape that is increasingly internationalized, transnational, and globally interpolated. Using concrete examples from my research on Indian immigration to Canada and associated transnational practices, I illustrate how multiculturalism, as a Canadian policy, interacts with transnational circulations of people, capital, and ideas, and in the process becomes unbound from the confines of Westphalian sovereignty. This unboundedness reflects both the spatial breadth of the labour search that migrant-receiving nations such as Canada engage in, as well as the cultural, economic, and political constrictions migrants face once within the receiving nation.

Bounded multiculturalism

Debating, exploring, bemoaning, and celebrating multiculturalism is a cottage industry in Canada, where we have made much of multiculturalism under the various arguments that multiculturalism makes much of us (as in official rhetoric), or that it divides the nation, or hollows out national identity, or acts as a subterfuge camouflaging inequality.[1] Recently Ley has written "in defence of multiculturalism," arguing that multiculturalism becomes a convenient target to blame for all kinds of social ills, from riots and terrorism to general cultural discord, when, in fact, poverty, social exclusion, and even unpopular government foreign policy should be the appropriate target.[2] Ley's argument, along with others, supports the idea that multiculturalism (in the citizenship-plus or structural multiculturalism model) is currently the only show in town when it comes to building inclusive communities within contexts of ethnic diversity.[3] As such, instead of *rethinking* immigrant incorporation in the face of dubious "evidence" that our multiculturalism model is failing, we should instead leave things as they are, or "let the dogs sleep"[4] – even if we don't eat them, as Stoffman suggests we might in a truly multicultural setting.[5]

For Canada, multiculturalism has protected the nation from the potentially fragmenting forces of difference presented by indigenous claims, Québécois separation pressures, and international migration. As a result, it has provided one option around which the Canadian state and its diverse population can attempt to cohere. As Audrey Kobaybashi argues, "multiculturalism policy, and the web of cultural relations that it engenders, is an important and effective means of mediation, and ties Canadian government to popular interests in ways seldom achieved in other countries."[6] The success Kobayashi attributes to multiculturalism depends upon the active participation of immigrants in citizenship practices, whether constituted institutionally, culturally, or materially.[7] Bloemraad argues that of the four dimensions of citizenship – legal status, rights, identity, and participation – participation is a vital concept for considering the interaction between individual immigrants and the sociopolitical community that grants membership.[8] But citizenship participation has tended to be interpreted somewhat one-dimensionally to denote political voting rights. This chapter goes beyond such a narrow frame to consider immigration itself as a process that engenders a number of opportunities for citizenship participation via rights that are transnationally, as opposed to nationally, constructed.

During the current era of post-national and transnational engagement, immigration raises fundamental questions that challenge the political status quo and demand an international perspective in order to frame effective analytical assessments and responses.[9] This can be seen in Saskia Sassen's observation that the immigration debate brings into focus a tension between a denationalizing of economic space on the one hand and a renationalizing of political discourse on the other.[10] She argues that

> the existence of two different regimes for the circulation of capital and the circulation of immigrants, as well as two equally different regimes

for the protection of human rights and the protection of state sovereignty, pose problems that cannot be solved by the rules of the game. It is in this sense that immigration is a strategic site to inquire about the limits of the new order: it feeds the renationalization of politics and the notion of the importance of sovereign control over borders, yet it is embedded in a larger dynamic of transnationalization of economic spaces and human rights regimes.[11]

The "new order" Sassen refers to is grounded in the ascendance of the global economy. In the Canadian case, this "new order" can be seen in the simultaneous transnational sourcing of migrant labour, and the material and rhetorical disaggregation of various rights within national space. Yet immigration and the increasing differentiation or "super diversity" it entails has not been forced upon Canada.[12] As Sassen asserts, "the state itself has been a key agent in the implementation of global processes" and as a result "sovereignty has been decentered and territory partly denationalized."[13] In addition, immigration has moved from being a domestic policy of nation-building to one that is primarily a response to international competition for talent.[14] Immigration, once sufficiently controlled from within the legal frameworks of the sovereign state, is now monitored by international human rights organizations and populations whose own immigrant backgrounds make them highly vocal contributors to issues of policy. "Immigration," Sassen contends, "is thus a sort of wrench one can throw into theories about sovereignty."[15]

Immigration policy, citizenship, and multiculturalism

In 1967, Canadian immigration policy shifted to the points system as Canada sought to decouple immigration from racial preference. This policy change, however, was not enacted for altruistic reasons. In the late 1960s, Canada faced a shortage of immigrants from Europe and the United States, the traditional preferred source regions, and in order to continue its economic expansion it needed labour. Thus the policy changes reflected the market logic of the day, and launched Canada into a new phase of reciprocal entanglement with the globalized circuits of human mobility. Moreover, Canada had also signed onto the Geneva Convention, a commitment that required some policy realignment in order for the country to meet its international obligations.[16]

Even with these changes to immigration policy, immigrant numbers were still constrained by the geographical distribution of Canadian immigration offices.[17] The machinery of the state needed time to catch up to the realities of the new sources of global labour market supply, a delay that permitted a lag to occur in transmitting the new "colour blind" nature of immigration policy into the reality of immigrant admissions. Such differentiations are still evident in current immigration policy as consulates in different countries exhibit different processing times that reflect a combination of source region demand, resource allocation, and the degree of application assessment required. Immigration has continued primarily to service Canada's economic and demographic needs, with the dominant makeup of permanent immigrants shifting away from sponsored family to point-based economic class immigrants. At the same time, there has been a gradual reduction in the percentage of refugees admitted, despite the fact that Canada has an international, legally mandated commitment to the most globally vulnerable (see figure 6.1). Today, Canadian immigration continues a trend that sees increased selection of the most qualified through the points system (even though their skills are devalued post-migration). The state has also increasingly turned to temporary workers to service labour needs, with the number of temporary foreign workers increasing 31 per cent between 2006 and 2010, compared to a 11 per cent increase in permanent immigrants over the same period.[18]

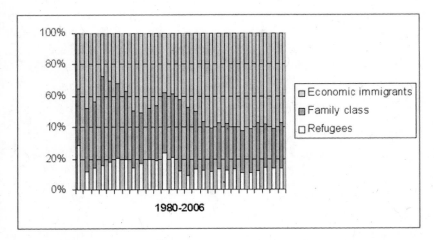

Figure 6.1: Immigrant category as percentage of total arrivals, 1980–2006 (source: CIC Facts and Figures, 2006)

Despite the increase in the number of economic-class immigrants, among the greatest challenges today with regard to immigration and migrant labour are labour market inequalities. Immigrants experience higher unemployment rates than Canadian-born persons, no return on pre-migration education, lower earnings, and lower labour market participation rates relative to Canadian-born workers.[19] Earnings inequality and instability has worsened for the 1990–2000 immigrant cohort compared to earlier cohorts.[20] Such outcomes are arguably beyond the jurisdiction of official multiculturalism policy.[21] Nevertheless, the equality and non-discrimination embedded in the idea of structural or deep multiculturalism requires that something be done about what is increasingly being recognized as a structural form of discrimination in the Canadian economy. Yet it is impossible to conclusively disentangle the variables that might account for these discrepancies in the econometric models that politicians and policymakers turn to for guidance. The tensions Sassen highlights between the denationalizing of economic space and the renationalizing of political discourse can be clearly identified in the debates surrounding the de-skilling of Canada's immigrant labour and the vexing problem of immigrants lacking "Canadian experience."[22] Rather than viewing this unevenness as something anomalous, it can instead be seen as a core component of neo-liberalization.[23] The multicultural rhetoric the state relies upon to nurture social cohesion and national identity appears to be a weak foil against the tendency of the labour market to discount foreign skills in order to gain forms of flexibility. But, rather than being an innocent bystander in this tragedy of immigrant human capital devaluation, multiculturalism might actually constitute one tool that enables this process of labour differentiation to occur.

Neo-liberalism in action: State management of difference

Multiculturalism can be seen as a key process by which the state manages difference by maintaining control over the power to name and annex "the other," thus reproducing itself and avoiding a crisis of citizenship. This scenario echoes Hage's criticism that multiculturalism creates a social field where the white manager manages the non-white, thereby securing the top positions for white management and placating white anxiety.[24] Goldberg puts it differently, demonstrating how a "traffic cop state" oversees, manages, and facilitates flows of information, goods, capital, and ideas.[25] Here, the rhetoric of multiculturalism does not necessarily contradict or undermine the neo-liberal agenda; in fact, it actively facilitates and reproduces the supply of flexible labour, one of the vital flows in the market economy.[26]

For Goldberg, this "traffic cop state" emerges alongside the neo-liberalization of race, where everything, including race, becomes privatized.[27] In the context of Canadian immigration, this might take the shape of professional immigration consultants who, faced with a system staggering under the weight of its own backlog, constantly seek out ways to capitalize on the latest loophole. Immigration consultants have become the expensive arbiters of the immigration application process for many, especially in nations where demand, and in turn, the rejection rate, is high. Even a cursory examination of immigration processing reveals distinct geographic inequities: while in London, England, 80 per cent of grandparent sponsorship applications are processed within eleven months, it takes forty-five months in New Delhi.[28] Once in Canada, immigrants are directed to under-resourced immigrant service providers mandated to deal with structurally embedded, systemic labour-market constraints. Indeed, many of these service providers are themselves immigrants who are underpaid and underemployed.[29] To enter the labour market using the skills for which they were poached, immigrants have to pay to have their qualifications and accreditations "translated" in order to convert their human and social capital for yet another Canadian audience (first the federal government gatekeeper, then the provincial professional association gatekeeper). Immigrants might then set up new Canadian homes, and in the process invest their savings (often transferred from outside Canada) into the real estate and consumer markets. Meanwhile, as Goldberg argues, the state does not have to be actively involved in this marginalization; it merely conserves what is already in place.[30]

Proponents of the current immigration system argue that the middle-class focus of immigrant selection criteria that has accompanied the rise in skilled migration selects individuals who will "hit the ground running," even as that ground is full of the metaphorical potholes of credentialism and "Canadian experience" requirements. In this regard, certain classes of immigrant, or "flexible citizens," to use Aihwa Ong's terminology, are able to articulate with neo–liberalizing tendencies that move state expenditure away from collective social programs, thereby enhancing the privatization of social services through the growth of the shadow state.[31] At the other end of the migrant stream, we see temporary labourers increasingly used to facilitate the labour force flexibility and restructuring required in the "race to the bottom" variant of globalization. Thus migrants, both permanent and temporary, at both ends of the skill spectrum, are willing and unwilling actors in the ongoing restructuring and globalization of the Canadian economy.

Canadian multiculturalism, then, is not a bulwark to neo-liberalism; rather it intersects with the retraction of state social investment while also enhancing international economic advantage. After all, the Canadian state has long viewed ethnic diversity and multiculturalism as an economic resource to the nation.[32] In the Australian context, Hage has critiqued the multicultural discourse of "productive diversity" for the way it exploits ethnicity "to make it yield a kind of ethnic surplus value."[33] Mitchell interrogates Canada's articulation with Asian capital in the 1980s, the related expansion of the business immigration program, and the resultant "multiculturalism means business" agenda that emerged. She argues that this discourse entrenched a neo-liberal political agenda that promoted self reliance and social cutbacks.[34] Such joining of multiculturalism and the economy has recently re-emerged in Canada, this time embedded in the argument that due to Canada's inertia and ignorance, the nation is not taking enough advantage of its multicultural talent – or "ethnic surplus value" – in order to succeed in the global economy.[35] This concern is evident in three other related areas: the high rate of Asian return migration from Canada; the argument that non-immigrant Canadians do not possess the innovative risk-taking nature immigrants have; and the constant concern over Canada's dominant trading relationship with the United States, which many argue is responsible for Canada's limited global trade exposure.[36] Multiculturalism offers a means to overcome the economic deficiency embedded in this provincial Canadian mentality because it forges global networking, the holy grail of the international business mindset. As Canada strives to "internationalize," immigration and multiculturalism become immense domestic resources, a situation that provides a fine example of Goldberg's "traffic cop state": since the management of flows both allows and disallows, it can be selective. The goal of flow management is to produce the best returns for the nation with the least public investment. For Canada, then, selecting people and managing their movement is sovereignty in action. Even if that practice is informed by international competition for talent, the state still determines the terms of the talent-for-citizenship exchange.[37] From this perspective, multiculturalism is a policy tool that supports the state's neo-liberalizing agenda insofar as it upholds the selective valorization of ethnic difference within the context of global migration.

This nexus between neo-liberalism and multiculturalism highlights an important critique of multiculturalism. Even if we interpreted it as the mostly benign public management of ethnic and racial difference that is relatively successful in a Canadian context, it would still have some major limitations from a social justice perspective. Multicultural-ism is officially bound to the state, while migration processes and migrants' rights are increasingly being unbound from state protection and social inclusion. To further social justice in a world that produces the migratory effects that inform Canada's immigration model, we must also unbound multiculturalism from its sometimes myopic nation-alism. I offer a provisional run at this issue from the perspective of work conducted on India–Canada immigration and transnational relations.[38]

Unbounding multiculturalism

The long view of India-Canada relations

Sovereignty, exclusive territory, and citizenship mark the specificity of the nation–state, and immigration poses challenges to all of these. My research has shown that while Indian immigrants (particularly Sikhs from Punjab in northern India) have played a role in unbounding mul-ticulturalism from its circumscribed Canadianness, this internationaliz-ing of the nation–state through immigration, particularly through Indian immigration, is not a new phenomenon.

Radhika Mongia has argued that the nineteenth-century develop-ment of a Canadian dominion distinct from the British Empire was rooted in the desire to deny entry to Indian immigrants.[39] The com-plexity of colonial relations in which Canada was embedded at that time made the country's exclusion of Indian nationals – then subjects of the British Empire – problematic. Mongia illustrates how Canada was able to enact a racist strategy of exclusion without naming race by demanding passports for all free Indian migrants in 1915. The emer-gence of the passport introduced a universality that "would function differentially" and which disguised both the Canadian government's blatant racism and the British colonial desire to prevent the unraveling of Empire due to the obvious differential treatment of its subjects along racialized lines.[40] Thus, Mongia asserts, "the emergence of the nation-state as the first state formation to exercise a monopoly over migration indicates not that control over mobility begins *after* the formation of the nation-state but that the very development of the nation-state occurs, in part, to control mobility along the axes of the nation-race."[41]

India's important role in the formation of the Canadian nation–state continues today. Numerous politicians now laud the "people-to-peo-ple" links that currently exist between the two countries.[42] Yet the relationship has seen its share of ups and downs in the century follow-ing the introduction of the free Indian passport. In 1998, observers

were optimistic that increasing connections emerging from India's economic growth would be the most likely way to overcome the relative
indifference existing between Canada and India. However, by 2002,
the lacklustre trade relations between the two nations "remain[ed] virtually stillborn."[43] Despite the relatively weak Indo-Canadian trade climate, India has consistently been one of the top two sources for
immigrants to Canada for over a decade, an association that has led to a
significant bureaucratic institutional relationship. If multiculturalism
allows the state to manage the difference it absorbs from outside its
borders, then the example of Indian immigrants provides an important
case to study. The following examples suggest that managing difference,
even if it were the explicit intention of the state, is not so easily
achieved.

The "traffic cop" state struggles to control

The overseas consular office, the front line of immigration operations,
is an important site for understanding the political processes that shape
human mobility and the practice of statehood. The overseas embassy or
consulate is typically experienced as a site of asymmetrical power relations where race and class heavily influence the treatment that "third
world" applicants receive. The obvious power imbalance and possible
discrimination linked to visa issuance have become prominent issues for
immigrant advocacy groups. Some of these groups represent what
Appadurai sees as "instances or incubators of a postnational global
order" who "work their way around the nation-state without directly
questioning its jurisdiction."[44] The Global Organization of People of
Indian Origin (GOPIO) is a prime example of such an incubator, since it
represents the interests of a deterritorialized, globally diasporic community. Yet it also directs its recommendations clearly at the national practices of both the "Mother" nation of India and the multiple sites of
Indian settlement around the world.[45] Since 1989, GOPIO has held various conventions and passed numerous resolutions that have, among
other things, demanded peaceful resolutions to conflicts affecting people of Indian origin in Fiji and elsewhere, encouraged all nations to
promote policies of multiculturalism, and advocated for dual nationality
for people of Indian origin overseas.[46] During the group's 2000 convention, held in Zurich, a resolution was passed on the "Adoption and
Promulgation of Guidelines to Preserve Human Dignity in Visa Application Procedures."[47] The resolution called upon the United Nations
to establish broad guidelines for foreign embassies regarding visa
issuance, such as ensuring applicants' comfort while waiting, and allowing visas to be granted by mail in order to avoid the need for personal

appearances. The final point of the resolution demanded that the "diplomatic mission must make every effort to act in a manner that purges the impression of irrationality and adhocism in the visa application procedure."[48] GOPIO's demands exposed the concern that many Indians harbour regarding their treatment at consular offices as well as the anxieties they bring to meetings with state officials.

In the case of Canada, Indian citizens, together with those from over 130 mostly developing nations, are required to secure a visitor visa in order to travel to Canada. In some cases, this may require attending an in-person interview at the Canadian High Commission in Delhi, or at one of the other ten visa application processing offices that have been established across India and Nepal. The Canadian High Commission in New Delhi, set back from the wide grassy boulevards of Shantipath, offers a haven from the chaotic streets of the busy metropolis. This area is home to most embassies in the city, and the space has been divided by dozens of micro-borders, designed to control the crowds of Indian nationals who line up against high, well-patrolled fences. Shantipath is a physical manifestation of the everyday struggle of global migrants against the borders of state sovereignty. The Canadian New Delhi High Commission enclosure has at least five gates, each of which is guarded. The entrance for those attending interviews for visas is marked by metal gates, which contain the early-morning queue in an orderly fashion, and booths with glass windows, behind which locally engaged staff offer tokens to the first people in line. Immigration officials assess the degree to which each interviewee presents a flight risk if she or he were given permission to visit Canada. High Commission figures in 2000 showed that up to a third of applicants each year were refused visitor visas.[49]

While Canadian multiculturalism may not appear to be relevant here, the multicultural reality of Canada is an important force that, through the processes of transnational social networks formed by decades of chain migration, directs potential immigrants to the walls of the Canadian High Commission.[50] In the case of Canada, social network migration produces spatial networks that consolidate the influence of the major sending region of the Indian state of Punjab. Punjabi-Canadians have long demanded a more substantial Canadian presence in the state, and gained this in the opening of a Consulate General in Chandigarh, Punjab, a development that was met by objections from senior Canadian bureaucrats and has been criticized by some members of the press as a Liberal party attempt to appease the Indo-Canadian community.[51] The Chandigarh case is interesting insofar as it reveals the lack of influence opposing Canadian officials had in the face of demands from a transnational community whose constituents had been emigrating to Canada for over a century. This event thus stands as an important example of how the Punjabi diaspora in Canada were able to mobilize multiculturalism to achieve their transnational aims.

A further incident of bureaucratic impotence in regards to influencing migration occurred when a delegation of university and college leaders from British Columbia were in India recruiting students and professionals. During a meeting with the chief visa officer in Canada's New Delhi High Commission, members of the delegation reported that he stated that:

> he did not understand why the heck we were recruiting in the Punjab; the state of the Punjab has the highest crime and forgery rate anywhere; the highest human-trafficking statistics in the world, and that we should be recruiting in South India.[52]

The incident was reported to a number of officials and resulted in British Columbia's Attorney General Wally Oppal expressing his concern that "all of this is starting to fester in the Indian community. I get calls from people in the Asian community suggesting perhaps our officials are racist."[53] Lost in this reaction is the fact that the chief visa officer's comments were not directed at Indians in general, but at a specific regional community with a historical and geographical connection to Canada. The officer was suggesting that other regions of India, not other nations, should be the focus of student recruitment. These geographical distinctions must be attended to because they reveal how the traffic cop state operates within specific spatial and historical relations in terms of what Goldberg has referred to as "racial regionalization": "The force of race assumes its power," he asserts, "in and from the thick contexts of the different if related geopolitical regions in which it is embedded, the specific conditions of which concretize the notion of race representing them."[54] The multicultural nature of Canada has become unbound in the various ways that these migratory channels from Indian Punjab to Canada reproduce themselves through channels of the state (the Consulate in Chandigarh is but one example), and the comments of the chief visa officer in New Delhi demonstrate the power of such networks and the seeming impotence of parts of the state to control them.

Before we become too engaged in self-satisfied castigation of Canadian bureaucratic officers, however, we must recognize that being a visa officer for Citizenship and Immigration Canada (CIC) today is a demanding job. Part of the reason for the backlog of immigration applications is the immense amount of due diligence required in screening applications (combined with the under-resourcing, deliberate or otherwise, of the department). The waiting rooms and back offices of Canada's overseas offices are important nodes where the traffic cop state is in action (or is not, which is also a form of state action), but the idea of an all-powerful state body in total control is absurd, and sometimes "seeing like a state" involves being overwhelmed by the work and the responsibility of protecting sovereignty.[55] Immigration officials estimate that Indian nationals comprise the fourth largest group of undocumented arrivals in Canada, which justifies their rigid approach to visa processing. This rigidity informs and is informed by racial regionalization. An example of this was clearly displayed during a High Commission social event I attended in December 1999. "The Club Canada Players," a social group composed of immigration staff from the Canadian High Commission in New Delhi, put on a pantomime called *Cinderellaji*. The performance was a public fundraising event held adjacent to the bar and swimming pool of the High Commission's social club area. The cast was made up of a variety of CIC officers, and the audience was mostly CIC's Canadian staff, families, and friends; as far as I could tell none were of Indian origin. One song in particular, sung to the tune of "Tie a Yellow Ribbon," was a cynical presentation of the typical Punjabi seeking a visitor visa for Canada.

I stood in line, got token five
Now, I've got to show that jerk I'm bonafide
If he believes my story, which consists of mostly lies
Then he'll know just what to do
Let me book my flight
Leave this place tonight. . . .

Put a student visa in my passport please
I spent 14 Lakh on these fake degrees[56]
If I don't get a visa with these fake degrees
I'll stay in the Punjab
Forget about Toronto
And blame it on CIC
If I don't get a visa with my fake degrees

Put a goddam visa in my passport please
It's been six long hours since I paid my fees
If I don't get my visa telling me I'll soon be free

I'll write to my M.P.
I'll file an appeal
And try a little bribery . . .
If I don't get a visa with my fake degrees

The lyrics of this song reflect the extent to which potential migrants are already embedded in transnational circuits; in particular the reference, "I'll write to my M.P. I'll file an appeal," suggests that the potential migrant has access to Canadian as well as Indian forms of representation, which many may have through kinship and other contacts. These lyrics suggest that Indo-Canadians can extend their Canadian citizenship rights to kin of Indian nationality, and how CIC officials are well aware of this connection.

I was initially surprised by the nature of this song; the unequivocal stereotyping of Indian visa applicants as liars, cheats, and potential fraudsters implies an entrenched bias, despite the personal commitment many officials express to an immigration system based on fairness and equity. It justifies GOPIO's demands for a humanization of the visa application process. But the song also demonstrates how the state is not always in control of what many consider the last vestige of sovereignty – the ability to determine who enters into their national space. The lyrics give voice to the futility that some visa officers experience with regard to their jobs. We need to recognize that the processes of admission are not always dehumanized and mechanistic, but are often the product of multiple power struggles informed by various political and public pressures. The development of the Canadian mission in Chandigarh and the challenges faced by visa processing officers in New Delhi and Punjab speak to that struggle and reflect the reality of Canada's unbounding multiculturalism. While Indian migration from Punjab has traditionally been rooted in family or chain migration, as Canadian immigration generally has shifted towards greater economic-class immigration, so too has migration from this region. This shift has been partly achieved through the increasing role of the immigration consultant, a development that also poses challenges to the state.

Talking back to the state
In 1997, CIC launched a global promotional campaign for skilled migrants, and immigration consultants emerged to meet the demand for intermediaries able to assess and file successful applications. The number of Indian immigration consultants ballooned in the 1990s in response to new immigration processing and Indian financial deregulation that permitted greater conversion of the Indian rupee.[57] In some

cases, these immigration consultants are Canadian citizens of Indian origin, and their active role in the expansion of immigration introduces a new balance of power into Canada's immigration system. The presence of such mediators is nowhere more clearly displayed than in the streets of Chandigarh, the capital of Punjab and Harayana, where the pages of daily newspapers and shop fronts display the encouraging words this growing sector of the Indian service economy deploys in its marketing mission.[58] In Chandigarh in December 1999, I spoke with representatives of World Wide Immigration Consultants Service (wwics), an agency that focuses on providing skilled applicants with immigration support that includes offices throughout India, as well as an office in Mississauga, Ontario, dealing with client settlement and employment placement in Canada. wwics' role in the immigration process illustrates the transnational strategies of negotiation that intermediaries bring to the immigration process. They act as the marketers of Canada overseas, and highlight the allure of Canada as an immigrant destination. At times such efforts are exuberant:

> Canada – A Heaven on Earth. The Canadian Government provides abundant welfare incentives, free medical, free education (up to 13th grade), highly subsidized university education, free houses for senior citizens and equal opportunities for all. It is a totally crime free country, ensuring a lifestyle devoid of any fear and apprehensions. It also offers a pollution free environment to live in.[59]

To Indian professionals worrying about their own and their children's future, this description is the heady stuff of dreams. For applicants with the right skills and $3,000 Canadian, plus the landing and processing fee, wwics promises it can help you succeed in Canada, and claims that it is the largest Canadian immigration consultancy in India.[60] The director of wwics, Colonel Sandhu, is an Indian ex-military man and now a Canadian citizen. In the 1980s, he owned a supermarket in Toronto, and was shocked by the number of undocumented Punjabi immigrants in the city. He encouraged a number of them to file with the Immigration Refugee Board, and based on the terrorism and police action occurring in Punjab at that time, many applications were successful. He began to work for an immigration law firm on an honorarium basis, and in 1993 decided to set up his own immigration consulting firm, which, at the time of my interview in the late 1990s, employed five hundred staff in offices across twenty-four Indian cities and fifty staff at its Canadian offices in Mississauga.

WWICS prides itself on its near total success rate. The director and staff claim that they offer a 99.9 per cent success rate; indeed their brochure advertises a "Zero Risk Factor, a written guarantee for refund of entire amount of professional fee if one doesn't get immigration."[61] In part, the consultants can offer this because they only submit applications that meet the required number of points, but they have also developed a system of appeals based on the knowledge they have gained as transnational actors familiar with the legal checks and balances Canadian federal departments are subject to. In cases where WWICS has submitted an application that has been rejected, they write a letter to the visa officer requesting an explanation within thirty days. Following this, they file a judicial review in the Federal Court of Canada using lawyers they retain in Toronto. If the case still fails, they re-file the application. The judicial review process determines whether there is any evidence of procedural unfairness, and the majority of cases, by CIC managers' estimates, are ruled in CIC's favour.[62] Though the CIC managers support the applicant's right to review, they are frustrated by the extra resources needed to deal with judicial reviews (which are priority cases with strict court appointed deadlines). An increase in judicial reviews also contributes to general processing backlogs. In this situation, Canada's Citizenship and Immigration Department is subjected to forms of external scrutiny initiated by immigrant actors who make full and active use of the rights available to non-citizens.

These examples illustrate how the immigration process is a site of struggle, and though the state is in control of legislation in setting targets and managing the process, it is disputable that they have total control, since potential migrants, in this case those from Punjab, have access to judicial oversight mechanisms through various third-party agents. Multiculturalism in these cases has created a sense of political empowerment for the significant Punjabi-Canadian population in Canada, who use their influence to strengthen Canadian institutional presence in the region, which in turn strengthens the type and nature of networks between the regions. Attempting to shift the efforts of Canadian officials away from a focus on northern to southern India, or indeed from one class of application to another, creates reaction at various public and state levels that can be utilized to reproduce the translocal networks between the two sites. The following example examines the post-migration experience in Canada, where the constrictions of settlement inform identity formation, and unbounded multiculturalism comes into play again.

The territorialities of diaspora and the multicultural nation

Despite the celebratory tone of recent explorations of diaspora, diasporic formations can operate to relay absolutist/essentialized versions of nation and identity. As Carter argues in the case of the Croatian diaspora, we must pay attention to the territorialities of the diaspora and not just the nation. In the case of the Punjabi migrants I have discussed above, the interaction between diasporic territorialities (in the case of the Punjabi diaspora) and a multicultural context (in the case of Canada) provides an opportunity to examine how seemingly countervailing ideologies and practices can be mapped onto each other with surprising and unpredictable outcomes.

Canada has had an uncertain strategy regarding its relations with India.[63] Canada's extended nuclear sanctions in the 1990s, past tensions over terrorism linked to Sikh separatists, and concern about Sri Lankan groups in the present, have all contributed to undermining diplomatic and trade relations.[64] The connection between Canada and India is especially interesting considering the important role of the Punjab as a traditional source of Indian immigration to Canada, since Punjab separatism has long been a concern for the Government of India.[65] Sikh demands for a separate territory known as Khalistan had been violently suppressed by the Indian government in the 1980s and 1990s during a period known as the Punjab "troubles." In my interview with the Indian then-Deputy Secretary, NRI (Non-Resident Indian) Affairs, in February of 2000, he commented that the Khalistan Sikh separatism issue had been contained and India had excellent cooperation from the United Kingdom, the United States and – considering the actions of Canadian-based Sikh separatists – "even" Canada in dealing with the threat of insurgency.[66] As Tatla has pointed out, the Khalistan problems in Punjab were initiated and sustained through transnational networks that worked through other states that were not immediately cognizant of the difficulties these networks would create for the central Indian state.[67] Gayer, echoing Dusenbery, has argued that the relationship between the politics of diasporic Sikh identity and the host nation's multicultural immigrant policies "legitimated such politics of identity in the private sphere but also in the public one."[68] Arguably, overseas political agitation has a longer history than multiculturalism, as it was already evident in the actions of overseas Indians involved in the Ghadar movement, which sought Indian independence from Britain at the turn of the nineteenth century.[69] Such nationalist movements born of dislocation and displacement are, of course, not new. Anderson recounts various historical examples of such long-distance nationalism that were encouraged with the rise of print capitalism.[70] But the reality of Sikh separatism today, as Gayer maintains, might be more usefully assessed as a form of Appaduria's "trojan nationalism" since it does not necessarily seek territorial nationalism.[71] Rather, it is more concerned with a politics of recognition within a diasporic or transnational landscape that compensates for the emotional anguish of dislocation. This has clearly been the view of many scholars who have argued that the politics of Sikh separatism is an outlet for a community who have been thwarted in their efforts to achieve sufficient status, economic or otherwise, both in their source and destination locations.[72] The case of Sikh separatism is an example where multiculturalism becomes unbound, since it is used as a vehicle for ethno-religious groups to build an officially acknowledged identity that can be used to activate their overseas resistance to homeland affairs.[73]

Canada can therefore be seen as one node within a global Sikh separatist identity that has been enabled, in part, by multiculturalism, but is also shaped by the lack of status afforded to immigrants via more orthodox routes such as the labour market. Likewise, the goal of organizations that support separatist movements may actually be less about the construction of Khalistan in Punjab, but more about building status and identity in Canada and across the global Sikh diaspora. Indeed Gayer argues that Khalistan is used by diasporic Sikhs to create a politics of recognition in the host state, but simultaneously generates "an exit reaction from Sikhs of the Punjab towards the Khalistan movement."[74] The resulting disconnect between home and host also extends to the relations between the Indian and Canadian government. The government of India monitors and blacklists any overseas associations that promote separatism, and if members of such organizations visit India, the central government maintains surveillance.[75] This surveillance has had a particular effect on Canadian Sikhs, and their lobbying efforts in Canada resulted in the Indian Government promising in the early 2000s to review controversial visa blacklists that might include Indo-Canadians who have never been involved with separatist action.[76] While the Indian government has been criticized for overreacting to Sikh separatist issues, in Canada there is still, even in the post-Air-India era, a naiveté demonstrated by politicians with regard to the presence and nature of Sikh separatism.[77]

Sikhs are traditionally presented as the fighters and farmers of India, and the religious and political culture of Sikhism celebrates those who take up arms for justifiable causes. It is in determining what is justifiable that controversy emerges. Under the aegis of multiculturalism, overt political activism has sometimes been staged by Sikh-Canadians, and interpreted by incognizant Canadian politicians merely as "red boots multiculturalism." Such was the case with the Sikh *Vaisakhi* parade, held in Vancouver, British Columbia, in 2007. Certain Canadian Sikh politicians avoided the event, aware of the fact that various parade floats would be celebrating Sikh "martyrs," some of whom had been linked to the Air India bombing and Indira Gandhi's assassination. Other, possibly less informed, politicians attended the parade only to offer embarrassing explanations later when publicly questioned about the event.[78] In such situations, state actors must manage reactions to events that are expressive of an unbound multiculturalism – local events that reproduce political concerns emanating from beyond the nation that, in the process of enunciation, embed themselves within a national dialogue. Thus, Sikh separatism can be viewed as an issue that is at least partly grounded in certain communities in Canada.

The Canadian state's management or mismanagement of these affairs suggests an ignorance of, or disinterest in, the complex political and cultural issues that are significant to Canadian immigrant communities with transnational political concerns. This unbound multiculturalism emerges from the state's need for labour, a need that has caused the state to expand its reach into international labour pools, while at the same time constricting settlement processes so that immigrant dislocation results in the experience of either marginality, or the lacuna of inhabiting an inauthentic place.[79] In both cases, the process of identity reconstruction becomes fraught. Canada currently lives with the huge void created by the lack of convictions from the Air India trials, and the horrendous missteps revealed in the Air India inquiry are still playing out in the public arena. Together they demonstrate the immense learning curve the state has been on in coming "to terms with the difference between being a land of immigrants and being one node in a post national network of diasporas."[80]

Conclusion

Discussions of multiculturalism must continue to consider the ways in which it engages not only with domestic preoccupations regarding Canadian identity, but also with the realities of global migration and labour circulation, which are structured by global systems of inequality. Canada both participates in and exploits these systems in order to service its own economic needs. When it is seen as prudent for the nation, Canadian multiculturalism is advertised globally to attract transnational entrepreneurs and skilled workers, who represent the epitome of productive diversity. Yet, when it comes to commoditized global, low-skilled labour inputs, the rights promoted in the rhetoric of multiculturalism suddenly become constrained and ruled out through the retraction of citizenship and the protection of privileged sections of the labour market. Labour-market constrictions work to diminish the agency of migrant actors, who may then turn elsewhere to find compensation for status deficits. It is a testament to multiculturalism's success that active political immigrant citizenship does articulate itself in the democratic political system and that immigrant communities do access resources and exert their influence alongside other actors in civil society.

This chapter has highlighted some examples where Canadian multiculturalism has become unbound and gone global through immigrant practices of community reproduction and identity/status building. Multiculturalism as an ideology of state-building reveals the state as being very careful to prescribe the type of belonging and the extent of inclusion. However, these restrictions are constantly challenged by transnational migrants who incorporate non-citizens into the state in order to reproduce community, and advance their own agendas from within national frameworks of belonging. Immigrants can insert themselves into the political process and demand recognition not only in Canada but also abroad, in terms of how their adopted nation officially relates to and services their homeland. State bureaucrats and civil servants resort to outbursts and pantomime in order to express their frustration at trying to direct externalized migration streams that are already deeply embedded in the transnational fabric of Canada.

What this chapter suggests is that Goldberg's traffic cop state has not been fully actualized in this instance, nor has multiculturalism fully annexed the ethnic other who resides outside of physical territorial boundaries. Immigration consultants take advantage of their own flexible citizenship to challenge state exclusion by employing the state's own mechanisms against itself. In the case of Canadian Sikhs, identity formation challenges the idea of the bounded body of the nation, both at home and abroad, and must be understood as a product of both the constrictions enforced by the immigration settlement process and the expansiveness evident in the international sourcing of skilled labour. Understanding and appreciating the intersections of these processes under the aegis of multiculturalism should encourage debate that is both more sophisticated and more grounded in relation to immigration, citizenship rights, and the role of multiculturalism in the national and transnational construction of Canadian identity.

Part 3

Lands

7 Recognition politics and reconciliation
fantasies: Liberal multiculturalism and the
"Indian land question"

Brian Egan

MULTICULTURALISM AS STATE POLICY IN CANADA is grounded in an attempt to come to terms with what is perceived as a problematic proliferation of "ethnic communities" in the nation, many of which are seen to be only loosely attached to any kind of distinctly "Canadian" identity.[1] This growing diversity of cultural groups within the nation is traced primarily to successive waves of immigration throughout the twentieth century, and particularly the arrival of non-white or non-European (i.e., "ethnic") peoples, which changed the face of the Canadian social body. By the 1970s, what had been long represented, according to dominant historical narratives of the nation, as the core Canadian cultural identity – Anglo-white – was in need of serious revision and reconstruction. Through the concept of multiculturalism, a new story of the Canadian nation was developed, one that recognized this diversity and sought to construct a unified Canadian identity through the harmonization or reconciliation of this ethnic difference – unity was to be found in diversity. Given the central importance of processes of recognition and reconciliation in the building of this new national identity, as elaborated in both official state discourse and in liberal academic theories of multiculturalism, this state-led multiculturalism initiative can be understood as a project of nation-rebuilding rooted in processes of recognition and reconciliation.

At the same time as it was constructing this new multicultural identity, the Canadian state was also seeking to come to terms with another kind of threat to its stability and integrity, the seemingly intractable "Indian problem."[2] The Indian problem, in this context, references the state's failure, after centuries of effort, to successfully amalgamate or integrate Indigenous peoples, as it sought to do, into the Canadian social fabric. By the 1970s, the Canadian state was beginning to realize

123

that this assimilationist project, at least as it had been formulated up to that point, would not succeed. The Indian problem, like the broader problem of ethnic diversity, was about the presence of problematic identities that did not fit within the dominant understanding of the Canadian identity and nation. This problem was much more deeply rooted in (indeed, inseparable from) Canada's history, however, and one that official multiculturalism was neither intended nor equipped to tackle. The Indian problem had a distinctly geographic or spatial dimension: central to it was the question of Indigenous rights to land and to self-determination within specific Indigenous territories. This meant its resolution would require the state to come to terms not only with problematic cultural identities but also with the way that these identities are grounded in rights or claims to specific places. As with official multiculturalism, the state's contemporary attempt to fix or "settle" the Indian problem, and more specifically to resolve the "Indian land question," would require some considerable reconstruction of the nation itself; to do so the state would rely on processes of recognition and reconciliation.

This chapter explores the parallels and divergences between these distinct but linked projects of national reconstruction: the state-led project of multiculturalism and the state's attempt to resolve the longstanding Indian problem. Both depend on processes of recognition and reconciliation to bring what are seen as problematic identities or entities within the bounds of the liberal capitalist state. Further, while liberal theory suggests that these processes are of mutual benefit to all parties involved, I draw on critical scholarship on multiculturalism and on recognition and reconciliation to argue that these processes tend to reinforce existing asymmetrical relations of power between the state and those groups most strongly attached to the state, on the one hand, and peripheral or marginalized groups on the other. As such, these projects serve to stabilize the Canadian state in its current form and to maintain existing structures of political and economic power. What primarily distinguishes these projects from each other is the spatial and material dimension inherent in the Indian problem, given the centrality of the land question. This question calls attention to the nation's colonial history and therefore requires from the state some measure of restitution or redistribution of wealth in the form of land or compensation for land taken away from Indigenous peoples. This territorial dimension forms a central theme in the chapter, and I explore its meaning and relevance for projects of recognition and reconciliation. My geographic focus is British Columbia, where the Indian land question is very much a live topic of legal and political discussion and debate.

A fitting entry point to the discussion of the Indian problem and the land question in British Columbia, as well as the mobilization of recognition and reconciliation processes in their resolution, is the government of British Columbia's proposal, first announced in early 2009, that it would develop groundbreaking legislation designed to fundamentally transform the relationship between the province and the Indigenous peoples (or First Nations) that live within the province's borders. The proposed new "Recognition and Reconciliation Act" (the R&R Act) was to provide blanket recognition of Indigenous land rights – or "Aboriginal title" – across the breadth of the provincial landscape and establish mechanisms that would allow for First Nations to be more directly involved in making decisions about, and sharing in the revenues that flow from, the management and exploitation of lands and resources in their traditional territories.[3] The R&R Act proposal also called for a restructuring of the province's history to more fully recognize its Indigenous nature and to aid in contemporary efforts to achieve reconciliation between Indigenous peoples and British Columbia's settler society. At the same time, the proposal involved a reworking of the province's geography to both reconstitute spaces of Indigenous nationality and to ease the province's administrative burden in working with the diversity of First Nations found in British Columbia. A closer examination of this proposal, and the reasons for its ultimate failure, provide insight into the possibilities and limitations of state-led projects of recognition and reconciliation, whether focused on Indigenous peoples or on ethnic communities.

Liberal multiculturalism and the "Indian problem"

In her critique of Canadian multiculturalism, Himani Bannerji is careful to distinguish between "elite multiculturalism" or a "multiculturalism from above," and "popular multiculturalism," which emerges from below.[4] Her focus is the former, which, she argues, is based on the idea that there is a "core cultural group" (Anglo-white) at the centre of the Canadian social body and a series of peripheral "Others" that occupy the margins of Canadian identity and society. In Bannerji's formulation, elite multiculturalism includes both "official multiculturalism" (i.e., multiculturalism as state policy) and "non-official elite multiculturalism," which refers to the intellectual groundwork on which the practice of official multiculturalism rests. Charles Taylor's essay, "The

Politics of Recognition," she suggests, is an excellent example of the latter. Richard Day makes a similar distinction, noting that multiculturalism as state policy "tends towards management, discipline, and uniformity" whereas multiculturalism as a "radical imaginary" emerges spontaneously.[5] Elsewhere, Day and Tonio Sadik define a field called "liberal multicultural theory and practice," which includes both multiculturalism as state policy and the work of liberal theorists – Taylor and Will Kymlicka being the most prominent – who develop and prescribe liberal multiculturalism as a model for pluralistic societies like Canada.[6]

Day argues that liberal multiculturalism is designed to deal with what he calls "the problem of Canadian diversity." This "problem" refers to a perceived proliferation of different ethnic identities within Canada as a result of a steady flow of immigrants into the nation throughout the twentieth century. The problem stems from the incoming "tide" of ethnic or non-white immigrants and the challenge this poses for a Canadian identity structured around an Anglo-white core cultural group. In the creation of the problem of Canadian diversity, Day points out, there is a clear division between "the naturally unproblematic Selves and the naturally problematic Others."[7] Defined as such, the very public problem of Canadian diversity was seen to have reached crisis proportions in the 1970s, requiring urgent state intervention in order to stabilize both Canadian identity and the Canadian state itself. If the myth of Canada as a unitary Anglo-white nation or, in some formulations, as a bicultural (English-French) nation, was no longer tenable, what would replace it? Official multiculturalism was devised to fill this gap, to smooth over the various "problematic fractures and fissures" in the Canadian social body.[8] It would function to bring these diverse "problematic Others" into the circle of the Canadian nation and state, ideally allowing for the construction of a coherent nation-state. Out of the raw material of a messy Canadian diversity, official multiculturalism would produce a "simulacrum of Canadian unity."[9]

Charles Taylor argues that in a modern pluralistic state like Canada, the full development of our identities relies on an affirmative recognition by others in society of who we are. This kind of positive recognition, Taylor asserts, entails "the acceptance of ourselves by others in our identity."[10] Nonrecognition or misrecognition, on the other hand, can inflict harm by deforming our identities. Further, Taylor argues that recognition of threatened minorities, such as Indigenous peoples and the Québécois, is particularly important and may involve some special forms of cultural and political accommodation. Proper recognition, in this sense, is key to overcoming the problem of many diverse and fragmented identities and to achieving Canadian unity, which, he argues, would ultimately come through a harmonization or reconciliation between both the individual and the nation, and between different nations (e.g., French, English) and the state. Will Kymlicka, another key theorist and proponent of Canadian liberal multiculturalism, argues that the differential allocation of collective rights among different social groups is key to the multiculturalism model. The claims of different groups within Canadian society – the main groups or categories he identifies in this context are "national minorities" (Indigenous peoples, Québécois), immigrants, and "colonizing forces" (English and French) – can be met through the allocation of different collective rights. As the dominant colonizing force and as the group most strongly articulated with the federal state, English-Canadians require no special rights, whereas national minorities may require special recognition and rights related to self-government within specific territories. Non-English and non-French immigrants, on the other hand, require no special cultural rights beyond those conferred by Canadian citizenship and are expected to integrate into one of the core or dominant (English or French) Canadian cultures.

These ideas about the recognition of different groups and identities, and of distinct societies or nations, within a pluralistic Canada, and of the differential allocation of rights between them, have been reflected in state law and policy over the past few decades. Most directly, of course, they have been incorporated into federal multiculturalism laws and policies, which recognize cultural and ethnic diversity as significant aspects of Canadian society and identify multiculturalism as "a fundamental characteristic of Canadian heritage and identity."[11] Official multiculturalism, however, was devised to address the proliferation of cultural identities that came about through transnational migrant flows. The ongoing presence of Indigenous peoples in Canada presented a problem of a different nature and would require a different kind of solution. Certainly, as Day points out, Indigenous peoples constitute part of the broad category of "problematic Others," a collection of ethnic or cultural groups that do not fit with – and refuse to melt into – the mythic idea of Canada and Canadian. But multiculturalism, at least in its official formulation, was not devised or well equipped to tackle the Indian problem, which is deeply rooted in the colonial constitution of the nation itself and in questions about attachments and rights to land and territory. The Supreme Court of Canada's 1973 decision in the *Calder* case provided legal support for the idea, long advanced by Indigenous peoples and their advocates, that Aboriginal peoples had certain unique rights to land and territory – "Aboriginal rights and, title" in legal parlance. Further, this decision raised the suggestion that these rights had never been extinguished and therefore continued to exist in many places.[12] These special land and territorial rights placed Indigenous peoples in a category and in a relationship with the state that was distinct from that of so-called ethnic communities.

The *Calder* case marked the start of a lengthy legal project focused on defining and delimiting Indigenous peoples' rights to land and territory, which led to the Court's ruling in the 1997 *Delgamuukw* case that Aboriginal title comprised the right to exclusive use and occupation of the land – something roughly equivalent to the Western idea of full land ownership.[13] The *Calder* decision spurred the federal government to scrap its assimilationist position, spelled out in the 1969 White Paper on Indian Policy, and to announce (less than seven months after the court decision) that it would begin to negotiate comprehensive land claims agreements with Indigenous peoples where their traditional land rights had not been extinguished by treaty or law. The federal comprehensive claims process opened the door to the negotiation of a range of issues of importance to Aboriginal communities. These included not only rights to land and natural resources but also provisions for economic development, protection of culture, and limited forms of self-government. Struck in 1991, the Royal Commission on Aboriginal Peoples was charged with tackling the so-called Indian problem more broadly and with identifying "the foundations of a fair and honourable relationship between the Aboriginal and non-Aboriginal people of Canada."[14] In the preamble to their report, the Commissioners note that Canada is a test case for the "grand notion . . . that dissimilar peoples can share lands, resources, power and dreams while respecting and sustaining their differences."[15] They note that this dream of living together in peace and harmony, however, was dependent on "the restoration of justice to the relationship between Aboriginal and non-Aboriginal peoples in Canada."[16]

The "Indian land question" in British Columbia

The Indian land question, in this particular geographic context, has its origins in the construction of British Columbia as a geopolitical entity, first as a British colony and later as a province within the Dominion of Canada. At this early stage, the question spoke to a key challenge in all colonial projects: how to take possession of Indigenous land and what to do with the Indigenous peoples displaced by European resettlement of their territories. In British Columbia, the Indian land question moved through several phases. During the early colonial period, officials and settlers often recognized Indigenous forms of ownership or title over extensive territories and sought to secure land for colonization through land purchase agreements. Fourteen such agreements or "treaties" were signed with Indigenous groups on Vancouver Island between 1850 and 1854.[17] By the early 1860s, however, colonial policy had shifted towards the denial of any Indigenous "claims" to extensive territories. Rather than securing land through agreements or treaties, officials of the Crown shifted to the creation of an Indian reserve system that would, according to their calculations, meet Indigenous community needs. The result of this policy, Cole Harris notes, was the division of British Columbia into "two vastly unequal parts . . . a tiny fraction of the land set aside for Natives, the rest available, in various tenures, for development."[18] Only a small portion of British Columbia came to be covered by historic land cession treaties; apart from a small part of Vancouver Island and the northeast portion of the province, which was included in the 1899 Treaty 8 extension, there was no formal ceding or surrender of Indigenous land title or rights to the Crown.

The state's denial of Indigenous land and territorial rights in British Columbia remained firmly in place until the 1970s, when persistent Indigenous pressure began to undermine this position. Over the past few decades, Indigenous protests against resource extraction in their territories, in combination with court rulings that provided support for their assertion of Aboriginal title and rights, has forced federal and provincial officials to acknowledge that the flat denial of Indigenous land claims is no longer viable.[19] Of particular importance in this respect have been Indigenous road blockades and court challenges, which have undermined the provincial government's ability to unilaterally authorize and regulate land and resource development in unceded Indigenous territories (i.e., almost the entire province). The disruption of this critical part of the province's economy and of the government's revenue stream convinced provincial political leaders that a new approach to dealing with the Indian land question was needed. By 1990, the centrepiece of this new strategy was in place as British Columbia and Canada agreed to engage in modern, comprehensive treaty negotiations with First Nations across British Columbia.[20] Through the B.C. treaty process, the old troubled relationship between First Nations and the Crown was to be cast aside and a "new relationship" developed based on the recognition of First Nations "as self-determining and distinct nations with their own spiritual values, histories, languages, territories, political institutions and ways of life."[21] Key to the development of this new relationship was the reconciliation of Aboriginal title and Crown sovereignty, which was to be achieved within each Indigenous territory in the province. Through this reconciliation, it was hoped, all parties could achieve "certainty" with respect to the land question.

The treaty process was beset by difficulties almost from the start and has failed to resolve, in any meaningful way, the land question. By mid-2010, after seventeen years of negotiations and more than $1 billion invested by the three parties – including hundreds of millions of dollars borrowed by First Nations from the federal government to pay for their share of the negotiation costs – only two treaties had been concluded while a handful of others were close to agreement. Meanwhile, talks at most of the four dozen other negotiation tables were proceeding only very slowly or were completely bogged down in deep division and disagreement.[22] The obstacles to treaties are numerous, including land and cash offers by the Crown that many First Nations consider wholly inadequate, disagreements over allocations of key resources such as fish, disputes over post-treaty legal regimes, and concerns about the constitutional status of lands that are to be included as part of treaty agreements.[23] At a more fundamental level, as the B.C. Treaty Commission pointed out in its 2001 annual report, the difficulty in negotiating treaties stemmed at least in part from the fact that the parties involved in the process seemed to have radically different, perhaps even contradictory, ideas about the nature of the treaties they were negotiating and about how certainty and reconciliation would be achieved.[24] Of equal concern is the fact that many First Nations view the treaty process as fundamentally flawed and have simply refused to take part in negotiations at all.[25]

With the treaty process floundering, in 2005 Premier Gordon Campbell moved to refocus his government's Aboriginal policy around the concept of developing a new relationship with Indigenous peoples. The province's commitment to this concept was articulated in a five-page "New Relationship" document, drafted in concert with the First Nations Leadership Council, a body representing the three main Indigenous political organizations in the province: the First Nations Summit, the Union of B.C. Indian Chiefs, and the B.C. Chapter of the Assembly of First Nations. The document begins with a statement of vision in which the parties "agree to a new government-to-government relationship based on respect, recognition and accommodation of Aboriginal title and rights."[26] Through this new relationship, the parties further "commit to reconciliation of Aboriginal and Crown title and jurisdictions." Importantly, the document also contained a commitment to "establish processes and institutions for shared decision-making about the land and resources and for revenue and benefit sharing."[27] The premier's commitment to the new relationship vision was seen as a positive step forward by a number of prominent Indigenous leaders, not least by those who made up the First Nations Leadership Council. Even Grand Chief Stewart Phillip – head of the Union of B.C. Indian Chiefs and traditionally a harsh critic of the provincial government's position on Indigenous matters – was gushing in his praise for the premier's leadership on the New Relationship front, describing Campbell as "an exceptional, extraordinary, visionary leader."[28] The New Relationship initiative offered hope that a resolution of the Indian land question was finally at hand.

The "Recognition and Reconciliation Act" proposal

A few years later, however, Phillip and other First Nations leaders expressed frustration that the vision they had helped develop had not been implemented. Nothing much had changed, it seemed, as the treaty process remained mired in seemingly intractable disagreement, the provincial bureaucracy struggled to make sense of the new relationship mandate, and First Nations communities and the Crown continued to seek resolution of land and resource disputes through lengthy and expensive court challenges. What was needed, a number of First Nations leaders began to argue, was a law requiring the implementation of the new relationship vision. By early 2009, with the release of the discussion paper containing "Instructions for Implementing the New Relationship" through new provincial legislation – what came to be referred to as the proposed "Recognition and Reconciliation Act" – it appeared that First Nations were about to get what they wanted: a law that would provide for full recognition of Indigenous land rights across the breadth of the province, and which would set up processes for Indigenous communities to be directly involved in making decisions about, and sharing the benefits from, land and resource management and development within their respective territories.[29] The legislation would be sweeping in its application, overriding all other provincial laws dealing with land use and resource management. According to Mike de Jong, the province's Minister of Aboriginal Relations and Reconciliation, implementation of the proposal would "represent change on a seismic scale."[30]

The proposal had several additional important elements. First, it called for the reconstitution of Indigenous Nations — essentially, the coalescing of the province's existing 200-plus First Nations (or "Indian bands," as they were defined under the *Indian Act*) into 23 "Indigenous Nations." Helpfully, the proposal contained a map delineating the territorial boundaries of what were referred to as the "Sovereign Indigenous Nations of British Columbia." The reconstitution or rebuilding of Indigenous Nations was described as central to the process of decolonization and a key vehicle for establishing the new relationship between Indigenous peoples and the Crown. Indeed, the proposal suggested that "the comprehensive application of recognition principles through shared decision-making and revenue-sharing agreements" in any particular place would be triggered by the reconstitution of the relevant Indigenous Nation. Second, the proposal also called for the province to issue a proclamation that would speak to the history of British Columbia "from pre-contact times through to the implementation of colonial policies that have had long-standing negative impacts and have served to create adversarial provincial Crown-Indigenous Nations relations." The proclamation, the discussion paper continued, would create a "huge opportunity to turn the page of history and establish a new relationship of respect and recognition."[31]

Not surprisingly given its scope, the R&R Act proposal generated considerable discussion and debate within the groups that would be most affected by the new law. Ed John, Grand Chief of the First Nations Summit and a member of the First Nations Leadership Council, suggested that there was both skepticism and optimism among First Nations leaders. Within the Indigenous community, the reconstitution of Indigenous Nations was viewed as particularly problematic.[32] The entire proposal was viewed with alarm from some within the province's "business community" and particularly from the mining industry, which argued that the law would essentially give First Nations a veto over every aspect of resource development in the province. There were also murmurs of dissent from within cabinet, including expressions of concern that such sweeping legislation was being pushed forward with undue haste.[33] Despite the opposition, the premier seemed intent on moving forward with the proposal. The proposal was withdrawn from consideration just prior to the provincial election, held on May 12th, 2009, and then, after the Liberals were returned to power, was brought forward again. With the support of the First Nations Leadership Council, by early summer the proposal was circulated and debated more widely in Aboriginal forums across the province.

By mid-summer 2009, however, it was clear that a number of prominent and influential First Nations leaders had found the proposal wanting in several respects. Most critical was the argument that the R&R Act proposal failed to adequately recognize Indigenous land and territorial rights. Indigenous concerns about the proposal were perhaps most fully and clearly articulated in an analysis by a group of lawyers with long experience working on Aboriginal legal cases.[34] The analysis, presented as a report to the First Nations Leadership Council's "Recognition Working Group," highlighted both the positive aspects of the proposal and its shortcomings. On the positive side, the authors of the report acknowledged that the proposal represented an important shift away from the denial of Aboriginal rights and title as well as a significant move towards the implementation of some form of shared decision-making and revenue-sharing, both of which have long been key First Nations demands. On the negative side, the lawyers' primary concern was that the form of Aboriginal title that would be recognized in the proposed legislation appeared to be "a significantly watered down version" of that which had already been recognized by the Supreme Court of Canada. In short, the concern was that the proposal would recognize a "non-exclusive" form of Aboriginal title, a version much weaker than that sought by many First Nations and much reduced from the "exclusive" form recognized by the courts.[35] The group also raised concerns about the linking of the proposal to the process of "reconstituting Indigenous Nations" and about the lack of detail regarding the meaning of terms such as "shared decision-making" and "revenue and benefit sharing." Without more detail about what this process and these terms meant, they pointed out, it was difficult to evaluate the extent to which the proposal represented a meaningful step forward.

There were other Indigenous critiques of the proposal circulating at the same time, which also focused on the failure of the proposed legislation to fully recognize Aboriginal title. In an article published in late July, for example, Arthur Manuel, a prominent Indigenous critic of the treaty process, argued that the proposal was a ploy designed by the Campbell government to both overcome the economic uncertainty that the province faced due to the Supreme Court of Canada's recognition of an exclusive form of Aboriginal title and to spruce up British Columbia's international image in the lead-up to the 2010 Winter Olympics.[36] The kind of recognition of Aboriginal title provided for in the proposed R&R Act, he noted, was contingent on the simultaneous recognition by Indigenous peoples of provincial Crown title. Manuel asserted that First Nations have historically rejected this approach and that the existing community-level opposition to the R&R Act proposal indicated a desire on the part of Indigenous peoples to be on an equal footing with the provincial government. With such mounting critique from within First Nations circles, the proposal was clearly in trouble. By the end of the summer, after a series of consultations with First Nations carried out by the First Nations Leadership Council, the Recognition and Reconciliation Act was pronounced dead – at least in the form that had been proposed. Most central to its demise was the failure to adequately recognize Indigenous peoples' rights to land and territories.

Recognition politics and reconciliation fantasies

In his chapter in this volume, Glen Coulthard argues that, over the past three decades, the Indigenous self-determination movement in Canada has been centrally mobilized around demands for recognition.[37] This desire for recognition on the part of Indigenous peoples, he points out, manifests itself in various demands, including for recognition of rights to land and territory, for self-determination and self-government, for recognition of their status as "nations" (or First Nations), and for being accorded a government-to-government relationship with the Canadian state. The Canadian state's engagement with Indigenous peoples on this basis, a process that began in the 1970s, represents an important shift away from the long-held state desire to see Indigenous peoples assimilated into a broader Canadian social body and towards the idea of a "mutual recognition" between the state and Indigenous peoples. This emphasis on recognition in the particular case of the Indigenous self-determination movement reflects a broader "politics of recognition" – a term drawn from Charles Taylor's work – which structures relations between different groups within contemporary Canadian society and forms the philosophical basis for the liberal concept of multiculturalism.[38] With respect to Indigenous peoples, Coulthard contends, the politics of recognition refers to a variety of models that emerge from a liberal pluralist political philosophy, and which "seek to reconcile Indigenous claims to nationhood with Crown sovereignty via the accommodation of Indigenous identities in some form of renewed relationship with the Canadian state."[39] These recognition models, including modern treaty and land claims negotiations and self-government initiatives, typically provide for the transfer of land, capital, and political power from the state to Indigenous communities.

In the case of both Indigenous peoples and ethnic communities, the mediation of state relations through a liberal politics of recognition is rightfully considered an improvement over past practices of exclusion and assimilation. However, such recognition processes have their limits. Perhaps most importantly, rather than leading to the state of peaceful coexistence and mutual recognition that its liberal proponents predict, the politics of recognition tends to perpetuate hierarchical relations of power between those who engage in such state-led processes. In the case of Indigenous peoples, Coulthard argues, the liberal politics of recognition tends "to reproduce the very configurations of colonial power that Indigenous peoples' demands for recognition have histori- cally sought to transcend."[40] Recognition processes of this form are often profoundly asymmetrical and non-reciprocal. The key point here is that these processes are typically not characterized by mutual recog- nition at all; they do not involve an equal and freely given recognition, but rather, as Day puts it, "a partial and grudgingly bestowed *gift* from a canonical Self group to a series of problematic Others."[41] Such recog- nition of the Other simply as different and ultimately subordinate is closer to tolerance than a full recognition of the equal value of different peoples and cultures. The politics of recognition requires that Indige- nous peoples and ethnic communities play within the rules established by the state and, further, that they recognize and identify with the state itself. Writing about Indigenous peoples in particular, Coulthard makes the point that their attachment to state-sanctioned forms of recognition is essential in reproducing the structures of colonial domination that persist in Canada. This argument can be extended to the full range of so-called problematic Others that seek recognition from the state.

Another important part of the critique of the politics of recognition is that it shifts attention away from the more structural or economic dimensions of social relations and towards more cultural concerns. This represents a move, in other words, from questions of redistribution to questions of recognition. Bannerji notes that official multiculturalism emerged during a period of heightened conflict among different groups within Canadian society, between the English and French in particular, and at a time when Indigenous land and self-determination struggles were gaining traction. These tensions were about culture but they were also centrally about material concerns, such as jurisdiction over land and territory and securing access to the economic benefits that flow from control over natural resources. Multiculturalism discourse, argues Bannerji, served to diffuse these claims and pressures, deflecting them into the cultural realm. Official multiculturalism, according to this per- spective, works not only to patch over diverse and fragmented identities, or contradictions in the cultural realm, but also to contain conflicts based in structural inequalities. Ethnic communities, for their part, were seeking economic and political rights from the state; what they got was multiculturalism. As Bannerji writes, "It was as though we asked for bread and were given stones."[42] Critical questions about the production and distribution of wealth within the nation – about employment and wages, social programs such as health care and education, and rights to land and natural resources – are depicted as less central to the politics of recognition. Thus, as Day notes, it is important to remember that the politics of recognition requires not only that Indigenous peoples and other ethnic communities be recognized as subordinate to the Canadian state but also that they be subordinate within a *capitalist* Canadian state.[43]

The politics of recognition are closely linked to ideas about reconciliation. These links are perhaps most clearly articulated through efforts to establish or construct a Canadian unity. The presence of a multiplicity of cultural identities across the Canadian landscape, especially ethnic communities and different Indigenous peoples, disturbs the "statist dream" of "a perfectly striated space of social order" and as such requires bringing them together and reconciling them to each other and to the state.[44] Ultimately, this is the work that official multiculturalism is called on to do: to achieve this reconciliation and harmonization of diverse and problematic entities. As noted earlier, Charles Taylor argues that Canadian unity is to be achieved through reconciliation on two levels simultaneously: between the individual and his or her people (his or her nation) and between different groups of peoples (cultures or nations) with the Canadian state. For Day, Taylor "stages a fantasy of a dual recovery: of the subject supposed to be lost, the Canadian; and the country supposed to be lost, Canada."[45] This is a fantasy, he continues, since it depends on the problematic idea that relations between French and English – and, more fundamentally, between Indigenous peoples and settlers – were once harmonious and that there had existed such a thing as a united Canada. This fantasy of reconciliation imagines Canada reaching a point of completion or rest, a time and place where identities and relations are fully realized and harmonized, and where there is a perfect congruence between individual, nation, and state.

Reconciliation has certainly become a key theme in state policy and political discourse with respect to relations with Indigenous peoples. At the national level, state references to reconciliation have come most often through efforts to address the legacies of the Indian residential school system. In 1998, for example, the Canadian government issued a "Statement of Reconciliation" as part of its response to the residential school debacle, expressing its "profound regret for past actions" and committing itself to an ongoing process of reconciliation.[46] In 2006, as part of a $4-billion residential schools settlement agreement, Canada agreed to the creation of a "Truth and Reconciliation Commission," which would provide former students with a public venue to share their experiences of residential schools. By shedding light on this dark corner of Canadian history, it was hoped, the Commission would foster reconciliation between Indigenous and non-Indigenous peoples in Canada.[47]

In British Columbia, the notion of reconciliation has played an even greater role in mediating state–Indigenous relations. Under Premier Campbell's leadership, achieving reconciliation with Indigenous peoples has been clearly identified as a key goal of government. Campbell and other provincial political leaders often use the term to refer to a broader aim of reconciliation between Indigenous and non-Indigenous peoples. More common, however, given that little of the province was formally ceded to the Crown through historic treaties, is its deployment in reference to Indigenous "claims" to jurisdiction over lands and natural resources. In its most common formulation, the objective is to achieve a reconciliation of Crown sovereignty and Aboriginal title. This objective permeates the legal, political, and bureaucratic language of Aboriginal relations in British Columbia, and is central to most of the provincial government's major Aboriginal policies and programs, especially the B.C. treaty process and the New Relationship initiative. From the province's perspective, what needs to be reconciled – above all else – are the competing claims to jurisdiction over the province's territories and the wealth of natural resources they contain. In this sense, through a process of reconciliation the province seeks "certainty" on the land question – certainty, that is, about who owns and has jurisdiction over lands and resources – so that it can get on with the business of land and resource "development" without fear of obstruction by Indigenous blockades or court challenges.

As is evident from this discussion, the notion of reconciliation is both politically potent and multivalent. For a settler society confronted with certain unpleasant truths about its colonial past, it offers a path to a form of redemption, through a "coming to terms with the past," and a means of reformulating attachment to a renewed national (or provincial) identity. However, as Carole Blackburn argues, all too often the discourse of reconciliation seeks to impose closure – to move beyond difficult yet essential discussions of colonial history and geography, for example – where such closure is unwarranted.[48] She describes how the reconciliation discourse around the negotiation and finalization of the Nisga'a treaty in the late 1990s moved very quickly from cursory acknowledgement of the past – "the past is the past, and we can't change it or what we did" – to a focus on a future ripe with promise, of "moving forward and building a modern relationship with Aboriginal people in Canada."[49] As Blackburn notes, this kind of reconciliation talk seeks to create a clear break with the past – and, perhaps more to the point, with a past tainted by colonial injustices – and, as such, functions to bolster the legitimacy of the state. Day and Sadik make a similar point about the B.C. treaty process, arguing that the unwillingness of federal and provincial negotiators to deal with history within that process serves to obscure "historical relations of power between Aboriginal peoples and the Canadian state as well as the concomitant obligation to deal with the illegal expropriation of lands and resources."[50] This unwillingness to consider British Columbia's colonial history and geography in treaty negotiations has been identified by Indigenous participants as a highly problematic aspect of the process.[51]

As noted above, over the past two decades, the treaty process has been seen as the key vehicle to achieving reconciliation. Its failure to do so, except in a very limited number of cases covering a tiny part of the province, indicates that the model is badly flawed. Most critically, the process is deeply asymmetrical in terms of the ability of the parties to affect the outcomes of the negotiations; backed with state resources and in no real hurry to shift from their fixed negotiating positions, federal and provincial negotiators hold almost all the cards. For Indigenous communities involved in the process – deeply impoverished and with negotiating teams funded through loans from the federal government – the pressure to settle is intense. This is a fundamentally unfair process. If the two central goals of the treaty talks are to achieve certainty on the land base and to achieve a measure of justice for Indigenous peoples, to date the federal and provincial governments have managed to shape the process so that it focuses primarily on certainty rather than justice.[52] In addition to the fundamental power imbalance between the negotiating parties, the state and Indigenous peoples seem to have fundamentally different notions of what reconciliation might look like through treaty. As James Tully notes, the state seems most preoccupied with reaching a final treaty agreement with Indigenous groups and views reconciliation as something that is achieved, once and for all, with the signing of the treaty. In this perspective, reconciliation does represent a kind of closure – a means of tying up loose ends and moving on. On the contrary, Tully argues, Indigenous peoples understand reconciliation as a process of opening up and continuing a dialogue.[53]

With respect to the specific objective of reconciling Aboriginal title and Crown sovereignty, the treaty model reflects a desire to maintain both highly asymmetrical power relations between the parties and a grossly unequal distribution of land and territorial rights. Reconciling Crown sovereignty and Aboriginal title, according to this model, involves the division of Indigenous territories into two unequal and separate spaces: the final treaty agreement allocates a small part (roughly three to five per cent) of the territory to the Indigenous group while the rest is designated (or confirmed) as "Crown land." Additionally, and of critical importance, the "burden" or Aboriginal title is removed from this larger Crown portion. Through this approach, the Crown is able to achieve certainty on the land base – that is, certainty that it can proceed with land and resource development without fear of further land or resource claims by Indigenous peoples. For their part, the Indigenous signatory to the treaty obtains fee simple ownership of Treaty Settlement Lands, a range of other treaty benefits (such as specific allocations of fish and wildlife, and cash transfers), and a limited form of self-government. Finally, as Blackburn points out, the treaty process functions to transform Indigenous land and territorial rights (or Aboriginal title and rights) into treaty rights that are recognized under section 35 the Canadian Constitution. Under this treaty model, Aboriginal title is reconciled *to* Crown sovereignty. In this way, Indigenous groups are incorporated into the Canadian state and it is incumbent on these groups, as Blackburn puts it, to "bear the brunt of accommodation" in order to achieve reconciliation and to ensure that Crown sovereignty remains unchallenged.[54]

Conclusion

What, in the end, can we take from this most recent attempt to settle the Indian land question in British Columbia? It is important to note, first of all, that although the R&R Act proposal ultimately collapsed, it went further than any previous state proposal in addressing a number of key Indigenous demands with respect to their lands and resources, including consideration of shared decision making and revenue sharing. The proposal represented an advance, in other words, in the broader Indigenous struggle to regain control over their ancestral lands and resources, and in unsettling the dominant colonial narrative of Canada as a lily-white nation-state. Also, the debates around the R&R Act proposal, and its eventual rejection by Indigenous groups, highlighted the contested nature of such recognition and reconciliation projects. Although these projects are mobilized by the state in a certain self-interested form, and are often supported by core cultural groups and dominant economic interests, they do provide a site for Indigenous peoples and their allies to critically engage with the state and with other groups in society on some of the issues of importance to them, and ultimately to reject or argue for a transformation of such proposals. With the collapse of the R&R Act proposal, Indigenous peoples will continue to push for a more accurate and full recognition of their rights to land and self-determination, and for an acknowledgement of the histories of displacement and discrimination that have been so central to their experiences of Canada. They will also be wary of continuing calls for reconciliation, as long as these are driven only by the desire of Canada's core cultural and political-economic group to recover a time and a place, a Canada, that never really was – a mythic land of peace and harmony – and to retain positions of power and privilege. Any kind of meaningful reconciliation depends on a much more open and full recognition of Indigenous rights than we have seen to date, and a much more meaningful approach to restitution, including a commitment to return Indigenous lands to their rightful owners and to compensate Indigenous communities for the resources that have been removed or despoiled. Without this, reconciliation remains only a fanciful idea.

The lessons from the R&R Act proposal apply to projects of recognition and reconciliation more broadly, including any kind of project of multiculturalism. An effective and just policy of multiculturalism must not be confined to the realm of culture – the recognition and tolerance (or even celebration) of cultural difference – but must be grounded in the material lives of those to whom it is targeted. For Indigenous peoples, the material dimensions and claims are clear: they were here first, living on the land and using resources before they were displaced by European newcomers or "settlers." The material claims of immigrants, the claim to a fair share in the nation's material wealth, are more difficult to make within the context of the modern Canadian liberal state, where the settlers now see themselves as "hosts" to these new newcomers and as gatekeepers of the nation's identity and political-economic institutions. Nonetheless, like the R&R Act proposal, liberal multiculturalism is an important site for resistance and contestation. Once the limitations of liberal multiculturalism are understood, both as an idea and as state policy, the temptation is to reject it altogether.

However, as Bannerji argues, such an approach is risky, particularly when reactionary forces are themselves calling for the dismantling of multiculturalism policy and retrenchment on the limited advances that have been made. Better to critically engage with liberal multiculturalism and seek advances through it. Approached critically, Bannerji asserts, multiculturalism presents "a small opening for making the state minimally accountable to those on whose lives it erects itself."[55]

Critically engaging with state-led projects of recognition and reconciliation, whether these are broader policies such as multiculturalism or more focused initiatives like the R&R Act, can expose the limitations of such projects and identify areas where there is possibility for movement and expansion. It is important to remember that working with and through state structures, policies, and initiatives can yield important material gains for those who occupy the cultural and political-economic margins, as evidenced by Indigenous peoples' use of Canadian courts to advance their land and resource rights. True, such gains are slow, partial, and fragile, being dependent on certain forms of state support and reaction, yet they can (and have) made a difference in the material lives of those who have won them. To acknowledge these incremental gains is not to discount the importance of exploring alternatives to those proposed by the state. Indeed, as Kay Anderson maintains, it is important to think both "beyond the limited frame of the state" and "*across* cultures," and in this way challenge the construction of distinct and separate sociocultural categories – such as those of Indigenous, settler, and immigrant – which are central to "modern colonial formations" like Canada.[56] Along similar lines, Bannerji argues for the importance of moving beyond the liberal model of multiculturalism, a model imposed from above, and for paying close attention to models that emerge spontaneously from below. Thrown together in a common space, different peoples find ways of recognizing and reconciling with each other, without need of political leaders or state programs telling them what this looks like.[57] For Richard Day, such a scenario heralds the possibility of a "more critical and radical multiculturalism," one that is based on a decisive shift away from the fantasy of reconciliation and a move towards openness and affirmation of difference.[58] These alternatives, centrally shaped by the perspectives of those who have long resided on the margins of Canadian society, suggest a different kind of project of national reconstruction, one that moves beyond the asymmetries and limitations of the colonial settler state and society and that explores the kind of truly multicultural Canada that *could* exist.

8 Reconciliation with Indigenous ghosts: On the politics of postcolonial ghost stories

Emilie Cameron

> The named marginal is as much a concealment as a disclosure of
> the margin. — Gayatri Chakravorty Spivak

THE STATUS OF INDIGENOUS PEOPLES WITHIN CANADIAN multicultural
policy and discourse has always been uneasy.[1] Developed in the context
of Québécois separatist movements and the "increased politicization of
cultural minorities" in the post-war era, multiculturalism was perhaps
first and foremost an attempt to integrate "difference" into the Canadian national imaginary so as to neutralize and institutionalize political
claims upon the nation-state.[2] Although celebrated as a form of state
accommodation, tolerance, and even benevolence, critics insist that
multicultural policies and discourse work to marginalize and depoliti-
cize the claims of racialized and colonized peoples in Canada.[3] More
specifically, they insist that the institutionalization of difference along
particular lines renders radical political claims illegible, and that the
emphasis on "culture" as the primary platform through which to gain
membership in the nation-state renders opaque the historical and
ongoing geopolitical and imperial contours of migration, colonization,
and racism.[4]

Will Kymlicka has argued that, in the Canadian context, "the term
'multiculturalism' is only used to refer to . . . the accommodation of
immigrant ethnicity" and that the "accommodation of our 'nations
within' [Indigenous peoples and Québécois] is dealt with by other
policies, under other government departments, and indeed under separate sections of the Canadian constitution."[5] Such a comment belies the
complex ways in which multiculturalism informs relations between

Indigenous and non-Indigenous peoples in Canada and, indeed, the ways in which colonialism shapes both the geographies of Indigenous peoples and those of diasporic, displaced migrants.[6] To the extent that liberal multicultural understandings of difference, inclusion, and citizenship have come to inform responses to the specific claims of Indigenous peoples, there is, as Sneja Gunew argues, "work to be done" in assessing the "interactions and multiple exclusions" of postcolonialism and multiculturalism.[7] This chapter contributes along these lines by considering how postcolonial ghost stories – stories that use the figure of the Indigenous ghost to make sense of colonial and postcolonial relations – incorporate the tensions, aspirations, and failings of liberal multiculturalism. Although the figure of the Indigenous ghost pre-dates the emergence of multiculturalism in Canada, the "spectral Native" has been mobilized in a distinctly multicultural register over the past several decades. Just as multiculturalism recognizes "difference" along specific lines, lines that render illegible the historical and ongoing geographies of migration and colonization, postcolonial ghost stories both register Indigeneity and undermine the specific claims of Indigenous peoples. As such, the use of haunting metaphors for conceptualizing Indigeneity demands critical interrogation.

Past and present hauntings

In her exploration of haunting and its role in the sociological imagination, Avery Gordon argues that the appearance of ghosts represents, above all, a claim upon us, an insistence that we acknowledge the role we play in present injustices. Ghosts notify us of our involvement and they "inaugurate the necessity of doing something about [that involvement]."[8] Ghosts, it seems, have a politics, and it should therefore come as no surprise, in an era of decolonizing and anti-colonial scholarship, that ghosts have increasingly occupied the imagination of those who aim to trouble, uncover, and interrogate the play of the colonial past in this ongoing colonial present.[9] Ghosts allude to the presence of that which has been excluded, marginalized, and expelled; although themselves immaterial and spectral, they gesture towards the materiality of colonized and abject bodies.[10] Ghosts unsettle the assumed stability and integrity of Western temporalities and spatialities and seem to embody the mismatch between the ideal and the real, the present and the absent.[11] Ghosts, Jacques Derrida reminds us, trouble any efforts to finish and close; it is only by living with, talking with, and accommodating our ghosts that we might "learn to live" in these "post" colonial times.[12]

In recent years, full articles and books have been devoted to the ghostly, the spectral, and the uncanny as a way of making sense of history, memory, materiality, and (in)justice.[13] But alongside this more focused interest in spectrality there has also been an increase in fleeting, metaphorical references to haunting in recent scholarship. It seems that everything these days is haunted, including memories, places, ideologies, and ontologies.[14] Haunting is a compelling metaphor for those engaged in studies of the emergent and immaterial, for those interested in identifying unnamed influences in contemporary thought, for studies into the textures of place and memory, and for general references to a present constituted by the non-linear enfolding of multiple, conflicting pasts. Scholars working within and across psychoanalytical, postcolonial, feminist, and post-humanist frameworks have all drawn upon haunting metaphors in recent years, and many have begun to incorporate adjectives like "spectral," "haunting," and "ghostly" into their writing. Haunting, it seems, has acquired a kind of tropological status in the social sciences and humanities, particularly among scholars concerned with the colonial and postcolonial.

But haunting is not, in fact, a wholly postcolonial trope. In a recent review of the proliferation of haunting metaphors in Canadian cultural production, Marlene Goldman and Joanne Saul cite Canadian settler-author Catharine Parr Traill's declaration that "ghosts or spirits . . . appear totally banished from Canada. This is too matter-of-fact a country for such supernaturals to visit."[15] Traill made this claim in 1833, but it was echoed by poet and critic Earle Birney in 1947 when he stated that "it's only by our lack of ghosts we're haunted."[16] Birney was referring to certain Canadians' preoccupation with their apparent "lack" of history in comparison to their American neighbours, a matter of particular nationalist concern that has defined Canadian cultural production for decades. Such claims to "ghostlessness," however, are more the exception than the rule. Margot Northey argues that ghosts have been at the centre of nation-building projects in Canada for a long while, beginning in the nineteenth century.[17] In particular, and of relevance to this chapter, D.M.R. Bentley argues that ghosts have been instrumental figures in efforts to connect Aboriginality with settler history, creating an aesthetic link between the "Indian past" and the settler present.[18] The Aboriginal ghost has been used to evoke a generalized sense of history in the Canadian landscape, but always with a sense of linearity and succession. It is assumed that Aboriginal ghosts are all that remains of the "disappearing Indian," and that settler-Canadians have inherited this rich land from those who have now "passed."

The spectral native was a particularly common figure among the Confederation poets, a group of writers working at the turn of the twentieth century who aimed to cultivate a uniquely Canadian literary voice and articulate the grounds for a budding Canadian nationalism.[19] One of their more celebrated members, Duncan Campbell Scott, also spent his career in the federal department of Indian Affairs and held the post of deputy superintendent from 1923 to 1932. Notably, some of the most restrictive and assimilative policies relating to Aboriginal peoples were crafted and implemented during Scott's tenure. While traveling into Northern Ontario to arrange for the surrender of Cree and Ojibway lands in 1905, Scott wrote a poem entitled "Indian Place Names" that begins:

The race has waned and left but tales of ghosts,
That hover in the world like fading smoke
About the lodges: gone are the dusty folk
That once were cunning with the thong and snare
And mighty with the paddle and the bow;
They lured the silver salmon from his lair,
They drove the buffalo in trampling hosts,
And gambled in the teepees until dawn.
But now their vaunted prowess is all gone,
Gone like a moose-track in April snow.
But all the land is murmurous with the call
Of their wild names that haunt the lovely glens
Where lonely water falls, or where the street
Sounds all day with the tramp of myriad feet.[20]

Scott wrote a number of mournful Indian poems like this one, lamenting the loss of the very cultures he was instrumental in undermining. Although literary critics like Stan Dragland have argued that Scott's poetry gave expression to his inner torment over the assimilation of Indigenous peoples into Canadian society, Laura Smyth Groening insists that Scott's poems supported and articulated his assimilationist agenda.[21] Ghostly, fading Indians, regrettable or not, were an essential component of Scott's vision as Deputy Superintendent of Indian Affairs. Scott was unequivocal that Indians should "progress into civilization and finally disappear as a separate and distinct people, not by race extinction but by gradual assimilation with their fellow citizens," and the motif of fading, spectral Indians in Scott's poetry worked to naturalize the policies he enacted as the deputy superintendent.[22] The portrayal of Indigenous peoples as fading ghosts did not originate or end with Scott, but the political implications of Scott's use of this trope are particularly stark given the context within which "Indian Place Names" was written. Scott was engaged in negotiations with real, live "Indians" when he wrote this poem, and this mismatch between the poem's aestheticized ghosting of Indigenous peoples and their embodied, material existence around the treaty table is remarkable. The discrepancy becomes all the more resonant from a contemporary vantage point: the Cree and Ojibway clearly did not "wane" after all. They were real then and they are real today, in spite of Scott's efforts, both poetic and bureaucratic.

Scott is clearly a unique case; his occupations as both a poet and a high-ranking bureaucrat demand that the relationship between his governmental and literary texts be interrogated. But the prevalence of ghostly Indigenous figures in Canadian cultural production extends far beyond Scott. Warren Cariou argues that spectral Indigenous figures are "part of the iconic vocabulary of Euro-American Gothic romances," citing the employment of such figures in prairie literatures from the 1930s to the present day.[23] Margaret Atwood has pointed to the importance of Aboriginal ghosts in constructions of the Canadian North as malevolent and mysterious, and Goldman and Saul identify an interest in haunting among contemporary writers such as Ann-Marie MacDonald, Jane Urquhart, Timothy Findley, and Michael Ondaatje, some of whom have made explicit links between Canadian history, Indigenous ghosts, and the politics of land and inheritance.[24] Ken Gelder and Jane Jacobs' important study of Indigenous ghosts as uncanny manifestations of settler unease, along with more recent work by Australian scholars, suggest that the ghost is a compelling figure in settler colonies more generally.[25] Indeed, Renée Bergland's comprehensive study of the Indian ghost in American literature traces the figuration of Indigenous peoples as "demons, apparitions, shapes, specters, phantoms, or ghosts" over the past three hundred years.[26] She notes the critical connection between Indigenous spectrality and colonial figurations of land and power. It seems that recent turns to the spectral as a metaphor for coming to terms with colonialism are by no means original.

The fact that settler colonies like Canada, Australia, and the United States are not "post" colonial in the sense of being beyond or after colonialism may explain the ongoing importance of the Indigenous ghost in the settler imagination. Yet whatever continuities may exist between past and present settler hauntologies, it is important to note that recent invocations of the Indigenous ghost are frequently understood to be postcolonial and even decolonizing gestures. The final report of the *Royal Commission on Aboriginal Peoples*, for example, a commission meant to address the foundations of contemporary conflicts between Aboriginal peoples and the Canadian state, frames Canadian history as haunted by colonial injustices:

> Studying the past tells us who we are and where we came from. It often reveals a cache of secrets that some people are striving to keep hidden and others are striving to tell. In this case, it helps explain how the tensions between Aboriginal and non-Aboriginal people came to be, and why they are so hard to resolve. . . . In our report, we examine that history in some detail, for its ghosts haunt us still. The ghosts take the form of dishonoured treaties, theft of Aboriginal lands, suppression of Aboriginal cultures, abduction of Aboriginal children, impoverishment and disempowerment of Aboriginal peoples.[27]

The report goes on to outline how these ghosts might be laid to rest and an era of "peace and harmony" might be initiated. Notably, this effort on the part of the commissioners to wrestle with the ghosts of the past was framed as a necessary step in the quest to achieve the promises of multiculturalism:

> Canada is a test case for a grand notion – the notion that dissimilar peoples can share lands, resources, power and dreams while respecting and sustaining their differences. The story of Canada is the story of many such peoples, trying and failing and trying again, to live together in peace and harmony. But there cannot be peace or harmony unless there is justice. It was to help restore justice to the relationship between Aboriginal and non-Aboriginal people in Canada, and to propose practical solutions to stubborn problems, that the Royal Commission on Aboriginal Peoples was established.[28]

Here, the claims of Indigenous peoples are understood as stubborn barriers to a multicultural ideal and resolution is envisioned as a restored state of cultural pluralism. Indeed, the "just" incorporation of Indigenous peoples into the multicultural nation-state is framed as specifically contingent upon a reckoning with ghosts.

Postcolonialism and multiculturalism interweave throughout the report. When describing the effects of assimilation policies, for example, the commissioners frame Indigenous survival in terms of the maintenance of pride in cultural difference, a hallmark of multicultural success. They note that, in spite of the assimilative aims of the state,

"Aboriginal peoples remain proudly different" and have "an enduring sense of themselves as peoples with a unique heritage and the right to cultural continuity." While assimilation policies "have done great damage, leaving a legacy of brokenness affecting Aboriginal individuals, families and communities," this "damage," note the commissioners, "has been equally serious to the spirit of Canada – the spirit of generosity and mutual accommodation in which Canadians take pride."[29] At stake in the Royal Commission report, it seems, is not simply redress for historical and ongoing injustice, but rather the restoration of a "grand notion" of Canada as a liberal multicultural state through a reckoning with the ghosts of the past. These ghostly metaphors seem to have taken hold; according to a recent *University of Toronto Quarterly* special issue devoted to "haunting" in Canadian cultural production, spectral accounts of Indigenous–settler relations have proliferated in the decade since the Royal Commission.[30]

One of the places from which such stories have emerged is a wilderness park in southwestern British Columbia. The Stein Valley Nlaka'pamux Heritage Park is a provincial park that was established to protect the "last unlogged, intact watershed" in southwestern B.C.[31] The park stretches from the Coast mountain range inland to the deep cuts of the Fraser Canyon. It is rugged, mountainous country, and was largely unknown to most non-Aboriginal British Columbians until the mid-1980s, when environmental activists realized that the valley was slated for logging. The valley has always been important to the Nlaka'pamux, whose traditional territory encompasses the watershed. It contains numerous rock paintings and the valley has been used as a source of food, as a travel route between inland and coastal territories, and as a site for vision quests and other activities.[32] According to an activist who was central in the campaign to protect the Stein, however, such uses were downplayed by the logging companies that were intent on extracting timber from the valley.[33] In the effort to protect the Stein, a coalition of First Nations, environmental activists, and scholars therefore self-consciously worked to "fill" the valley with signs of Aboriginality, emphasizing its spiritual significance and insisting on the integrity of the valley as a whole, charged space.[34] T-shirts, posters, and flyers were emblazoned with rock art images and a coffee table book was assembled to showcase the Stein and raise funds for its protection.[35] Wilderness concerts were staged to draw attention to the plight of the valley and the Stein Rediscovery Program – a program aimed at reacquainting Lytton, Lillooet, and Mt. Currie Band youth with their traditional culture through extended journeys into the Stein Valley – was launched.[36]

Ultimately these multiple conservation efforts were successful. By 1995, a park co-managed by the provincial government and the Lytton First Nation had been declared. The park, named "Stein Valley Nlaka'pamux Heritage Park: A Living Museum of Cultural and Natural History," was one of the first parks in Canada to highlight its Indigenous heritage. As Bruce Braun has argued with regards to Clayoquot Sound, however, a particular kind of Indigeneity was emphasized in the creation of the park.[37] Notions of a pure, static, ancient Indigeneity aligned with a pure and untamed nature predominated. This was a Stein of "living, loving arms," with "laughter on the breeze,"[38] a charismatic space that was characterized by David Suzuki as palliative for a society "desperately in need of environmental and spiritual restoration."[39] Descriptions of the Stein as a benevolent and healing spiritual place predominated in the many articles, flyers, reports, and images produced to protect the valley from logging.[40] Notably, the universally welcoming and protective nature of the "spirits" of the Stein was emphasized in these publications through the words of people such as Okanagan Elder Napoleon Kruger. "In truth," he asserted, "ancestors still sing in the Stein, using words which have remained unchanged throughout centuries. In truth, there is laughter on the breeze, and each tree, each stone, is alive. That the ancestors have always protected the Stein, and always will, is true; and the Stein, in turn, protects all."[41]

Efforts on the part of the Lytton, Mt. Currie, and Lillooet Bands to protect the Stein were embedded in a broader political movement to regain control over their traditional territories, a movement that began to gain some momentum in the mid-1990s. After over a century of demands on the part of the province's First Nations for official treaties and land claim settlements, the British Columbia treaty process finally resulted in a settlement in 1998, when the Nisga'a Nation successfully regained title over a portion of their traditional territory in northern British Columbia.[42] Suddenly, or so it seemed to a number of non-Aboriginal British Columbians, the entire province was open to similar claims, and a great deal of anxiety and uncertainty over land tenure began to emerge.[43] It was in this context that the spirits of the Stein began to figure in different terms than those celebrated by the coffee table books, and the notion of the Stein as "haunted" by Aboriginal ghosts began to appear.

"*Everyone* knows that the Stein is haunted," noted one former resident of Vancouver, when asked about his understandings of the Stein's spectrality, but the valley's hauntings remain an unsubstantiated urban legend.[44] Interviews conducted with non-Aboriginal informants who have hiked in the Stein Valley since the late 1990s nevertheless reveal a number of haunting stories ranging from a vague sense of unease in the Valley to accounts of ghostly apparitions.[45] Importantly, all those I interviewed characterize these spectral experiences as frightening, unsettling, and scary, and describe an impression of being unwelcome trespassers in what is ostensibly a public park. One hiker asserted that "the site gave us a sense that we were trespassing somehow, and that there was still a presence there."[46] Another suggested: "I think it was just feeling like we were intruding on somebody, and they were threatening in some way."[47] Much like the postcolonial ghost stories Gelder and Jacobs discuss in *Uncanny Australia*, these are stories about being unwelcome, illegitimate, and vulnerable to malevolent Indigenous ghosts. Although the Stein was set up as a "living museum" to showcase the Valley's cultural history, Gelder and Jacobs argue that such museological containment has become increasingly untenable in decolonizing settler nations like Canada and Australia. Museologically framed exhibits like Asking Rock, described below, take on a whole new resonance for a settler society experiencing "growing anxiety . . . regarding the legitimacy of their claims to belonging on what they call 'their' land."[48] As a park brochure instructs visitors:

> There are many rock paintings sites in the Stein Valley. A good example is the one known as "Asking Rock" situated near Stryen Creek. At this site Nlaka'pamux people stop, recite a prayer, and ask permission to travel through the valley in safety. Some people leave offerings of burnt sage and tobacco to accompany their prayers.[49]

Although the brochure implies that only Nlaka'pamux need ask for permission to travel through the valley, non-Aboriginal British Columbians have become increasingly aware of their failure to ask for permission to traverse and settle the province's lands. Sites like Asking Rock, then, are no longer read by non-Aboriginal British Columbians as neutral, museological exhibits. Indeed, the presence and claims of Aboriginal peoples in the Stein Valley – a presence that was purposely highlighted throughout the 1980s to ensure the Valley's conservation as a wilderness space – seem to undercut the legitimacy of non-Aboriginal wilderness enthusiasts traversing the Stein in the more politicized climate of contemporary treaty-making.

Drawing on Gelder and Jacobs, one might interpret contemporary hauntings in the Stein as manifestations of a certain uncanny, unsettled sense of place for those non-Aboriginal British Columbians who are struggling to come to terms with their (il)legitimate presence in the province.[50] Aboriginal ghosts represent the "return of the repressed" for settler-colonists, an uncanny reminder of the illegimicacy and injustice at the heart of land resettlement in the province.[51] But whether or not one finds a psychoanalytic reading of the Stein Valley ghost stories compelling, one might more productively query the ways in which these stories manage to write out the bodies and voices of living, politically active Indigenous peoples. In spite of the implicit recognition of Aboriginal "presence" in these stories, postcolonial hauntings in the Stein do not seem to account for *living* Indigenous peoples any more than Scott's poems did a century ago.

Not only do these ghost stories jar against Nlaka'pamux accounts of the spirits of the Stein as universally protective and welcoming, they also continue a long-standing practice of relegating Aboriginality to the immaterial and spectral past. Hikers do not recount stories of live, angry Nlaka'pamux asking them to leave, but rather tell stories of disembodied "spirits" emerging from an evocative landscape. These ghosts do not speak or act; they haunt by virtue of their very existence. As the peoples of the Mt. Currie and Lytton Bands declared during the "Save the Stein" campaign, they are too frequently engaged with on spectral terms:

> As we live through our daily lives as Indians, eventually we become accustomed to the fact that non-native people can see right through us. We don't mean that these people understand us fully or somehow sense the innermost workings of the Indian heart, because it seems to us that most non-native people don't take the time to come to this kind of knowledge. We mean simply that the majority of the non-natives view us as invisible peoples who really should not exist outside museums.[52]

These comments highlight the specific, lived experience of ghostliness as opposed to a generalized, metaphoric condition of Indigenous spectrality. The distinction between these two forms of spectrality is worth probing, as Gayatri Chakravorty Spivak has argued in her discussion of the singular and the general in postcolonial contexts.[53] She emphasizes the importance of understanding the singular not so much as an instance of the general, but rather as that which marks, in Ian Baucom's words, a "cryptic, secretive space . . . discloses the presence of that withheld space, but 'guards' its secret."[54] In other words, as Baucom has argued in reference to the generalized sense of haunting evoked by stories of the drowning of 132 slaves on the Atlantic crossing of the *Zong* in 1781, postcolonial scholars must pay attention to the ways in which singular, specific historical experiences and events are translated into generalized allegories of a reprehensible colonial past. He insists that the specificity of these histories must be stripped away in order for them to circulate as evocative signs of certain "kind" of history, and that the value of a specific history is only legible in this generalized state.

There is a certain violence, then, in the evocation of a general sense of haunted (un)settlement in places like the Stein Valley. It is a haunting that speaks not to the particular ways in which Nlaka'pamux have experienced and objected to colonial policies and practices (experiences and concerns that they specifically articulated, for example, to Gilbert Malcolm Sproat, Joint Indian Reserve Commissioner, as he traveled through their territory in the summer of 1878, tasked with allotting small reserve lands for the use of the Nlaka'pamux and thus clearing the way for non-Aboriginal settlement),[55] but rather to a generalized sense of the contemporary resonance of "that kind" of history. This generalized and allegorical understanding of the colonial past inevitably leads, Baucom argues, to an equally generalized "fantasy" of postcolonial justice, to the notion of reconciliation with ghosts rather than a reckoning with the specific and ongoing violence of colonialism.[56] "In poll after poll," reports the *Royal Commission on Aboriginal Peoples*, "Canadians have said that they want to see justice done for Aboriginal people, but they have not known how," in spite of the fact that Aboriginal peoples have consistently and forcefully articulated their specific demands for justice.[57]

What does it mean, then, to be haunted in a decolonizing settler colony like British Columbia? *Who* is haunted in these stories, and who or what is doing the haunting? What kind of future might these hauntings demand? Do they signal, as Derrida intended, a recognition of the always unfinished and *unfinishable* in our relation to the present and past and, by extension, a sense of generosity and hospitality towards ghosts? Or do they, as Sarah Ahmed has argued in relation to white guilt in postcolonial Australia, constitute yet another self-referential engagement with the colonial past, in which the experiences and desires of the settler occlude consideration of other desires and possibilities?[58] Postcolonial ghost stories risk perpetuating a kind of endless "dancing around a wound" that Daniel David Moses identifies among liberal, left-leaning Canadians, who anxiously replay their complicity in an ugly colonial past while failing to mobilize effectively for change in the present.[59] The ghosts of the Stein do not seem to me to represent the Nlaka'pamux with very much dignity or agency, and surely any postcolonial trope that scholars and citizens might mobilize ought at the very least to figure Indigenous peoples with dignity. If, as Donna Haraway notes, we inevitably read the world through tropes, we can still choose "less-deadly version[s] for moral discourse,"[60] and haunting has the potential to function as a particularly "deadly" trope, one that requires the death and immateriality of Indigenous peoples to make both an effective and affective claim on non-Indigenous British Columbians. It is a trope within which today's living descendents of the generalized spirits haunting the Stein, people like Chiefs Leonard Andrew and Ruby Dunstan, seem to have no place:

> As the direct descendents of those aboriginal peoples who have inhab-ited, shared, sustained, and been sustained by the Stein Valley for tens of thousands of years down to the present, our authority in this water-shed is inescapable . . . Under the cooperative authority of our two bands we will maintain the Stein Valley as a wilderness in perpetuity for the enjoyment and enlightenment of all peoples.[61]

Conclusion

At a time when (primarily non-Aboriginal) scholars, among others, seem to have taken an interest in ghostly matters, it is critical to acknowledge that ghostliness is a politicized state of being. Many schol-ars have interpreted these politics as a function of visibility – that is, they suggest that the uncovering and exposure of the ghosts of the past is an emancipatory act. In many cases this may be true, but there is also a politics of vision involved in these hauntologies. Those who see and imagine ghosts are as deserving of interrogation as the ghosts them-selves, and the ghosts of the Stein are profoundly self-referential. So, while the spectral does seem to offer a means of conceptualizing that which we cannot easily see, and even of giving some voice to colonial traumas, confining the Indigenous to the ghostly also has the potential to re-inscribe the interests of the powerful upon the meanings and memories of place.

Further, while in this chapter I have bracketed out the possibility that non-Aboriginal hikers truly are connecting with a complex spiri-tual world in the Stein, I think Métis scholar Warren Cariou's comments on postcolonial ghosts are worth considering. In contrast to the horror, anxiety, and sense of punishment or revenge conveyed by Indigenous ghosts in settler literatures, Cariou points out that "for Native readers and writers, there is no reason that . . . Indigenous ghosts or spirits should be frightening. Native people already have plenty of evidence in their daily lives of how the legacies of colonialism have been passed down through the generations; they do not need to summon specters to fulfill that function." He notes, however, that

> Native writers do represent spirits in their work nonetheless; it is just that these spirits are not necessarily figures of uncanny terror. They may be malevolent beings such as the wihtiko or the skeleton-spirit Pahkakos, but they may also be figures of healing, ceremony, or political action. Or they may simply be ancestors. And while many such spirits do seem to address the transgressions of the colonial past, they usually do so as part of a call for some kind of redress or change in the present.[62]

Haunting need not be about forgetting, avenging, and lurking; richer understandings of both spectrality and colonialism are available, and I would suggest that scholars might reconsider the political potential of haunting tropes in their accounts of the colonial and postcolonial. While the figuration of Indigenous peoples as ghosts haunting the Canadian state seems to be offered as a gesture of recognition in these "post" colonial times, such hauntologies dwell more upon the anxieties of settlers than they do upon the specific claims and experiences of Indigenous peoples.

As such, postcolonial ghost stories expose some of the risks of reducing matters of recognition, redress, and justice to a form of "difference" that might be accommodated by the powerful.[63] The spirits of the Stein Valley have been both celebrated as figures of multicultural inclusion and feared as signifiers of pluralistic excess; they function today as "haunting" reminders of the illegitimacy underpinning settler colonialism. Indeed, if "the figure of the ghost is often used as a means of apprehending that which we cannot explain, do not expect, understand, or struggle to represent,"[64] then postcolonial ghosts exemplify an almost willful refusal to recognize the claims of Indigenous peoples in Canada. Indigenous claims to land and self-determination are neither unexpected nor inexplicable; to represent them as such only serves to defer a truly "post" colonial condition.

Part 4

Bodies

9 Resurfacing landscapes of trauma: Multiculturalism, cemeteries, and the migrant body, 1875 onwards

Laurie K. Bertram

The land I live on, according to local history books, was never occupied by aboriginals. My ancestors came to Canada early in this century with little more than the clothes on their backs. They survived by hard work. They never stole anything from anyone. There must be millions of other Canadians with similar backgrounds. Taxing us to compensate the aboriginals for past wrongs, suspected or proven, is not correcting an injustice – it's inflicting a new one.   – Karen Selick, 1997

Consider the obituary as an act of nation-building.
                              – Judith Butler, *Precarious Life*

WHILE RESEARCHING ICELANDIC-CANADIAN COLLECTIVE MEMORY in 2006, I made a strange, somewhat grisly discovery at a neglected small-pox cemetery with my uncle and cousin in Riverton, Manitoba. Riverton lies at the northern-most boundary of "New Iceland," the block settlement where almost 25 per cent of Iceland's population migrated in the late nineteenth century. The migrants contracted smallpox in the Quebec City immigration sheds en route to Manitoba and transmitted the disease to their Aboriginal neighbours, the Sandy Bar Band, in 1876. The migrants and band members were in the midst of a heated land claims contest before the disease overwhelmed and killed 70 per cent of the band and about 10 per cent of the Icelanders.[1] According to historical records, the wooded fringes, grassy fields, and marshy land of a place just outside of town, a place the Icelanders called *Nes*, is the unmarked resting place for up to eighty Icelandic and First Nations victims of that epidemic.[2]

I had already heard ghost stories about the now vacant stretch of land where a morbid Icelandic farmer had decided to build a house a few years following the epidemic. Nes is short for this site's longer name, *Graftarnes* (Burial Point) or *Náströnd* (Corpse Strand), a reference to the graphic description of Norse hell found in the Poetic Edda, where the bodies of the dead were strewn about on a shore and devoured after the end of the world.[3] Stories about the farmer's gory death, ghosts of epidemic victims, and the appearance of black animals on the walls of the house at night illuminate the emotionally charged cultural history of the space, one that both conceals and preserves unsettling memories of the past. Nes is a marginal space that community members have avoided and neglected for many years. The continual surfacing of human remains as a result of riverbank erosion has also contributed to its unpleasant reputation. The day we decided to visit, the river had been high for many days but had suddenly dropped. When we reached the grassy outline of the foundation of the old house, we looked down onto some debris scattered along the beach. My uncle first spotted a large skull, tinged green with algae, lodged upside down in the muddy river shore (figure 9.1). Climbing down from the eroding bank, we found many more fragments from Nes's unsettled inhabitants: disembodied jaws, stray teeth, vertebrae, ribs, clavicles, and arm bones. Later an archaeological team would identify these remains as belonging to at least eight different Icelandic women and children who had died from smallpox and been buried in shallow winter graves close to the rapidly fluctuating river.

I thought often about this compelling and grotesque display of Icelandic-Canadian forgetfulness so close to the town itself. Why did community members neglect these otherwise celebrated "pioneers," a group of people usually canonized and mythologized in the community as "the descendents of the high mettled warriors and matriarchs of the Icelandic sagas, whose feats were no less heroic"?[4] I was also startled by the breach in the traditionally concealed space of the cemetery, a space usually associated with gates, markers, and neatly kept lawns. This unexpected sight prompted me to investigate the dual process of resurfacing, or the re-emergence *and* revision of traumatic histories in Canadian history. How can we account for the neglect of nineteenth-century skeletal mementos of catastrophe and the pervasive twentieth-century celebration and commemoration of migrant suffering? How

Figure 9-1

and why are certain bodies, histories, and spaces of trauma celebrated, while others are ignored and forgotten?

Human bodies are unusual and compelling historical texts. Achille Mbembe writes that in gazing upon skeletons, one is struck by both their simplicity and "undifferentiated generality" as "simple relics of unburied pain, empty meaningless corporealities, strange deposits plunged into cruel stupor." Despite the "strange coolness" of the skeletal body, Mbembe also asserts that skeletons possess a "stubborn will to mean, to signify something."[5] Yet, as the uncomfortable history and exposure at Nes suggests, the "stubborn signification" of bodies does not mean that all bodies become "memorable." This chapter explores the role of the nineteenth-century Canadian migrant-settler's body in both the colonial project and multicultural depictions of the past.

Beyond the simple commemoration of dates of arrival and pioneer names, multicultural heritage campaigns broadcast through the media since official multiculturalism's implementation in the 1970s have employed histories and memories of migrant-settler trauma in particular ways. Such campaigns create a potentially neutralizing set of nationalist narratives that place migration and ethnic memory in a larger tradition of shared suffering. Though motivated by social historians' desire to incorporate marginalized populations, such as poor migrant women and children, the new commemorative emphasis on migrant-settler suffering and oppression simultaneously depopulates Canada's colonial project. Proceeding from recent American scholarship on race and gender in the commemoration of mass migration, including that of Matthew Frye Jacobson and Erica Rand, this chapter resituates the redemptive image of nineteenth-century Canadian migration into its proper historical context and argues that such "sympathetic" nineteenth-century migrant bodies, including women and children, were still enmeshed in a range of activities that secured colonial boundaries and claims.

Beyond providing an analysis of the role of migrant families in the colonial project, a close reading of the unsettling landscape at Nes also speaks to the disruptive and productive potential of revisiting underground landscapes of trauma and the uneven ways in which they are reworked, enshrined, or ignored aboveground. Far from a neutral or mute force, landscapes can fail to silently contain painful pasts by preserving and occasionally allowing traumatic ethnic and colonial memories to surface. The complexity and unfaithfulness of underground landscapes also provide opportunities for the emergence of postcolonial historical understandings in the Canadian West by disrupting colonial regimes of "meaningful" trauma – regimes that continue to invest certain lives with value and others without.

European migration and settlement are pivotal moments in popular and academic histories of the Canadian West, occupying an essential role in what Library and Archives Canada terms "Making the West Canadian."[6] Indeed, this is typical of the popular Canadian vision of migration to the West, one that emphasizes migration as a creative drive with beneficial and productive personal, cultural, economic, and political effects. Central to this vision is the multifaceted figure of the migrant him- or herself as a nation builder who is both "rescued" by and labours within the project of "making Canada." The settler-centric chronology of "making the West Canadian" frequently infers substantial temporal distance between First Nations dispossession and European migrant arrival in the West, attempting to disconnect these often historically simultaneous processes.

Previously under the jurisdiction of the Hudson's Bay Company, the newly formed Dominion of Canada acquired the title to Rupert's Land (modern-day Southern Manitoba and broader regions within the Northwest Territories, Northern Manitoba, Saskatchewan, Alberta, and British Columbia) in 1870. The purchase ignited long-standing grievances among existing Métis and First Nations inhabitants regarding rights to land, governance, and economic activity, resulting in the Red River Rebellion of 1869–70. Responding to the grievances set forth by the provisional government head and rebellion leader, Louis Riel, the Dominion of Canada entrenched Métis land rights into the Manitoba Act of 1870, guaranteeing 1.4 million acres for Métis families and their descendents. Unfortunately, the government failed to enforce the legislation. The resurrection of armed Métis struggle and the ensuing military engagement with the Canadian state in 1885 during the North-West Rebellion, more than ten years after the arrival of the first large waves of migrants to the prairies, further illustrates that the land claimed by migrant settlers was by no means vacant, nor uncontested.

While the federal government may have focused on containing First Nations and Métis communities with a range of either poorly implemented or marginal settlements, it negotiated more generous block settlements for European populations. Driven by business and railroad interests, the government provided land deals to Mennonite and Icelandic communities. These groups arrived en masse in Manitoba in 1874 and 1875 and settled in regions also still occupied by Métis and First Nations communities.[7] Early European block-settlement groups enjoyed preferential treatment by the Canadian government based on state notions of their racial, religious, and cultural compatibility with Anglo-Saxons.[8] Hoping beneficial terms would entice large numbers of their kin to follow them to Manitoba, the government offered the Mennonites and Icelanders semi-autonomous zones of land with promises of cultural, linguistic, and spiritual freedom, including the rights to establish their own schools and municipal governments.

The Icelanders received a 600-square-mile land package along the shores of Lake Winnipeg where they formed a block settlement in

1875. The land was actually located North of the existing provincial border and was still inhabited by the Sandy Bar Band. Chief John Ramsay contested this expansion but his claims to the land, as well as official recognition of his band, were rejected by the government.[9] The decision to refuse recognition of the Sandy Bar Band while simultaneously granting autonomy to a group of European migrants demonstrates the early expression of sovereign power through the creation of race-based states of exception, or the erosion or suspension of the rights of a certain population as part of a larger attempt to eliminate that population.[10] Conversely, European block-settlement agreements slowed settler integration and assimilation into Anglo-Canadian society, but the federal and provincial governments assumed this risk in order to attract the maximum number of settlers. This emphasis on maximum European population growth had a disastrous effect on the negotiation of settlements and land grants for Aboriginal peoples in Manitoba. As Anne Brydon and Olive Dickason note, "the pressure of incoming settlers made officials move quickly to force land surrender in situations bereft of equality – officials seem to have regarded the exercise as little more than a formality."[11] In addition to Chief Ramsay's exclusion from official channels for redress, the onset of Icelandic-introduced smallpox devastated the band's numbers. Surviving members dispersed and joined newly formed reserves in the region.

Sick migrant families and epidemic cemeteries seldom appear in analyses of Canadian colonial history. In contrast to more clearly problematic colonial cemeteries that contain celebrated male adult officials, Nes and other early migrant settler cemeteries on the prairies often contain the remains of women and children. Because of the subjugated positions of these populations within nineteenth-century Western Canadian society, scholars have only recently begun to analyze the role of these groups and the spaces they inhabited in the colonial project. The emphasis on health, population-creation, and management in biopolitical analysis provides an effective framework for the exploration of the role of families in the state-coordinated population transformation known as the "peopling of the Prairies." Used here to assess the state's attempt to produce or encourage preferred populations and discourage and eradicate others, biopolitical analysis helps illuminate the connections between colonialism and mass migration to the West in the nineteenth century. Rather than resorting to the more overt use of punishment, incarceration, and execution to control populations, biopolitical governance shrouds itself through a broad network of actors and the subtle manipulation of what it deems "natural" forces, achieving its goals through fostering or abandoning certain populations. Biopolitical analysis has the potential to seriously inflect popular and academic understandings of Canadian colonialism, which have traditionally limited their condemnation to well-known, explicit instances of genocide and state violence such as the American Battle at Wounded Knee, the popular history surrounding the Riel Rebellion and, to a lesser extent, the tragedy of residential schools and legally entrenched inequalities. As the narratives of Canadian multicultural campaigns and popular Prairie identity illustrate, the Native/non–Native contests over land, status, and history over the past 130 years have involved far more intricate power relations. As Mary Ellen Kelm argues, colonial power structures also affect the spread of communicable disease while hiding the racism of government health care policies behind the façade of "faceless pathogens."[12]

In addition, the settler's body itself must be understood as an active biopolitical agent, one that simultaneously "made live" through the production of children in young families and "let die" through the introduction of disease, the enforcement of white land claims, and the disruption of First Nations food production and economies. Apart from transmitting disease, settlers themselves attempted to reinforce the province's claims to the land during conflicts with Aboriginal inhabitants by occupying contested land. An examination of European settlement-era accounts reveals the overlapping geographic and temporal proximities between migration and the forcible and violent removal of Aboriginal people. The use of settler bodies in Aboriginal displacement was a sometimes very intimate and direct affair, as evident in Sandy Bar Chief Ramsay's discovery that Icelandic settlers had moved next to Ramsay while he was away on a hunting trip.[13] Ramsay's conflict with the Icelandic settlers, and the death of his wife in the ensuing smallpox epidemic, stand in stark contrast to popular depictions of vacant prairies and noble pioneers, and further illuminate the central role of migrant settlers in a range of activities that displaced First Nations people:

> Three settlers rowed across the creek to their work. Ramsay was awaiting them with an angry look, and when they attempted to land he pushed the boat out again, making it very clear by his actions that he was forbidding them to step ashore . . . the three put into shore a second time, and once again Ramsay shoved the boat away, but the third time Ólafur [who had recently moved in next to Ramsay] walked to the bow with an axe and instructed the others to row in. They succeeded in getting ashore.[14]

While this Icelandic account emphasizes bravado and the "pioneer spirit," other settler tales express concern over the "restlessness of the Indians and the half-breeds," particularly after the Battle of Little Bighorn in 1876 and the North-West Rebellion in 1885.[15] Though migrants often appear in popular histories and commemorative campaigns as hapless bystanders in First Nations displacement, migrant groups were very cognizant of and dependent on the violent repression of organized Aboriginal resistance. A closer examination of settler ties to the state reveals a lack of distinction between armed, violent enforcers of colonial boundaries and the officially sanctioned bodies charged with maintaining colonial borders. Migrant settlers could invoke state enforcement of their land claims; as Brydon notes in her investigation of First Nations and Icelandic encounters, representatives from the Icelandic group notified Lieutenant-Governor Morris of the Icelanders' and the Sandy Bar Band's competing claims to the land and its resources.[16] First Nations people certainly understood migrant settlers as closely aligned with, if not sometimes indistinguishable from, state agents. Thorstína Walters writes that Icelanders travelling from Manitoba to a new settlement in North Dakota avoided a potentially violent confrontation with a large group of First Nations warriors. According to one man, the Icelanders had been spared by virtue of their likeness to local militia members who were notoriously "quick on the trigger" in enforcing new legislation prohibiting "Indians (from) gathering in large groups on the Prairies."[17]

While adult male migrants were largely responsible for formal and informal connections to the state, scholars must also be mindful of the role of individual settlers who did not participate in the negotiation of official claims and provincial and national boundaries. An exploration of how women, children, and domestic space contributed to the construction of settler land claims illuminates the significant role that these understudied players had in the colonial project. As Eyal Weizman asserts in his discussion of Israeli suburbs, domestic space and the gaze of the settler can be "hijacked for strategic and geopolitical aims."[18] He argues that the home itself is a point of surveillance on disputed land in which living room windows and the eyes of settler family members provide an opportunity for constant surveillance and the continual reassertion of personal and political claims to land. Popular Icelandic-Canadian and other Prairie narratives of settlement told by first-generation Canadians also often reference domestic space in the reinforcement of spatial and social boundaries between First Nations and white populations, particularly in the recurring narrative of "the Indian guest." These narratives generally describe an unwelcome First Nations male "guest" descending on a fearful migrant mother and her children while their father is away.[19] Guttormur J. Guttormsson, a poet whose farmstead bordered Nes, recalled that "a greater discomfort was felt when they came, many at a time, uninvited and without knocking, to an Icelandic home. They would sit themselves down without saying a word, and stay put for many hours, often when only a woman was at home alone with her children."[20] These narratives describe white women and children as targets of unwanted Native male physical affection and the corruptive, threatening, and unhealthy touch of their skin – a striking notion given the role of migrant families in the transmission of disease to First Nations.[21] Stefanía Magnússon recalled her mother's horror at the decision of her unwelcome guests to touch her newborn daughter.

> Indians started coming in droves to get a look at her (new) white child . . . And the Indian chief he – Mother said he had been so black and ugly. It wasn't enough for him to look at me, rather he had to hold me, and then he had been stroking me with his fingers about the face – and body, with his coal-black fingers.[22]

By depicting the First Nations neighbours as both "unwelcome" and "guests," these narratives speak to a broader motif in migrant-settler society and narratives, one that identifies First Nations men as unpleasant, vaguely menacing, transitory figures, who rudely disrupt the inherently more permanent and legitimate migrant-settler claims to racially and sexually segregated homogenous space. They also reveal an intriguing relationship between motherhood, gender, and colonialism, most notably the boundaries of migrant-settler women's hospitality and the enforcement of race-based social and spatial distance from the unwelcome guest. Such narratives speak to the desire to establish an exclusive, intimate space only open to family or community members. Settlers attempted to police these spaces not only by invoking the power of the state or threatening violence, but also through unfriendliness and the refusal of hospitality.

The Indian guest narrative was most popular with the first- and second-generation descendants of mass-migrants. The decline of such narratives and other references to racial tensions between migrants and First Nations, including unresolved land claims, Canadian white supremacy, and underlying threats of post-settlement violence, coincided with the implementation of pluralist heritage campaigns following the Canadian government's official adoption of multicultural policy in 1971. In keeping with the policy's focus on cultural diversity and equality, more recent images of the past set forth in school curricula, monuments, museum exhibits, Historica's "Settling Canada" series, and Library and Archives Canada's "Making the West Canadian" campaign depict the settlement of the West as part of a larger tradition of pluralism and humanitarianism instead.[23] This shift resembles the rise of the Ellis Island and ethnic history movement in the United States in the 1970s, in which the cultural diversity of migrants became central to narratives of American nation-building and notions of "meaningful" history. Matthew Frye Jacobson argues that the pressure of the civil rights movement inspired this shift in the 1970s, resulting in the replacement of Anglo-American narratives of privilege and pedigree, such as the Plymouth Rock story, with commemoration of white ethnic mass migration and suffering.[24] This new focus simultaneously fossilized racial injustices, he writes, imbuing modern white Americans with a sense of "just off the boat innocence."[25] Twentieth-century Canadian heritage campaigns have similarly altered their focus, moving away from older Anglocentric narratives, such as the arrival of the Loyalists, in favour of histories of mass migration, which included the creation of heritage parks at Pier 21 in Halifax and Grosse Île in Quebec. The centrality of migration in these new narratives is particularly evident in the transformation of First Nations into "fellow migrants" in public history campaigns such as the Manitoba Museum's exhibit, *Mass Migration to Manitoba*. Created in connection with the province's centennial celebrations in 1970, the exhibit opens with the lone figure of a female mannequin sitting amid a stack of trunks (figure 9.2). The text above the mannequin reads

> First the Indians and the Inuit came.
> Then came the European fur traders and Red River settlers.
> In 1870 a massive influx of peoples began.
> This brought to Manitoba people from virtually every corner of the world.[26]

The Royal Ontario Museum similarly constructs a migration-centric creation narrative in its Daphne Cockwell Gallery of Canada: First Peoples. Visitors to the gallery are greeted with an excerpt of a Mi'kmaq narrative about crossing the ocean in a giant canoe beside Norval Morrisseau's painting of a large group in a canoe entitled *The Migration*. While acknowledging Morrisseau's own rejection of the Bering Strait theory, the ROM's audio guide reminds visitors that "sci-

Figure 9-2

entific research suggests that North America was first populated thousands of years ago, when migrants crossed over from Asia during the Ice Age."[27] Such narratives impose modern narratives, histories, and identities related to mass migration, in some cases complete with boats and oceanic travel, over an array of long-standing First Nations chronologies that insist on a pre-Ice Age presence and seldom locate migration as a point of origin. While migration may work well as a nation-building framework and point of origin for non-Native Canadians, superimposing this narrative onto First Nations peoples has meant collapsing even the most conservative estimate of 13,500 years of First Nations presence (scholars from the long chronology school assert a presence of up to 100,000 years) on North American soil to fit into a largely 130-year-old mass-migration Canadian creation narrative.

Beyond being anachronistic, migrant-centred chronologies, Western heritage narratives also demonstrate their deeply entrenched biases in the way that sympathetic historical figures and "grievable" trauma are constructed. Most Canadians are familiar with an image of the largely economic migrants of the nineteenth-century as heroic but destitute quasi-refugees fleeing oppression and poverty. Far from simply providing the public with the historical details of settlement, school curricula, museums, memorials, and media representations of migrant and settler trauma create a historically selective image of the past based on an imagined collective experience of tragedy and a complementary, redemptive tradition of Canadian humanitarianism. *The Newcomers* television miniseries, which aired on CBC from 1977 to 1980, focused on migrant poverty and suffering, including "the constants of separation, hardship, domestic conflict, homesickness, the search for freedom, and crisis," in order to orient the public in "today's search for a Canadian identity."[28] Historica's Heritage Minutes, the brief advertisements/ miniature dramas that have been widely broadcast on Canadian television and radio since 1991, also frequently use migration history to depict "our country's defining moments and personalities."[29] The minute, *Underground Railroad,* presents an emotionally charged depiction of Black slaves escaping to Canada by hiding in a wagon shipment of furniture while the narrator explains "between 1840 and 1860 more than 30,000 American slaves came secretly to Canada and to freedom. They called it the underground railroad."[30] The minutes *Soddie* and *Orphans* similarly present dramatic depictions of European migrant settler hardship. *Soddie* begins with operatic choral music announcing the arrival of a young Ukrainian couple expecting their first child on their new homestead on the prairies, following them as they work, sometimes through the driving rain, to build their first home out of sod.[31] The minute's choral music reaches a pitch as the unnamed wife clutches her stomach and stumbles, referencing the toll of settlement labour and harsh living conditions on women. In contrast, *Orphans* tells the story of migrant Irish children who have lost their parents to disease. With a slow, sad violin solo as its soundtrack, the minute opens on the children's arrival and adoption by Québécois families.[32] At the insistence of the children, the Québécois parents allow the newcomers to keep their Irish names. The minute closes with the sound of cheerful music as the narrator comments on this moment of tolerance and diversity that established an enduring Irish presence in Quebec. In each minute, the final scene celebrating the triumph of the beleaguered migrant is marked with the words "a part of our heritage."

While such visions respond to the demand for inclusivity characteristic of multicultural heritage campaigns, they remain deeply problematic due to their fixation on the construction of a Canadian humanitarian tradition, one that fails to seriously engage with the subtleties of power and discrimination in Canadian history. *Underground Railroad* ignores the persistence of slavery in Canada into the nineteenth century, while *Orphans* re-inscribes an English-speaking presence onto Quebec's hotly contested history. The emphasis on birth, redemption, and survival in depictions of migration are also striking in contrast to several of the minutes depicting First Nations peoples' history. These minutes are devoid of the family bonds that are central to migration-themed minutes and, most interestingly, begin or end with the actual death (versus the endangerment) of the featured protagonists, Sitting Bull, Louis Riel, and Tommy Prince.[33]

The depiction of nineteenth-century migrants as quasi-refugees has been popular with both Anglo and ethnic communities on the Canadian prairies. The popularity of this narrative is evident in the celebration of ethnic European trauma in more recent commemorative campaigns of settlement, and in the suppression or revision of histories that reference the role of social, economic, or racial privilege in shaping an ancestor's arrival in Canada. As Kirby Miller observes of Irish Canadians, the vast majority of whom migrated as middle-class Protestant farmers before the Irish Famine, stories of exile may not reflect the historical reality of individual Irish families, but are instruments in the performance of cultural identity.[34] Multicultural heritage campaigns have similarly suggested certain narratives to help Canadians to "understand" or reframe their own families' pasts. However, the use of traumatic images, or images of physical endangerment, injury, or death with which the viewer identifies and empathizes, has had specific effects. Relating this process to the larger body of scholarship on memory and trauma is useful insofar as it demonstrates how such a fixation on settler hardship and trauma relates to post-traumatic stress disorder (PTSD). Studies of PTSD link sufferers' obsessive mental reperformance of traumatic incidents to the unique way in which the brain records and processes trauma. Ruth Leys asserts that "the experience of the trauma, fixed or frozen in time, refuses to be represented as past, but is perpetually re-experienced in a painful disassociated, traumatic present."[35] Central to this theory is the brain's failure to successfully integrate the traumatic incident as a normal memory. Traumatic memories and the landscape through which they are imagined and remembered refuse the traditional historicity of the past, occupying instead a painful present that must be repeatedly addressed. This process is not only a response to first-hand experience of trauma, but can also be caused by witnessing trauma. Wulf Kansteiner argues that images can play a particularly potent role in the adoption of second-hand trauma by collapsing the gap between first- and second-hand experience.[36] Thus, the images of migrants in multicultural media campaigns stand in for the absent ancestor, potentially reminding audience members of existing family

history narratives or creating new visions of ancestral suffering and sacrifice.

Understanding the popularity of the traumatic migrant-settler
"memories" that infuse personal and public representations of the past
requires attention to the way in which images and "memories" of
trauma are organized within larger regimes of "meaningful" and
"meaningless" suffering. Beyond museum displays and film, landscapes
and the material world relate to the traumatic past in uneven ways,
both enshrining and protecting spaces and bodies related to productive
trauma, and containing and suppressing those from less redemptive
pasts. The centrality of settler/migrants' bodies in imagining Canadian
history also speaks to the importance of the physical sites associated
with their bodies and experiences of trauma. Space plays a particularly
important role in the recognition of and respect for the suffering
migrant-settler body, even in death, a fact evident in the creation of
monuments and careful lawn maintenance of certain migrant-settler
cemeteries on the prairies. As Brian Osborne writes, the "collective
remembering – and, if necessary, collective amnesia – " involved in the
construction of "imagined communities" are grounded in "imagined
geographies."[37] Migrant-settler graveyards and monuments must then
be understood not as simple spaces containing bones, but as sites of
power with complex effects. These spaces legitimate the images of settler sacrifice set forth in Canadian heritage campaigns by providing dis-
creet, emotionally charged spaces that can be easily invoked as proof of
suffering. In their merging of the migrant body with the land, the
migrant-settler graveyards can also be seen as illustrative of what Terry
Goldie has called an indigenization "through which the 'settler' population attempts to become as though indigenous, as though 'born' of
the land."[38] Additionally, the bodies in settler graveyards and monuments also function as a point of origin while simultaneously reminding visitors of the role of endangerment and death in settler survival.
The migrant-settler cemetery may be employed, then, as an expression
of both victory and tragedy in which migrant-settler bodies are privileged in a way that simultaneously absolves migrant-settler Canada of
any association with unfair/racist privilege in Canadian colonial history.

The focus on migrant trauma in multicultural heritage campaigns
has also transformed popular responses to previously neglected histories
of migration. During the first half of the twentieth century, sites of
mass trauma such as Nes were abandoned in favour of promoting more
celebratory lives and spaces associated with settlement, including "The
White Rock," a monument to the "first" Icelandic child born in New

Iceland. Unveiled at Willow Point, Manitoba in 1950, the large white stone actually commemorated the birth of the third child born in the settlement, while omitting two others who were born earlier but died from disease several months later.[39] Previously relegated to unmarked or impermanently marked corners of municipal cemeteries, farmyards, and fields, sites of migrant-settler child trauma and death have re-emerged into the public consciousness and commemorative landscape of many rural ethnic communities on the prairies. In addition to federally funded historical sites of trauma, volunteer committees in numerous communities have begun to reclaim and care for previously abandoned and neglected sites. Nes itself is currently undergoing a community-initiated transformation into a heritage park. This project will address bank erosion and protect additional graves while converting the surface into a well-kept cemetery featuring a proposed monument of a woman cradling a baby. This site, once relegated to the margins of community memory due to its painful contradiction with celebratory narratives of pioneer endurance and success, has re-emerged as a habitable and memorable place since an emergency archaeological visit from Manitoba's Historic Resources Branch in 2006. Townspeople now visit the site on hikes and picnics, mow the grass there, and have organized several fundraising campaigns for the site's protection. While these commemorative projects – often funded by the community and by individuals – speak poignantly of the attempt to reconcile enduring memories of trauma, the corresponding silence surrounding the victims of colonial violence speaks to their complex and ambiguous function.

Other sites of child mortality involving contagious disease from the same time period in the same province have been excluded from commemorative efforts, based on their potential to undermine redemptive nationalist narratives. In Birtle, Manitoba, stands the crumbling edifice of the district's residential school, where over 50 per cent of the First Nations student body succumbed to tuberculosis between 1912 and 1917.[40] This space, along with dozens of unmarked mass grave sites on residential school property in the Canadian West, has been neglected by heritage agencies. Other schools in Manitoba, such as the Brandon Indian Residential School, one of the largest in Canada, have been demolished while still others have been left to slowly collapse. First Nations people in Canada are in the midst of instituting a public grieving and reconciliation process, which is evident in several ways, including their successful pursuit of a formal apology to residential school survivors from the federal government, the establishment of the Truth and Reconciliation Commission of Canada, the endurance of familial commemoration at school sites, and a series of media reports on residential schools.[41] The need for the recovery, protection, and reconciliation of First Nations sites of trauma are evident in personal and intergenerational memories of residential school experiences, which include frequent references to unusually vivid memories, open wounds, and feeling "haunted" by the past.[42] The public testimony by residential school survivors and their descendents that coincided with the 2008 apology illuminates the ways in which residential school trauma also appears to refuse historicity, occupying instead a painful present in which many experience recurring and intrusive thoughts about children and family members who experienced trauma or died at residential school. Beyond the reconciliation of painful family and community histories, however, the responses to the legacy of residential schools have also begun to imagine an anti-colonial historical landscape capable of contesting, and arguably, ultimately disrupting the migrant–settler-centric mentality above and below ground on the prairies.

Though neglected cemeteries may offer a slightly morbid venue for a discussion of multiculturalism, landscape, and memory on the prairies, it is the power of these spaces and memories associated with them that speaks to their importance and critical potential. In *Precarious Life*, Judith Butler argues that bans on mourning, including for example the censoring of Iraqi casualty photographs in the United States, must be understood as an expression of power that attempts to contain the subversive potential of mourning as a transformative process. Confronting the lack of recognition for traumatic histories, Butler asks: "what is the relation between the violence by which these ungrievable lives were lost and the prohibition on their public grievability? Are the violence and the prohibition both permutations of the same violence?"[43] Kansteiner similarly notes that "memory is valorized where identity is problematized,"[44] a relationship that is particularly evident in the troubling and inadequate discussion of colonialism in multicultural history campaigns. Rather than pursuing an anti-racist approach to historical understanding that critically engages with the endurance of colonial structures in contemporary Canada, multicultural heritage campaigns have instead complicated the relationship between colonialism and nationalism by recasting historical colonial agents as mournable co-victims with First Nations in a distant Canadian past. As Karen Selick's words indicate, personalized narratives of settler suffering have complex effects, including the erosion of Canada's popular and official acknowledgement of its colonial past. Non-Native Canadians can invoke memories of migrant-settler trauma or hardship to claim status as nation builders, while simultaneously negating the ownership or admission of participation in the colonial project. Rather than simply recalling a family's traumatic past, the complex origins and loaded usage of "memories" of trauma – that is, memories that are shaped by multicultural narratives, visual culture, and regimes of meaningful trauma – must be understood, in this case, as a tool for consolidating national power.

Paul Gilroy notes that meaningful multiculturalism must traverse "bloody histories" to address the power structures that facilitate racism's tenacious grasp.[45] In the Canadian West, meaningful multiculturalism must also untangle the ways in which those bloody histories are organized, particularly since the fixation on settler trauma often surfaces in rebuttals of First Nations claims to suffering and demands for reconciliation. Migrant–settler cemeteries and "memories" of migrant–settler suffering are compelling examples of the power of trauma as a political tool and a geographical boundary marker. These sites are indicative of the role of traumatic memory in legitimating settler land claims. However, they also construct both a physical and ancestral claim to colonial territory by establishing a persistent and arguably irrevocable white presence on the land. This biological, political, and territorial lineage is further legitimated by a Canadian colonial chronology and geography that privilege histories inscribed with Euro-Canadian notions of development, settlement, and permanence. As Goldie asserts, history before a literate colonial presence occupies an alternate chronology, one resembling what Frantz Fanon has termed "an unchanging dream."[46] Fanon writes that the vision of the settler is encased in an alternate view of time: "the settler makes history; his life is an epoch, an Odyssey. He is the absolute beginning . . . he is the unceasing cause."[47]

Though the migrant settler's body has performed a variety of tasks in the establishment and eventual denial of colonial governance in Canada, the erosion at Nes and the power of traumatic memories that contradict nationalist historical narratives also demonstrate the possibilities of commemorative campaigns on the prairies and the instability of the settler–centric landscape. Underground landscapes, bodies, and histories also have the power to make themselves visible in disruptive ways. Anders Swanson offers an eloquent reassessment of the possibilities of the subterranean prairie in his painting, *The Three Sisters* (figure 9.3). His work envisions the prairies as dominated by an often hidden but incredibly complex subterranean landscape, home to a dense and diverse population of which the three sisters, the only live bodies on the canvas who occupy a mere sixteenth of its surface, are unaware.[48] This vision, like Nes and other unmarked, unmaintained gravesites on

Figure 9-3

the prairies, has the power to prompt Canadians to reconsider their relationship to landscapes below ground. Such spaces suggest that concealment and forgetting are potentially impermanent states and push us towards the reconciliation of pasts constructed above ground and the complex archive below. This vantage point reframes prairie history and disrupts the silences upon which the major Western Canadian myths and chronologies of colonization depend. By reimagining underground landscapes as complex spaces that demand a sometimes painful but crucial historical democracy, commemorative campaigns in Canada can move towards a more meaningful multiculturalism able to unsettle nationalist historical narratives that attempt to contain or forget such spaces.

10 Mere "song and dance": Complicating the multicultural imperative in the arts

Natasha Bakht

THE MEANING OF MULTICULTURALISM IN CANADA is multifaceted. For some, multiculturalism is a descriptive term that simply captures the social phenomenon of Canada's racial, ethnic, cultural, religious, and sexual diversity. As a normative concept, multiculturalism suggests that this diversity is a positive development and that the appropriate policy response is to "accommodate difference" in the public sphere. Legally, this is achieved through provincial and federal human rights codes, employment standards acts, and the Canadian Charter of Rights and Freedoms.[1] Multiculturalism also refers to the official policy of multiculturalism advanced by the Liberal government in the 1970s and enacted in 1985.[2] Though Canada's Multiculturalism Act offers little in the way of substantive rights to minorities, it does indicate the government's symbolic policy preference for integration over assimilation. However, this framework has since changed because Canada's policy of multiculturalism was criticized for, among other things, its emphasis on the mere "song and dance" aspect of cultural pluralism, its failure to improve the living conditions of many new immigrants, and the promotion of fragmentation rather than a common vision of values for all Canadians.[3] As a result of this criticism, the language of anti-racism has infiltrated discussions of multiculturalism.[4] In 1982, the Canadian Charter of Rights and Freedoms entrenched the concept of multiculturalism in the Constitution. Section 27 reads: "This Charter shall be interpreted in a manner consistent with the preservation and enhancement of the multicultural heritage of Canadians."[5] Section 27 does not independently confer any rights, but legal scholars have interpreted it as modifying or adding meaning to the other rights contained elsewhere in the Charter.[6]

However one understands multiculturalism in Canada, one of the shared features of its multiple definitions is diversity – what many would describe as the undisputed success of a multicultural policy. This chapter is a personal reflection on what diversity means in this context, with a particular and serious focus on the "song and dance" aspect of multiculturalism. While multiculturalism encourages cultural diversity, it correspondingly seeks to contain it. This chapter is intimately connected to some of the goals of multiculturalism while still being wary of its consequences, including the rigid classification of individuals and groups into predetermined categories.[7] My experience as an Indian classical and contemporary dancer in Canada has shown me that while multiculturalism has partially furthered artistic production and appreciation in Canada, the corresponding categorization of certain art forms and modes of performance as "multicultural" fetishizes and essentializes cultural difference.[8]

Culture or art?

I am a South Asian woman and a naturalized Canadian. I came to Canada with my immigrant parents as a young child. I grew up doing the things that many middle-class kids do, including extracurricular activities such as swimming lessons and skating classes. In addition, my parents were keen to ensure that I was connected in some way to Indian culture, so they enrolled me in a south Indian classical dance class focusing on a technique called *bharata natyam*. Neither of my parents is south Indian; they come from the north of India. Thus, they do not speak any of the south Indian languages. When they have traveled to the south of India, they have had to rely on English because Tamil, Kanada, Malayalam, and Telegu are as foreign to them as Mandarin.

Thus, in enrolling me in bharata natyam classes, their intention was not so much to preserve a cultural form that had a long history in my family (or indeed even in my north Indian culture). Rather, it was about the transfer of an art form that they believed would make me a better developed, more whole person.[9] So, they sent me off to learn dance from Toronto's Dr. Menaka Thakkar, who as it happens, is also a north Indian teaching and performing a south Indian classical dance style. The recurring adoption of south Indian dance forms by north Indians suggests that the fact of dancers practicing the art form, both in India and in the diaspora, does not reliably indicate a linear, intergenerational transmission of culture, or cultural patrimony, that is uniquely or authentically one's own. Yet white Canadians commonly assume that young Indian children learn Indian art forms in the disapora as a way of maintaining cultural traditions. In fact, learning Indian dance, at least in my family, was less about maintaining ties to a community back home, and more the result of a strong connection to the beauty, rigour, and value of the arts in the day-to-day development of a person. My parents enrolled me in Indian dance because this was a form of dance to which they had been exposed, just as many in Canada and elsewhere in the West are exposed to ballet.

Too often, certain forms of artistic pursuit and training are readily conflated with a desire to retain an authentic ethnic heritage, however inaccurate the lineage of this heritage may be. This assumption is steeped in the belief that some cultures produce art while others simply practice culture. Marlene NourbeSe Philip has drawn a distinction between the maintenance of "tradition for tradition's sake in an alien environment" versus an "attempt to build on what . . . individual cultures have passed on . . . in the possibility of creating something new."[10] Multiculturalism in the arts presupposes that racialized artists or artists working outside of dominant artistic traditions are necessarily replicating the creations of the past rather than innovatively generating fresh artistic works.[11] One of the problems with the rhetoric of multiculturalism is the assumption that we racialized, "outsider" artists are easily categorizable, that as individuals we have some sort of causal connection to "core cultural characteristics,"[12] and thus, that multiculturalism in the arts must necessarily be about cultural preservation. In my case, it was a little more complicated than that.

The benevolent side of the liberal idea of multiculturalism recognizes and celebrates cultural difference by asserting that belonging to another culture does not necessarily imply inferiority or exclusion, but merely "difference." When my dance teacher, Menaka Thakkar, came to Toronto in the 1970s, she began to make a career for herself as a performer and teacher. She was very successful, receiving critical acclaim for her performances, and her school grew in size with each passing year. She had heard that the provincial and federal governments provided arts funding to dance companies and individuals engaged in artistic practice. When she approached the dance divisions of the various arts councils she was told that, while the dance departments would not be able to fund her, the department of multiculturalism might be willing to receive her application.[13] My dance teacher knew then that multiculturalism was not working for her. She was practicing dance and she wanted to be funded by the departments that supported dance.[14] At that time, only ballet and modern western dance were supported by arts funding.

The message was quite clear: ballet and modern western dance are *bona fide* art forms deserving of arts funding. While dance associated with a different culture might be recognized, it would not be given the status of "real dance." Indeed, the categories of "modern" or "contemporary dance" were implicitly defined to exclude non-western (or integrated) cultural forms, suggesting that "Indian dance" was frozen in time and could never be "contemporary." This colonialist logic divided the realm of art from the realm of culture.[15] Arts councils, not surprisingly, had larger budgets than departments of multiculturalism. If multiculturalism was the "catch-all trough"[16] to which all but Ontario's Anglophone and Francophone artists were expected to apply,[17] then racialized and minority artists were always perceived as separate – read substandard – from artists of the dominant culture. As Philip has noted, the work of Black artists often gets labeled as "folk" or "multicultural," which contributes significantly to the funding problems that Black artists often face.[18]

Much has changed since the 1970s, and most arts councils are now far more inclusive in their funding criteria.[19] These changes are the result of many people – including my dance teacher – having fought long and hard battles to reveal how racist these exclusionary policies were, despite the existence of a multiculturalism policy. However, while arts councils can no longer be criticized for completely excluding minority artists, the frequency and degree to which these artists are funded relative to their majority counterparts is of ongoing concern.[20]

The multicultural learning experience and the onus of teaching

My early experiences of performing bharata natyam took place in two kinds of venues. First, local school shows or South Asian community events and second, multicultural festivals or events such as Caravan,[21] Carabram,[22] the CNE, and Expo '86. The first kinds of performances were typically self-produced by dance teachers or local organizations in churches, high school auditoria, or other non-prestigious theatres. The media never covered these events unless they were pursuing some obscure human interest story that rarely had anything to do with the arts. Nonetheless these performances had an important function in that they offered Indian migrants, like my family members, a positive sense of belonging. While I have noted that my parents did not enroll me in bharata natyam to preserve a specific south Indian heritage (that in any case was not our own), such cultural events and public performances were important in a diasporic context. They established a shared

"Indian" identity to which Canada's Indian minority community could lay claim, and around which we could form a sense of communal belonging. Adopted practices like bharata natyam could thus become a locus for a sense of "Indianness" that, in the diaspora, developed around practices and in configurations that may not have been shared at "home." Indeed, the kind of shared identity these performances fostered was a necessary response to the multiple experiences of racism that we encountered in the dominant culture.

The second type of venue, the CNEs and Caravans, were places that people came to in order to experience the "food, fun, and dance" of multiculturalism. One would rarely see ballet performed there. As a child, I liked performing at the CNE; I especially liked when the performance was over and I could run around freely with my friends. But as I got older, my attitude changed. When I was young, I was happy to explain the purpose of the red decorative markings on our hands and to point out that not every hand gesture that we made meant something. As I got older, I grew impatient with the questions and began to tire of explaining to wide-eyed white people what this charming form of dance was. This is the load that multiculturalism insists that some of us carry, while allowing other Canadians to take no responsibility for their own learning. What amazes me when I attend these events today is that the questions have not changed. The burden of educating people about bharata natyam still rests on the shoulders of young women, usually women of colour. Today, when someone asks me "what is bharata natyam?" I feel like saying, "google it."[23]

In addition to general audiences' ignorance of bharata natyam, there are mainstream dance critics who assume that their knowledge of specific western dance traditions is easily transferable to all dance. Of a four-day festival of Indian dance in Manhattan in August 2008, one critic wrote of a Canadian dance company:

> One issue invariably arises when traditional Indian dances are shown here: *the works seldom illustrate their supposed subjects with anything like the clarity that Western audiences, trained by three centuries of belief in narrative dance drama, usually expect.* You watch a dance that's gorgeous in detail and architecture, but you can't see how it's supposed to be about Krishna and the cow girls (a favorite subject), as the program note tells you. Accompanying words may explain what's missing, but they aren't translated.[24]

Amazingly, this critic, savvy in the ways of western dance drama, assumes that his inability to comprehend the unfolding narrative is the result of a pervasive lack of clarity in Indian dance, rather than in his own interpretive deficiency. Thus, even when Indian dance is explained to white audiences, their inability to understand also becomes our responsibility.

Predictable reponses to unpredictable identities and artistic choices

I believe art is a very important tool with which one can effect change. Artists can provide critical social commentary on the world in which we live. And by creating new configurations, art pushes at the "edge of semantic availability,"[25] enabling new meanings to be imagined, and hence new possibilities for identification. As a medium, dance differs from theatre or poetry, for example, where the artist can use words to express her intention. While some dances rely on text to assist in expressing a message, most dance work relies on movement vocabulary and the inherent emotion of the body to express intention. Indeed, many people claim to shy away from dance for fear of "not getting it." One of the challenges then, for a dance artist, is the abstract medium in which we work. To be fair, then, some of the failures of comprehension that I am describing here indicate the challenges of the dance medium generally. However, the formal challenges that dance presents are heightened for those dancers whose practice is not marked as mainstream. For these artists, the failure of the audience to comprehend is also sometimes a failure of imagination, since the cultural projections of audience members and critics are, at times, virtually unshakeable. In response to their confusion, these spectators interpret the dance by resorting to received stereotypes and assumptions about cultural practices. So while many people might avoid dance for fear of not getting it, when it comes to non-dominant forms of dance, critics and audiences frame the shared formal challenges of the medium as problems of cultural comprehension, thus rendering non-dominant practices as unreadable racialized ciphers.

A revealing example of this occurred when I worked with the Shobana Jeyasingh Dance Company, one of the most successful dance companies in Britain. Shobana Jeyasingh is known internationally for her groundbreaking Indian contemporary choreography.[26] From 1995–1999, when I was with the company, its funding from the British Council was the fourth largest among all dance companies in Britain. We toured mainly through the United Kingdom and Europe, but we also traveled to North America. In 1997, we danced at the Joyce Theater in New York as part of the curated program for that year, and were the first-ever South Asian dance company to perform at this prestigious venue.[27] We performed a piece called *Palimpsest*. An archaeological artifact, a palimpsest is a document that has been written on more than once, with the earlier writing incompletely erased and often still legible. Using the layered metaphor of the palimpsest, Jeyasingh depicted the multiple identities that people carry with them, a theme that was in keeping with her interest in migration. The piece further explored the multiple lenses through which a migrant sees the society in which she lives.[28]

Marketing material produced by the Shobana Jeyasingh Dance Company described the performance as follows: "*Palimpsest* – a new piece – captures the resonance of many stories told simultaneously. The present is layered with memory, the public with the private, for a dramatic, sometimes explosive exploration of space, reality and identity."[29] Despite such a clear articulation of the work's narrative and conceptual framework, the *New York Times* arts critic described *Palimpsest* this way: "One might have been looking out a London window onto a street crowded with workers hurrying home, eddying around a sari-clad woman slowly returning from the shops to cook the family dinner."[30] The dance critic must literally have been looking out the window, since none of the performers wore saris, but rather fitted trousers with matching tops. The critic's reference to food is an instance of the ubiquitous association of Indian food with Indian dance imagined by many non-Indians.[31] Scenarios such as this demonstrate how some audiences are studiously missing the point. Artistic criticism of this sort has hidden within it the values, assumptions, and dispositions of the dominant culture that both propose and impose a specific identity on "others."[32]

This phenomenon was similarly illustrated in the critical reception to *Obiter Dictum*, an original dance work I created in 2002. The piece emerged after I had spent three years in law school, immersed in case law. Obiter dictum is a Latin phrase that refers to comments made by a judge in a decision that are not entirely on point. They are "remarks made in passing,"[33] as it were. As a law student, I was fascinated by how some of the judiciary's most interesting comments were often relegated to the unauthoritative realm of obiter. As a lawyer, I was taught that making a legal argument that relied on obiter was dangerous. As a dancer, I saw a clear relationship between obiter dictum and the kind of dance that I do. I wanted to reposition my marginalized dance practice and centre it. My intention was to make obiter dictum – in this case, Indian contemporary dance – authoritative.

Despite my best efforts, however, the *Globe and Mail*'s dance critic, while appreciative of the look of the piece, wrote that *Obiter Dictum* "could be called anything."[34] For me, the title and what it signified were key. Yet clearly, my piece remained inaccessible to the critic, who rather than expressing the common complaint about dance ("I don't get it"), declared the work incoherent. The movement was deemed meaningless or at least unintelligible to a western framework of dance. Ironically, *Obiter Dictum* was relegated to the realm of irrelevance and, as the Latin phrase literally translates, deemed of no great weight.

Thus, even as multiculturalism encourages cultural diversity, it correspondingly seeks to contain it. In a multicultural framework, as Homi Bhabha has observed, other cultures are permitted to coexist so long as they can be located within the appropriate cultural grid.[35] The media responses I have cited here speak poignantly to the conditions under which Indian dance is located as multicultural.[36] Either the work means nothing at all and the body of colour is dehistoricized, or in order to comprehend the work, one must rely on cultural caricature. And little lies in between.

As Sanjoy Roy has argued, the ghettoization of " 'other' cultures into different compartments does not take into account the traffic which crosses the borders between them, both in historical and social terms."[37] Individuals and groups in a diverse society are not living in silos. They are influenced by each other, they form alliances with one another, and their artistic works are fed and transformed by the dynamism of their encounters while living in close urban spaces together. Indeed, the recent history of bharata natyam, its nineteenth-century decline and twentieth-century rejuvenation, is intimately interwoven with the British presence in India.[38] Yet this sociohistorical context, which complicates the landscape of Indian dance, is rarely acknowledged because it obscures the neat, compartmentalized story of multiculturalism. It is much simpler for Indian dance in Canada to be persistently associated with food, Bollywood, or arranged marriage.

Conclusion

The arts play an important role in contesting and complicating categorizations of peoples and their histories. New artistic formations can prefigure new social identities. Emergent social groups that have yet to be positioned within dominant regimes of representation may find points of identification in the emergent meanings articulated in art.[39] The literal "song and dance" of multiculturalism could have a profound impact on reshaping preconceived notions of difference: "Art can be, and often has been, seminal in changing the way people think and feel. . . . [T]he arts can be dangerous because they help people to think independently."[40] However, many artists get co-opted into multiculturalism's tendency toward cultural fetishization. They unwittingly become the makers of "dances of curry and spices" helping to create, perhaps, the multiple and contradictory demands for "authenticity" that come from within and outside their communities. To impugn such artists is difficult when these dances of curry and spices are what presenters and consumers of dance want to see. Moreover, the reality is that artists are among the most marginalized and poverty-ridden groups in the country, a trend that is aggravated if the artist is racialized.[41] In order to make a viable living, artists often have more than one job; that is, they engage in paid employment beyond their artistic practice. In addition to their artistic practice and other work, artists are typically also involved in several hours a week of art-related administrative work and art-related volunteer work.[42] The tremendous demands on artists and the constant financial and personal sacrifices that they make might explain their decisions to create art that will be presented (and therefore remunerated) versus art that will be ignored yet that is true to their voices – a dilemma that characterizes art production generally, but that is particularly poignant when it demands that artists inhabit or embody racialized identities in order to make their work legible.

The rhetoric of multiculturalism in Canada has often stifled Indian dance artists, or at least this one. It has not allowed us to be unpredictable because it has insisted upon categorizing us, usually inaccurately. The "*Canadian*-Canadians," to rely on Eva Mackey's terminology, "sustain dominance by refusing categorization as other than just 'normal' and 'human.' "[43] The rest of us look forward to the day when such a refusal is a possibility for everyone.

11 The colour of poverty

Uzma Shakir

I DON'T NORMALLY GET TO BE INVOLVED in academic institutions. I am a frustrated researcher whose need to make a living means I can't go to school anymore. The last time I went to school was for law and diplomacy. The registrar, when she gave me my degree, said, "Miss Shakir, you learnt neither law nor diplomacy, but you've got a degree." This pretty much summed up my academic career, so I ended up being a professional immigrant.

I am what they call a "minority-racialized woman." I came to Canada to find out that the only qualifications that were of any concern to Canadian society were ones that I actually had no hand in: I'm brown, I'm a woman, and I'm multilingual (I can speak more than English and French). It also helped that after 9/11, I became terribly exotic because I'm Muslim. I have found that these factors have shaped my entire career for the twenty-one years that I've been in Canada. What matters is who I am and where I come from and not my skills – indeed, these factors have created a little space in society just for me. I am told this is because we in Canada are so wonderfully multicultural.

Multiculturalism

What multiculturalism does to you as an individual is to create that little space for you. It's a ghettoized space because it remains perpetually outside the mainstream norm. This little space is where you end up permanently rotating. The fact that you can speak a South-Asian language, the fact that you can also speak English and so you can navigate society a little better than others means that at best you become a cultural translator, or what I call a "native informant," to the mainstream but never a part of it. You become a cultural interpreter, and you end up working with ethno-racial communities because that's where your expertise seems to lie. That's what multiculturalism does to you – it distances you from the mainstream but never changes the mainstream itself. However, the fact that you are ghettoized can be a great advantage: first, because you get a job that pays (albeit not very well) and that only you can do, and second, because you have the possibility of finding other ghettos where there are people with whom you can work towards solidarity. This has been one of the most enlightening elements of my experience in Canada: building a sense of solidarity with people I might not have met or worked with otherwise. That is the most wonderful and unexpected benefit of being in Canada.

Ever since the day I landed in Canada I've been working with the "South-Asian" community. This is really very funny, because in South Asia we don't actually like each other. Indeed, we didn't actually think we were "South Asians" until we landed at Toronto's Pearson Airport. In South Asia, if you are Indian, Pakistani, Sri Lankan, or Bangladeshi, you hate each other's guts and for very good reason: you've had hundreds of years of history of conquest and colonization that has engendered hatred. But when you come to Canada, it's wonderful: racism suddenly makes you like each other because everybody else likes you even less. Here, I run organizations where I bend over backwards to make sure that all the religious, cultural, country of origin, and linguistic diversity of South Asia are represented. In Canada, you can start to create an identity that you actually never had.

Racialization and the Colour of Poverty campaign

In Toronto, poverty seems to have a colour to it. To talk about this, I would like to discuss a project I am involved in called the Colour of Poverty Campaign. Those of us involved in this project were very much influenced by people like Michael Ornstein and his 1999 report (updated in 2006), as well as Grace-Edward Galabuzi's work around economic apartheid and the racialization of poverty. Of course, all of us who work in the social service sector have very little time to read whole books. We do, however, read chapters. We connect those chapters to our personal realities and to those of the communities that we serve – given the fact that most of us who are involved in this campaign come from the ethno-racial community-based sector. Ornstein's and Galabuzi's research and scholarship resonated with us because they showed in stark statistical terms what we had been aware of for at least ten years. They validated our struggles. Given that the media, public discourse, and policy pundits all seem to require particular "authoritative" types of empirical "evidence" to legitimize the attention given to an issue, these research publications have lent us the credibility that people's lived realities never quite seem to achieve. The fact that Ornstein made a clear connection between race and both poverty and income insecurity, and that Galabuzi extended that connection to race and un/underemployment, race and negative health outcomes, race and higher rates of criminalization, and race and systemic experience of marginality, suddenly changed the advocacy landscape for us in the social justice sector. Now we had "evidence." Our campaign is the most recent outcome of actions that have been undertaken in the last several years.

The Colour of Poverty Campaign was born from a legal clinic environment. The Metro Chinese and Southeast Asian Legal Clinic got some money from – irony of ironies – the Department of Canadian Heritage to start the project. They initially also pulled together the South Asian Legal Clinic of Ontario and the African Canadian Legal Clinic. The reason legal clinics took an interest is because, in Ontario, they are set up to specialize in poverty law. We have a mandate to serve low-income people. Legal Aid Ontario decides the income threshold within which a person is considered low-income and then legal clinics can provide free legal education and representation. So, by definition we deal with people with low incomes.

One of the things that we repeatedly observe is that the reasons for many of our clients' legal problems are twofold: they are poor and they are racialized. This is ever clearer since 9/11. The legal problems that poor, racialized immigrants have when they come here – whether they are landed immigrants, refugees, or people without status – have worsened. Suddenly all of their legal issues are compounded by the fact that they are poor, racialized, living in this environment of heightened security, and questioning of multiculturalism. What were once simple legal issues are now extremely complicated.

The other day, for instance, a woman called me at the legal clinic and said: "I'm locked up in my house. My husband won't let me go out." She was speaking to me in Urdu – she can't speak English. She can't go out, she doesn't have a bank account or her husband controls it, and she wants help but she doesn't know how to get it. We at the clinic are not in the business of walking into her house, opening her door, and saying, "You are free now." However, if you don't do that, and if you talk about it too much in public, it reinforces the stereotype that "these ethno-racial types, they oppress their women." The reason she's oppressed is partly because her spouse is a jackass, but also partly because of her immigration status: she's sponsored by him. Further, it's to do with the fact that her access – or lack of access – to this society is predetermined by her economic status and by her immigration status, both of which are complicated by the fact that she can't speak English. As a legal clinic, we struggle to deal with this at only a legal level because that's our mandate.

Another day a woman called me to say: "I know you think I am crazy. I know. But I'm going to tell you something." She said she was a university graduate from South Asia, had several years' work experience, and had tried everything to find a job in Canada. She'd been to all kinds of job retraining and "re-retraining," but still could not find a job. "So I'm going to tell you right now," she said, "I'm going to commit suicide and you're going to tell me that I should actually go and see a doctor, but I'm not going to see a doctor. I am not insane. I'm just going to commit suicide and I want somebody to know." In such instances, our job becomes not just legal service provision, but the bearing of witness. That's what we are doing. We, as service providers, have become people who are bearing witness to people's desperation because our ability to create concrete change is so limited.

This work of bearing witness led us to believe that it was our moral obligation to do something about the issues we kept seeing. If we couldn't provide people with services (and "service" is defined in a very limited manner by our mandate) then we had to do something else. Out of these experiences came the Colour of Poverty Campaign, an attempt to articulate and organize around the so-called "coincidence" between race and poverty.

The "we" I refer to encompasses a group of ethno-racial legal clinics, community-based planning bodies, immigrant/refugee-serving organizations, and academics who have made a commitment to social justice through their research. Our aim is to raise awareness of the racialization of poverty, as well as to make a conscious effort to produce accessible information that can be used by the very people who face the daily challenge of being poor and racialized. We hope this will not only provide much needed information for communities themselves to push for policy shifts and structural change, but also that it will create a means for diverse ethno-racial communities to connect with each other on a shared and common platform to build solidarity.

Since we don't ultimately know how to produce actual change ourselves – after all we are limited by what we can do – our first idea was to produce some basic information: simple, one-page fact sheets that could be easily translated into different languages (to date we have identified fifteen languages). Although there's a cost attached to all of this translation work and our resources are severely limited, we have tried to be as inclusive as possible. After all, limited resources and "too much" diversity are not excuses for exclusion.

In terms of content for the fact sheets, we had to keep in mind the realities of the "immigrant/refugee mindset"; just because people are racialized and living in poverty doesn't necessarily mean they acknowledge that they're poor, or that it's a great ambition on their part to hail their poverty as a badge of honour. In fact, often poverty and marginality are a source of intense feelings of failure and loss of self-worth. Also, in our experience, our communities do not necessarily make the connection between their particular reality and structures of racism and marginality in society. They do, however, know what issues they face and how they would like to change their situation. Hence, we had to pitch our message in terms of issues and solutions, while providing a race-based lens to understand how these issues are created and reproduced. Our logic was to create a one-page document that would define and contextualize the experience of racialized poverty, and provide some facts, figures, and useful information about who to connect with in order to move the issue forward, which would then be followed by a number of subsequent fact sheets articulating the multiple dimensions of this experience. Our purpose was to create something that would be useful for people in our communities to organize around, rather than to spend our time making policy submissions and writing papers and books about it which nobody – and certainly not the people with whom we are working – was going to read. We think positive change can result if we organize communities around their own issues, keeping firmly in mind that whether the subject is the criminal justice system, education, or health, we need to foreground the racialized dimension of each.

The reason we are particular about racialization is because there is a strong perception that poverty is a newcomer phenomenon. There is this comfortable discourse in Canada that we were all immigrants once and that, over time, we all do well. That is, of course, not quite true: Aboriginal people might have something to say about the continued reality of colonization and marginality, but the myth is that we were all immigrants, and if you stay here long enough, you'll be fine. The myth states that all immigrants/refugees come and struggle but that within ten to fifteen years they catch up to the Canadian average, or even surpass it, and therefore their children eventually do better. As the narrative goes, since the newcomers who are coming now are coming from non-traditional countries, they happen to be people of colour, so they happen to be poor. In reality, however, what we are finding is that over the past fifteen years that is not what is happening. People who are coming in now are very different. Yes, they are coming from what are considered "non-traditional" countries, which is basically a euphemism for "racialized." They are coming from Africa, Asia, Latin America, but they are coming – because of Canadian immigration requirements – from a much higher economic and educational stratum than immigrants in the past. Contrary to popular belief and historical experience, fifteen or twenty years after they come, their lot is not getting better. It's in fact getting worse; this has been clearly shown through statistics by Ornstein. A series of staggering facts quoted in our first fact sheet state:

• Ethno-racial minority group members – other than Aboriginal persons (i.e., people of colour) – make up over 13 per cent of Canada's population (in Ontario, 19 per cent); by 2017, this will rise to 20 per cent (in Ontario, 29 per cent);
• By the year 2017, well over half of Toronto's overall population will be people of colour;
• Children from ethno-racial minority communities (i.e., communities of colour) constituted 67 per cent of all children in low-income households in 1995, this increased to 75 per cent in the year 2000;
• Ethno-racial minority (i.e., non-European heritage) families make up 37 per cent of all families in Toronto, but account for 59 per cent of poor families;
• Between 1980 and 2000 in Toronto, the poverty rate for non-racialized (i.e., white, or people of European or caucasian heritage) population fell by 28 per cent while poverty among racialized families rose by 361 per cent;
• 32 per cent of children in racialized families and 47 per cent of children in recent immigrant families in Ontario live in poverty.

So today's myth that "I will suffer and I will work hard and my children will do better" is working itself out in the opposite manner. Now the reality goes: "I used to do better, I have worked very hard, I'm going to do even worse, and my children will be worse off."

What is happening is that people of colour are disproportionately impoverished and this is persisting over time and status (whether long-term residents or newcomers). The one unchanging fact seems to be that they're poor because they are people of colour, irrespective of their time of arrival or their educational background. This poverty, therefore, is entrenched. It's systemic. It's not going away. Recent immigrants are not the only people affected. Many who have been here much longer, Aboriginal peoples, indigenous black populations, and various other racialized communities who have been here for well over twenty years are also continuing to remain in poverty and marginality. Thus racialization of poverty, contrary to common assertions, is not a newcomer phenomenon. It is a much more deeply entrenched and systemic issue.

The Colour of Poverty Campaign fact sheets lay out information on education and learning, health and well-being, employment, income levels and social assistance, justice and policing, immigration and newcomer settlement, housing and homelessness, and food (in)security. We plan to use these fact sheets to create conversations with different communities who are actually living and going through these problems and are experiencing all of those multifaceted aspects of racialization of poverty. We hope to create a shared framework for action – which essentially is a nice way of saying that we don't want to come up with a poverty reduction strategy that we dreamt up in our living rooms. Rather, we want to have community conversations that feed into a comprehensive poverty reduction – if not poverty elimination – strategy in which communities can get involved by organizing to change individual policies, create public discussions, and hold different departments, government institutions, and policymakers accountable. As I see it, this would do a number of things. First, it would create that level of engagement that is required for communities to actually take ownership of any poverty reduction/elimination strategy. Second, since the campaign truly is grassroots, it should lead to the creation of critical relationships. Recall what I mentioned at the beginning – that one of the good things about the ghetto is that you realize there are many more ghettos and people like you who are similarly ghettoized, even though you might not initially know about them. If you participate in these conversations and discussions you will come to realize that other people are in exactly the same situation. This is our way of saying, "we can work together."

Activism and the academy: A plea for solidarity

I would like to end with a request, and by naming the groups who are involved in the Colour of Poverty Campaign and describing how they came together. The groups participating in this particular project chose to come together because they have a common agenda. They include the Metro Toronto Chinese and Southeast Asian Clinic, the South Asian Legal Clinic of Ontario, the African Canadian Legal Clinic, the Council of Agencies Serving South Asians, the Hispanic Development Council, Chinese Canadian National Council Toronto Chapter, Midaynta (an umbrella Somali organization), the Ontario Council of Agencies Serving Immigrants, the Canadian Arab Federation, Sistering, and others. Grace-Edward Galabuzi has provided critical analytical information and research leadership to the group. It is therefore a broad-based association of individuals and umbrella organizations representing as many ethno-racial communities facing these issues as possible, with the purpose of achieving inclusive and widespread conversations, making alliances and, ultimately, organizing.

The reason I am presenting this strategy is not to tell you how wonderful we are. It is because I wish to harness your support. As academics – as people who are socially, politically, and intellectually involved in issues like this – you must get involved with our campaign. Not to take ownership of it – please don't do that. Not to debate the finer points of whether we have described the experience of racialization of poverty in a correct conceptual manner. Quite frankly, people in our communities couldn't give a shit whether we spelled racialization correctly or incorrectly, or whether our definition is conceptually defensible. What I would like you to do, and I encourage you to do, is to help us by being animators in the community. If you have any interest in this, join us, be the animators, hold these discussions in the community, be the recorders, and most importantly, help us develop that eventual plan of action by assisting us to devise the best strategies to mobilize communities. We can mobilize a lot of communities because our clients come from those communities. We would like you to help us mobilize as many people as possible at the grassroots level, and then record their ideas, feeding them into that common plan of action so we can all take ownership of it and make a difference. Bring your skills to the table but check your egos and careers at the door! Such are the demands of solidarity for social justice.

Notes

Introduction: Labours, lands, bodies

1 For some readers, our title may resonate with that of another anthology, Barnor Hesse's *Un/settled Multiculturalisms: Diasporas, Entanglements, Transruptions* (New York: St. Martin's Press, 2000). Both volumes engage with the persistence of multi-cultural discourse, despite episodes of crisis in the field and periods of unpopularity in academic and political circles, and both take stock of anti-racist critiques from the Left that challenge multiculturalism's salience. However, there are significant differences between the two books. Most significantly, Hesse's framework stresses the interruptive potential of multiculturalism by way of what he terms "multicultural transruptions," which "put into question, particularly in unexpected places and at unforeseen times, matters deemed in hegemonic discourse to be settled, buried and apparently beyond dispute" (p.18). Hesse ascribes a productively unsettling quality to multiculturalism and thus partially recuperates the term and its critical potential – an orientation reflected in the "Un/*settled* Multiculturalisms" of his title, which implies multiculturalism's latent or emergent disruptiveness. In contrast, this volume is deeply skeptical about multiculturalism's productive disruptiveness or its capacity to unsettle hegemonic discourses. Our focus is on "un*settling* multiculturalism" itself, by challenging its commonsensical, naturalized, or dominant status. These differences spring partly from the two books' very different geographical domains: Hesse's volume focuses on Britain, while ours addresses Canada.

2 See chapter 1.

3 Thus, in 1963, Prime Minister Lester B. Pearson formed a Royal Commission on Bilingualism and Biculturalism designed to explore Canada's linguistic and cultural divisions.

4 Will Kymlicka offers an account of these developments and their influence on the emergence of official multiculturalism in "Marketing Canadian Pluralism in the International Arena," in *International Journal* 59, 4 (Autumn 2004), pp.829–852. See especially pp.840–841.

5 For a critique of this recasting of Aboriginal peoples as the third founding nation, see Sunera Thobani, *Exalted Subjects: Studies in the Making of Race and Nation in Canada* (Toronto: University of Toronto Press, 2007). Thobani argues that this formulation homogenizes disparate Aboriginal communities and overlooks the violence of the colonial encounter and the persistence of a colonial relation in the present, p.40.

6 See for instance Himani Bannerji, *The Dark Side of the Nation: Essays on Multicultur-alism, Nationalism and Gender* (Toronto: Canadian Scholars' Press, 2000), and Eva Mackey, *The House of Difference: Cultural Politics and National Identity in Canada* (London: Routledge, 1999).

7 In Canada, multiculturalism and the politics of recognition are generally described as a strategy for coping with immigrants, ethnic minorities, and "newcomers." Multiculturalism's functions for regulating Aboriginal claims about land and status are less explicit and less visible. Anthropologist Elizabeth Povinelli has offered a sustained account of how, in Australia, multiculturalism largely takes as its project the recognition of Aboriginal peoples. She argues that such recognition works to mark the limits of what is acceptable and what is repugnant, and in the process determines the nature of reconciliatory projects and shapes indigenous subjectivities. See Elizabeth Povinelli, *The Cunning of Recognition: Indigenous Alterities and the Making of Australian Multiculturalism* (Durham: Duke University Press, 2002).

8 See Sherene Razack, *Casting Out: The Eviction of Muslims from Western Law and Politics* (Toronto: University of Toronto Press, 2008).

9 Allan Gregg, "Identity Crisis," in the *Walrus* Magazine (March 2006), pp.38–47. The final quote appears on page 39 of Gregg's article. Pronouns such as "we" and "our," which are never defined but seem to refer to a cohesive population of Canadians, are scattered throughout the article, such as when Gregg writes of the events of 9/11, which "brought grievances from distant lands to our doorstep" (p.47).

10 Margaret Wente, "End of the Multicultural Myth," *Globe and Mail* (Toronto), March 18, 2006.

11 Rex Brynen, paper presented in "Muslims, Political Violence and the Security Establishment," *Muslims in Western Societies* (Vancouver, British Columbia, November 2006).

12 Rinaldo Walcott, *Black Like Who? Writing Black Canada* (Toronto: Insomniac Press, 1997), pp.79.

13 Bannerji, *The Dark Side of the Nation*.

14 Eva Mackey, *The House of Difference*; Carol Tator, Frances Henry, and Winston Mattis, *Challenging Racism in the Arts: Case Studies of Controversy and Conflict* (Toronto: University of Toronto Press, 1998).

15 See here Marlene NourbeSe Philip, *Frontiers: Essays and Writings on Racism and Culture* (Stratford: Mercury Press, 1992).

16 Bannerji observes that, by invoking multiculturalism, English Canada depicts itself, as well as French-Canadians and Aboriginal peoples, as just three cultures among a multitude of cultures, without acknowledging the way that these other cultures are assimilated to it as the cultural "core." See Bannerji, *The Dark Side of the Nation,* pp.9–10, 94. Mackey puts it thus: the "unmarked, unhyphenated, and hence, normative Canadian-Canadians who are . . . implicitly constructed as the authentic and real Canadian people" define and authorize culture, "while all others are hyphenated and marked as cultural." Mackey, *The House of Difference*, p.89.

17 Razack, *Casting Out*, p.3.

18 Neil Smith, *Uneven Development: Nature, Capital and the Production of Space, Third Edition* (Athens: University of Georgia Press, 2008), p.291.

19 Derek Gregory, *The Colonial Present* (Maldon, MA, Oxford, and Victoria: Blackwell Publishing, 2004), pp.13, 28.

20 Gregory 2004, *The Colonial Present,* p.16.

21 For a profound critique of tolerance as a, or even *the,* key term in the politics of

liberal multicultural democracies, see Wendy Brown, *Regulating Aversion: Tolerance in the Age of Identity and Empire* (Princeton: Princeton University Press, 2006).

22 Chapter 2, "Subjects of Indigenous Empire: Indigenous Peoples and the 'Politics of Recognition' in Canada," by Glen Coulthard, was originally published in *Contemporary Political Theory* 6 (2007), pp.437–460. It is reproduced here with the permission of Palgrave Macmillan.

Chapter 1: Disgraceful: Intellectual dishonesty, white anxieties, and multicultural critique thirty-six years later

1 The idea that Western conceptions of freedom and democracy are the best way to live a life has been perpetuated by various people, from George W. Bush to Irshad Manji to Tarek Fatah.

2 Toni Morrison, *Playing in the Dark: Whiteness and the Literary Imagination* (Cambridge: Harvard University Press, 1992), p.37.

3 Morrison, *Playing in the Dark*, p.38.

4 Susan Buck-Morss, "Hegel and Haiti," *Critical Inquiry* 26, 4 (2000), p.821.

5 Paul Gilroy, *The Black Atlantic: Modernity and Double Consciousness* (Cambridge: Harvard University Press, 1993), p.5.

6 Buck-Morss, "Hegel and Haiti," p.821.

7 Both Trouillot and Fischer provide accounts of modernity and particularly its discourses of freedom, which allow for understanding how deeply unfreedom is embedded in European emancipatory discourses. Their work helps us to make better sense of how post-Enlightenment ideas of freedom are founded on the denial of freedom to racialized and enslaved others who exposed Euro-American contradictions concerning freedom.

8 Stuart Hall, "Universities, Intellectuals, and Multitudes," in *Utopian Pedagogy: Radical Experiments against Neoliberal Globalization*, eds. M. Coté, R. Day, and G. de Peuter (Toronto: University of Toronto Press, 2007), p.123.

9 Charles Mills, *The Racial Contract* (Chicago: University of Chicago Press, 2007).

10 K. Onstad, "Exploring Humanity, Violence and All," *New York Times*, September 16, 2007 http://www.nytimes.com/2007/09/16/movies/16onst.html.

11 Ibid.

12 Allan Gregg, "Identity Crisis," *Walrus Magazine* (March 2006), pp.38–47; Michael Bliss, "Has Canada Failed," *Literary Review of Canada* (March 2006), pp.3–5; Janice Stein, "Living Better Multiculturally," *Literary Review of Canada* (September 2006), pp.3–5; Cecil Foster, "Pierre Trudeau would have approved our new G-G," *Globe and Mail* (Toronto), August 5, 2005; "A regal statement about gender and race," *Globe and Mail* (Toronto), September 7, 2006.

13 John Ibbitson, "Canada's Tolerance Conundrum," *Globe and Mail* (Toronto), September 6, 2006; Haroon Siddiqui, "Charter, Gender Equity and Freedom of Religion," *Toronto Star*, September 7, 2006.

14 See Foster's "Somewhere, Over the Rainbow," *Globe and Mail* (Toronto), June 20, 2006.

15 David Scott, *Refashioning Futures: Criticism after Postcoloniality* (Princeton: Princeton University Press, 1999), pp.8.

16 Janice Stein et al., *Uneasy Partners: Multiculturalism and Rights in Canada* (Waterloo: Wilfrid Laurier University Press, 2007).

17 Cecil Foster, *Where Race Does Not Matter: The New Spirit of Modernity* (Toronto: Penguin Canada, 2005), pp.120.

18 Ibid.
19 Cecil Foster, *Blackness and Modernity: The Colour of Humanity and the Quest for Freedom* (Montreal and Kingston: McGill-Queens University Press, 2007), pp.103–4.
20 Stuart Hall, "Conclusion: the Multi-cultural Question," in *Un/settled Multiculturalisms: Diasporas, Entanglements, Transruptions*, ed. Barnor Hesse (London: Zed Books, 2006), p.209.
21 Sylvia Wynter, *Do Not Call Us Negros: How Multicultural Textbooks Perpetuate Racism* (San Francisco: Aspire Books, 1992), p.31.
22 Charles Taylor, "Multiculturalism and the Politics of Recognition," in *Multiculturalism*, ed. A. Gutman (Princeton: Princeton University Press, 1994), p.132.
23 See the work of Angela Davis, Ruth Wilson Gilmore, and Julia Sudbury as examples.
24 Ayaan Hirsi Ali, *The Caged Virgin: An Emancipation Proclamation for Women and Islam* (New York: Free Press, 2006), p.x.
25 Ibid., p.xi.
26 Judith Butler, "Endangered/Endangering: Schematic Racism and White Paranoia," in *Reading Rodney King Reading Urban Uprising*, ed. R. Gooding-Williams (New York: Routledge, 1993).

Chapter 2: Subjects of empire: Indigenous peoples and the "Politics of Recognition" in Canada

This chapter was originally published in *Contemporary Political Theory* 6 (2007), pp.437–460. It is reproduced here with the permission of Palgrave Macmillan.

I would like to express my appreciation to Taiaiake Alfred, Richard J.F. Day, Rita Dhamoon, Duncan Ivison, John Munro, Robert Nichols, and James Tully for helping me clarify the ideas and arguments expressed in this paper. I would also like to thank the editorial board and anonymous reviewers with *Contemporary Political Theory* for their helpful comments and suggestions on earlier drafts of this chapter.

1 In the Canadian context, I use the terms "Indigenous," "Aboriginal," and "Native" interchangeably to refer to the descendants of those who traditionally occupied the territory now known as Canada prior to the arrival of European settlers. I also occasionally use these terms in an international context to refer to those peoples that have suffered under the weight of European colonialism more generally. I use the term "Indian" and phrase "First Nation" to refer to those legally recognized as Indians under the Canadian federal government's *Indian Act* of 1876.
2 Dene Nation, "Declaration of the Dene Nation," in *Dene Nation: The Colony Within,* ed. Mel Watkins (Toronto: University of Toronto Press, 1977), pp.3–4.
3 Assembly of First Nations, *Our Nations, Our Governments: Choosing Our Own Paths* (Ottawa: Assembly of First Nations, 2005) p.18.
4 Assembly of First Nations, *Our Nations, Our Governments*, pp.18–19.
5 Charles Taylor, "The Politics of Recognition" in *Multiculturalism: Examining the Politics of Recognition,* ed. Amy Gutmann (Princeton: Princeton University Press, 1994).
6 On the reconceptualization of Canada's relationship with Aboriginal peoples, see Alan Cairns, *Citizens Plus: Aboriginal Peoples and the Canadian State* (Vancouver: UBC Press, 2000); Alan Cairns, *First Nations and the Canadian State: In Search of Coexistence* (Kingston ON: Institute of Intergovernmental Relations, 2005). On federal Indian policy, see Canada, *Royal Commission on Aboriginal Peoples. People to*

People, Nation to Nation: Highlights from the Report of the Royal Commission on Aboriginal Peoples (Ottawa: The Commission, 1996); Department of Indian Affairs and Northern Development, *Gathering Strength: Canada's Aboriginal Action Plan* (Ottawa: Published under the authority of the Minister of Indian Affairs and Northern Development, 1997); Department of Indian Affairs and Northern Development, *A First Nations–Crown Political Accord on the Recognition and Implementation of First Nation's Governments* (Ottawa: Published under the authority of the Minister of Indian Affairs and Northern Development, 2005); also see James Tully, *Strange Multiplicity: Constitutionalism in the Age of Diversity* (Cambridge: Cambridge University Press, 1995); James Tully, "The Struggles of Indigenous Peoples for and of Freedom" in *Political Theory and the Rights of Indigenous Peoples*, ed. Duncan Ivison and Paul Patton (Cambridge: Cambridge University Press, 2001).

7 In the following pages I use the terms "colonial" and "imperial" interchangeably to avoid repetitiveness. However, I do so acknowledging the important distinction that Edward Said, Robert Young, James Tully, and others have drawn between these two interrelated concepts. In their work, a colonial relationship is characterized as a more *direct* form of imperial rule. Imperialism is thus a broader concept, which may include colonialism, but could also be carried out indirectly through non-colonial means. Following this logic, a significant amount of the world's population can now be said to live in a post-*colonial* condition despite the persistent operation of *imperialism* as a form of "political and economic" dominance. Canada, of course, remains a settler colony in which indirect imperialism has never typified the relationship between Indigenous peoples and the settler-state and society. See Edward Said, *Culture and Imperialism* (New York: Vintage, 1994); Robert Young, *Postcolonialism: An Historical Introduction* (Oxford: Blackwell Publishing, 2001); James Tully, "The persistence of empire: a legacy of colonialism and decolonization." Paper presented at the international conference, *Colonialism and its Legacies*, University of Chicago, 22–25 April, 2004.

8 Richard Day, *Multiculturalism and the History of Canadian Diversity*, (Toronto: University of Toronto Press, 2000); Richard Day, "Who is this we that gives the gift? Native American Political Theory and The Western Tradition," *Critical Horizons* 2, 2 (2001), pp.173–201.

9 See Frantz Fanon, *Black Skin, White Masks* (Boston: Grove Press, 1967) and G.W.F. Hegel, *The Phenomenology of Spirit* (Oxford: Oxford University Press, 1977) respectively.

10 Frantz Fanon, *The Wretched of the Earth* (Boston: Grove Press, 2005), p.148.

11 Nancy Fraser and Axel Honneth, *Recognition or Redistribution? A Political Philosophical Exchange* (New York: Verso, 2003), p.11.

12 Hegel, *The Phenomenology of Spirit*, p.178.

13 Robert Pippin, "What is the Question for which Hegel's Theory of Recognition is the Answer?" *European Journal of Philosophy* 8, 2 (2000) p.156.

14 Hegel, *The Phenomenology of Spirit*, pp.191–192.

15 Ibid.

16 Ibid., p.195.

17 Robert Williams, "Hegel and Nietzsche: Recognition and Master/Slave," *Philosophy Today* 45, 5 (2001), p.167.

18 Ibid.

19 Markell, *Bound by Recognition* (Princeton: Princeton University Press, 2003), pp.22–25.

20 Ibid., p.25.
21 Taylor, "The Politics of Recognition."
22 Ibid., pp.61 and 40.
23 Ibid., p.61.
24 Ibid., pp.32–33.
25 Ibid., pp.33–34.
26 Ibid., p.33.
27 Taylor, *The Sources of the Self* (Cambridge, UK: University of Cambridge Press, 1989), p.27.
28 Taylor, *The Malaise of Modernity* (Toronto: Anansi, 1991), pp.45–46.
29 Taylor, "The Politics of Recognition," p.25.
30 Ibid., p.26.
31 Ibid., p.36.
32 Ibid.
33 Taylor, "The Politics of Recognition," p.64.
34 Ibid., p.26.
35 Taylor, "The Politics of Recognition," p.40; Charles Taylor, *Reconciling the Solitudes: Essays on Canadian Federalism and Nationalism* (Montreal: McGill-Queen's University Press, 1993), pp.148, 180.
36 Taylor, *Reconciling the Solitudes*, p.180.
37 Taylor, "The Politics of Recognition," p.40.
38 First quote from Richard Day and Tonio Sadik, "The BC Land Question, Liberal Multiculturalism, and the Spectre of Aboriginal Nationhood," *BC Studies* 134 (Summer 2002), p.6. The terms "recognition" and "granted" are from Taylor, *Reconciling the Solitudes,* p.148. The term "accorded" is found in Taylor, "The Politics of Recognition," p.41.
39 Taylor, "The Politics of Recognition," pp.65–66.
40 See Fanon, *Black Skin, White Masks,* p.12; Taylor, "The Politics of Recognition," pp.65–66; Charles Taylor, *Philosophical Papers, Volume 2: Philosophy and the Human Sciences,* (Cambridge, UK: University of Cambridge Press, 1985), p.235.
41 A number of studies have mapped the similarities and differences between the dialectic of recognition as conceived by Fanon and Hegel, but relatively few have applied Fanon's insights to critique the groundswell appropriation of Hegel's theory of recognition to address contemporary questions surrounding the recognition of cultural diversity. Even fewer have used Fanon's writings to problematize the utility of a politics of recognition for restructuring hierarchical relations between disparate identities in colonial contexts. For a survey of the available literature, see: Irene Gendzier, *Fanon: A Critical Study* (New York: Grove Press, 1974); Hussein Bulhan, *Frantz Fanon and the Psychology of Oppression* (New York: Plenum Press. 1985); Lou Turner, "On the Difference between the Hegelian and Fanonian Dialectic of Lordship and Bondage," in *Fanon: A Critical Reader,* eds. Lewis Gordon et al. (Oxford: Blackwell, 1996); Beatrice Hanssen, "Ethics of the Other," in *The Turn to Ethics,* eds. Marjorie Garber et al. (New York: Routledge, 2000); Sonia Kruks, *Retrieving Experience: Subjectivity and Recognition in Feminist Politics* (Ithaca: Cornell University Press, 2001); Kelly Oliver, *Witnessing: Beyond Recognition* (Minneapolis: University of Minnesota Press, 2001); Nigel Gibson, *Fanon: The Postcolonial Imagination* (Cambridge, UK: Polity Press, 2003); Anita Chari, "Exceeding Recognition," *Sartre Studies International* 10, 2 (2004); and Andrew Schaap, "Political reconciliation through a struggle for recognition?" *Social and Legal Studies* 13, 4 (2004).

42 Louis Althusser, "Ideology and Ideological State Apparatuses" in *Mapping Ideology*, ed. Slavoj Zizek (London: Verso, 1994).
43 Fanon, *Black Skin, White Masks*, p.84, emphasis added.
44 Ibid., pp.111–112.
45 Ibid., p.109.
46 Ibid., p.111.
47 Ibid., p.112.
48 Ibid., p.109.
49 Ibid., pp.11–12.
50 Ibid.
51 Ibid., p.11.
52 Ibid., p.202.
53 Ibid., p.11.
54 Fanon, *The Wretched of the Earth*, p.5.
55 Himani Bannerji, *The Dark Side of the Nation: Essays on Multiculturalism* (Toronto: Canadian Scholar's Press, 2000); Richard Rorty, *Achieving Our Country: Leftist Thought in Twentieth-Century America* (Cambridge, MA: Harvard University Press, 1998); Richard Day, "Who is this we who gives the gift?"; Day and Sadik, "The BC Land Question"; Brian Barry, *Cultural and Equality: An Egalitarian Critique of Multiculturalism* (Cambridge, MA: Harvard University Press, 2002); Fraser and Honneth, *Recognition or Redistribution?*
56 Fraser and Honneth, *Recognition or Redistribution?*
57 Ibid.
58 Ibid., pp.12–13.
59 Ibid.
60 Day, "Who is this we that gives the gift?" p.189.
61 Howard Adams, *Prison of Grass: Canada from a Native Point of View* (Saskatoon: Fifth House Publishers, 1975); Howard Adams, *A Tortured People: The Politics of Colonization* (Penticton: Theytus Books, 1999); *Dene Nation: The Colony Within*, ed. Mel Watkins (Toronto, University of Toronto Press; 1977); Marie Smallface Marule, Traditional Indian Government: Of the Peoples, by the People, for the People," in *Pathways to Self-Determination: Canadian Indians and the Canadian State*, eds. Little Bear et al. (Toronto: University of Toronto Press, 1984).
62 Lee Maracle, *I am woman: a native perspective on sociology and feminism* (Vancouver: Press Gang Publishers, 1996); Taiaiake Alfred, *Peace, Power, Righteousness: An Indigenous Manifesto* (Don Mills: Oxford University Press, 1999); Taiaiake Alfred, *Wasase: Indigenous Pathways of Action and Freedom* (Peterborough: Broadview Press, 2005); Andrea Smith, *Conquest: Sexual Violence and American Indian Genocide* (Boston: South End Press, 2005).
63 Alfred, *Peace, Power, Righteousness*, p.60.
64 Alfred, *Wasase*, p.133
65 Fraser and Honneth, *Recognition or Redistribution?*, p.29.
66 Ibid., p.31.
67 Ibid.
68 Fanon, *Black Skin, White Masks*, p.11.
69 Ibid., p.219 emphasis added.
70 Ibid., p.217.
71 Hegel, *The Phenomenology of Spirit*, pp.113–114.
72 Fanon, *Black Skin, White Masks*, p.220.

73 Ibid., p.18.

74 Ibid., p.12.

75 Turner, "On the Difference between the Hegelian and Fanonian Dialectic of Lordship and Bondage," p.146.

76 Ibid.

77 Fanon, *Black Skin, White Masks*, p.221.

78 Ibid.

79 Kelly Oliver, *Witnessing*.

80 Fanon, *Black Skin, White Masks*, p.221.

81 Frantz Fanon, *The Wretched of the Earth*, p.9.

82 Fanon, *Black Skin, White Masks*, pp.220–222.

83 Taylor, "The Politics of Recognition," p.50, emphasis added.

84 Fanon, *Black Skin, White Masks*, p.220.

85 Will Kymlicka, *Multicultural Citizenship: A Liberal Theory of Minority Rights* (Don Mills: Oxford University Press, 1995); Will Kymlicka, *Finding Our Way: Rethinking Ethnocultural Relations in Canada* (Don Mills: Oxford University Press, 1998); Will Kymlicka, *Politics in the Vernacular: Nationalism, Multiculturalism and Citizenship* (Don Mills: Oxford University Press, 2001).

86 Todd Gordon, "Canada, Empire, and Indigenous Peoples in the Americas," *Socialist Studies* 2, 1 (2006), pp.47–75.

87 Isabelle Schulte-Tenckhoff, "Reassessing the Paradigm of Domestication: The Problematic of Indigenous Treaties," *Review of Constitutional Studies* 4, 2 (1998), pp.239–289.

88 Michael Asch, "From 'Calder' to 'Van der Peet': Aboriginal Rights and Canadian Law, 1973–96" in *Indigenous Peoples' Rights in Australia, Canada and New Zealand,* ed. Paul Havemann (New York: Oxford University Press, 1999); Patrick Macklem, *Indigenous Difference and the Constitution of Canada* (Toronto: University of Toronto Press, 2001); James Tully, "The Struggles of Indigenous Peoples for and of Freedom."

89 Quoted in James Tully, "Aboriginal Peoples; Negotiating Reconciliation" in *Canadian Politics, 3rd edition,* eds. James Bickerton and Alan G. Gagnon (Peterborough: Broadview Press, 2000), p.413.

90 Ibid.

91 Elizabeth Povinelli, *The Cunning of Recognition: Indigenous Alterities and the Making of Australian Multiculturalism* (Durham: Duke University Press, 2002).

92 Eduardo Duran and Bonnie Duran, *Native American Postcolonial Psychology* (Albany: State University of New York Press, 1995).

93 Isabel Altamirano-Jimenez, "North American First People: Slipping into Market Citizenship," *Citizenship Studies* 8, 4 (2004), pp.349–365; Alfred, *Wasase*; Paul Nadasdy, *Hunters and Bureaucrats: Power, Knowledge and Aboriginal-State Relations in the Southwest Yukon* (Vancouver: UBC Press, 2005).

94 Nadasdy, *Hunters and Bureaucrats.*

95 Bill Ashcroft, *Post-Colonial Transformation* (New York: Routledge, 2001), p.35.

96 Ashcroft, *Post-Colonial Transformation*; David Scott, *Refashioning Futures: Criticism after Postcoloniality* (Princeton: Princeton University Press, 1999); David Scott, *Conscripts of Modernity: The Tragedy of Colonial Enlightenment* (Durham: Duke University Press, 2004).

97 Fanon, *Black Skin, White Masks*, p.222.

98 Fanon, *The Wretched of the Earth*, p.148.

99 Fanon, *Black Skin, White Masks*, p.222.
100 Ibid., p.221.
101 Sonia Kruks, "The Politics of Recognition: Sartre, Fanon and Identity Politics" in *Retrieving Experience: Subjectivity and Recognition in Feminist Politics* (Ithaca: Cornell University Press, 2001), p.101.
102 Fanon, *Black Skin, White Masks*, p.222.
103 Young, *Postcolonialism*, p.275.
104 Jorge Larrain, "Stuart Hall and the Marxist Concept of Ideology" in *Stuart Hall: Critical Dialogues in Cultural Studies,* eds. David Morley and Kuan-Hsing Chen (New York: Routledge, 1996), p.48.
105 John Scott, *Power* (Cambridge UK: Polity Press, 2001), p.10; Stuart Hall, "The Problem of Ideology: Marxism without Guarantees" in *Stuart Hall: Critical Dialogues in Cultural Studies,* eds. David Morley and Kuan-Hsing Chen (New York: Routledge, 1996).
106 Larrain, "Stuart Hall and the Marxist Concept of Ideology," p.49.
107 Fanon, *Black Skin, White Masks*, p.183.
108 Fanon, *The Wretched of the Earth*, p.8, emphasis added.
109 Young, *Postcolonialism*, p.295.
110 Fanon, *The Wretched of the Earth*, p.44.
111 Ibid., p.51.
112 Ibid., p.54.
113 Ibid., p.44.
114 Ibid., pp.58 and 30.
115 Fanon, *Black Skin, White Masks*, p.221.
116 bell hooks, *Yearning: Race, Gender, and Cultural Politics* (Boston: South End Press, 1990), p.22.
117 Taiaiake Alfred, Glen Coulthard, and Deborah Simmons, eds., *New Socialist: Special Issue on Indigenous Resurgence* 58 (2006).

Chapter 4: Hegemonies, continuities, and discontinuities of multiculturalism and the Anglo-Franco conformity order

Epigraph: Robert Cox, "Ideologies and the New International Economic Order: Reflections on Some Recent Literature," *International Organization* 33, 2 (1979), pp.257–302.

1 I refer here to a multicultural regime for managing the social relations between white and racialized populations using Puchala and Hopkins' understanding of the concept of regime as "normative structures" representing "a set of principles, norms and rules and procedures around which actors' expectations converge – thereby channelling political action within a system and giving meaning to it." Regimes reflect the actors' understanding, expectations and convictions about legitimate, appropriate, and moral behaviour in a given environment. Multiculturalism can be seen to generate a convergence of expectations, constraints, and patterned behaviour on the part of various actors within a system of institutions or society. See D. Puchala and R. Hopkins, "International Regimes: Lessons from Inductive Analysis" in *International Regimes*, ed. Stephen Krasner (Ithaca: Cornell University Press, 1983); and O. Young, "International Regimes: Problems of Concept Formation" in *World Politics* 32 (1980), pp.331–356.
2 Antonio Gramsci, *Selections from the Prison Notebooks of Antonio Gramsci* (New York:

International Publishers, 1971). Gramsci's work on hegemony suggests that particular institutional processes within and beyond the state become available for the development of dominant norms, modes of behaviour, and expectations consistent with the hegemonic social order.

3 J.L. Kunz and S. Sykes, *From Mosaic to Harmony: Multicultural Canada in the 21st Century* (Ottawa: Government of Canada PRI Cultural Project, 2007).

4 Antonio Gramsci refers to the build-up of the social power of subordinate social forces to contend with established formations that become unsettled in periods of crisis. In the case of Canadian multiculturalism, this would mean building up intellectual resources, developing alternative institutions, and organizing alternative modes of managing difference that are anti-racist and anti-colonial to contend with the colonial Anglo-Franco conformity order. See Gramsci, *Selections*.

5 Gramsci, *Selections*, p.180.

6 "Visible minority" represents a Canadian construction of a category that approximates what is otherwise referred to as "racialized peoples" (members of non-caucasian groups who are not Aboriginal people). While increasingly discredited, the category and the "naming" are instruments of regulation developed under the Canadian official multiculturalism regime.

7 Harold Palmer, "Social Adjustment of Immigrants to Canada: 1940–1975" in *Immigration and the Rise of Multiculturalism*, ed. H. Palmer (Toronto: Copp Clark, 1975).

8 Eva Mackey, "Settling Differences: Managing and Representing People and Land in the Canadian National Project" in *The House of Difference: Cultural Politics and National Identity in Canada*, ed. Eva Mackey (Toronto: University of Toronto Press, 2002).

9 Will Kymlicka, *Multicultural Citizenship: A Liberal Theory of Minority Rights* (Oxford: Clarendon Press, 1995); Charles Taylor, "The Politics of Recognition" in *Multiculturalism and the Politics of Recognition*, ed. A. Gutman (Princeton: Princeton University Press, 1992).

10 See Himani Bannerji, *The Dark Side of the Nation: Essays on Multiculturalism, Nationalism and Gender* (Toronto: Canadian Scholar's Press Inc., 2000); Richard Day, *Multiculturalism and the History of Canadian Diversity* (Toronto: University of Toronto Press, 2000); K. Moodley, "Canadian Multiculturalism as Ideology," *Ethnic and Race Studies* 6, 3 (1983), pp.320–332; Sunera Thobani, *Exalted Subjects: Studies in the Making of Race and Nation in Canada* (Toronto: University of Toronto Press, 2007); Yasmin Abu-Laban and Christina Gabriel, *Selling Diversity: Immigration, Multiculturalism, Employment and Globalization* (Toronto: Broadview Press, 2002), among others.

11 See Neil Bissoondath, *Selling Illusions: The Cult of Multiculturalism in Canada* (Toronto: Penguin Books, 1994); Daniel Stoffman, *Who Gets In: What's Wrong with Canada's Immigration Program . . . and How to Fix It* (Toronto: McClelland & Stewart, 2002); Martin Collacot, *Canada's Inadequate Response to Terrorism: The Need for Policy Reform* (Vancouver: Fraser Institute, 2006); Gerard Bouchard and Charles Taylor, *Building the Future: A Time for Reconciliation. The Report of the Quebec Consultation Commission on Accommodation Practices Related to Cultural Differences* (Quebec City: Government of Quebec, 2008).

12 K. Moodley, "Canadian Multiculturalism as Ideology"; Laverne Lewycky, "Multiculturalism in the 1990s and into the Twentieth Century: Beyond Ideology and Utopia" in *Deconstructing a Nation: Immigration, Multiculturalism and Racism in '90s Canada*, ed. Vic Satzewich (Halifax: Fernwood Publishing, 1992), pp.359–97.

13 K. Moodley, "Canadian Multiculturalism as Ideology," p.326.

14 Esteve Morera argues that Gramsci's work prefigures many of the debates on cultural politics and social diversity inherent in discussions of multiculturalism today. See E. Morera, "Gramsci's Critical Modernity," *Rethinking Marxism* 12, 1 (2000), pp.17–46.

15 Himani Bannerji, *The Dark Side of the Nation*.

16 Karl Peter, "Multicultural Politics, Money and the Conduct of Canadian Ethnic Studies," *Canadian Ethnic Studies Association Bulletin* 5 (1978), pp.2–3.

17 See Robert Cox, "Gramsci, Hegemony and International Relations: An Essay in Method," *Millennium Journal of International Studies* 12, 2 (1983), pp.162–175.

18 Mark Rupert, *Producing Hegemony: The Politics of Mass Production and American Power* (Cambridge: Cambridge University Press, 1995).

19 Barry Smart, *Foucault, Marxism and Critique* (New York and London: Routledge, 1986).

20 Gramsci, *Selections.*

21 Barnor Hesse (ed.), *Unsettled Multiculturalisms: Diasporas, Entanglements, "Transruptions"* (London: Zed Books, 2000).

22 The Canadian Labour Congress played a pivotal role in advocating for a racism-free Canadian immigration policy. Canadian Labour Congress then-president Dennis McDermott is quoted as lashing out at the federal labour minister at a labour union conference, saying that "a government that endorses the Universal Declaration of Human Rights should clean up its own policy . . . as far as Negroes are concerned." See Bromley Armstrong and Sheldon Taylor, *Bromley: Fireless Champion of Just Causes* (Toronto: Vitabu Publishing, 2000), p.107.

23 See also Bromley Armstrong's account of the advocacy of the Negro Citizenship Association (NCA) in the 1950s. Armstrong quotes federal immigration directives to the effect that "persons of African origin from the Caribbean, or of colour any place in the Commonwealth, were not deemed to be British subjects . . . only White Commonwealth citizens were considered to be eligible for entry to Canada as immigrants." See Armstrong and Taylor, *Bromley*, p.102.

24 Evelyn Kallen, "Multiculturalism: Ideology, Policy and Reality" in *Multiculturalism and Immigration in Canada*, ed. E. Cameron (Toronto: Canadian Scholars' Press Inc., 2004), pp.75–96.

25 Robert Cox, *Production, Power and World Order: Social Forces in the Making of History* (New York: Columbia University Press, 1987).

26 J. Burnet, "Myths and Multiculturalism" in *Multiculturalism in Canada*, eds. R. Samuda, J. Berry, and M. Laferriere (Toronto: Allyn and Bacon, Inc., 1984), pp.18–29.

27 Elliot Tepper, *Changing Canada: The Institutional Response to Polyethnicity* (Ottawa: Carleton University, 1988).

28 Kallen, "Multiculturalism: Ideology, Policy and Reality"; Moodley, "Canadian Multiculturalism as Ideology."

29 Abu-Laban and Gabriel, *Selling Diversity.*

30 Harold Palmer (ed.), *Immigration and the Rise of Multiculturalism* (Toronto: Copp Clark, 1975); J. Burnet and H. Palmer, *Coming Canadians: An Introduction to the History of Canada's Peoples* (Toronto: McClelland and Stewart, 1988); J. Elliot (ed.), *Two Nations, Many Cultures: Ethnic Groups in Canada* (Scarborough: Prentice-Hall, 1981).

31 The Royal Commission on Bilingualism and Biculturalism, *Report of the Royal Commission. Book IV: The Cultural Contribution of Other Groups* (Ottawa: Government of Canada Publishing, 1969).

32 John Porter, *The Vertical Mosaic: An Analysis of Class and Power in Canada* (Toronto: University of Toronto Press, 1965).

33 Bonita Lawrence and Ena Dua, "Decolonizing Anti-Racism," *Social Justice* 32, 4 (2005), pp.20–25.

34 Mackey, *The House of Difference;* T. Alfred, *Peace, Power, Righteousness: An Indigenous Manifesto* (Don Mills, ON: Oxford University Press, 1999); J. Frideres, "Policies on Indian People in Canada" in *Race and Ethnic Relations in Canada,* ed. Peter Li (Toronto: Oxford University Press, 1990); M. Boldt and J. Long, "Native Indian Self-Government: Instrument of Autonomy or Assimilation?" in *Governments in Conflict,* eds. M. Boldt and J. Long (Toronto: University of Toronto Press, 1988).

35 Abu-Laban and Gabriel, *Selling Diversity.*

36 Michael Dewing and Marc Leman, *Canadian Multiculturalism,* Current Issue Review 93–6E (Ottawa: Library of Parliament – Parliamentary Research Branch, 2006).

37 Department of Canadian Heritage, *A Canada for All: Canada's Action Plan Against Racism* (Ottawa: Public Works and Government Services Canada, 2005).

38 Kunz and Sykes, *From Mosaic to Harmony.*

39 Canadian Heritage, *Annual Report on the Operation of the Canadian Multiculturalism Act, 1999–2000* (Ottawa: Heritage Canada, 2001).

40 Will Kymlicka, *The Current State of Multiculturalism in Canada and Research Themes on Canadian Multiculturalism, 2008–2010* (Ottawa: Minister of Public Works and Government Services Canada, 2010).

41 Porter, *The Vertical Mosaic.*

42 See R. Breton "Multiculturalism and Canadian Nation Building" in *The Politics of Gender, Ethnicity and Language in Canada,* ed. A. Cairns and C. Williams (Toronto: University of Toronto Press, 1986); Peter Li, *Ethnic Inequality in a Class Society* (Toronto: Wall and Thompson, 1988).

43 Grace-Edward Galabuzi, *Canada's Economic Apartheid: The Social Exclusion of Racialized Groups in the New Century* (Toronto: Canadian Scholars' Press Inc., 2006).

44 Ibid.

45 Michael Adams, *Unlikely Utopia: The Surprising Triumph of Canadian Multiculturalism* (Toronto: Penguin Books, 2008).

46 Economic Council of Canada, *New Faces in the Crowd* (Ottawa: ECC, 1992).

47 G. Gauld, Multiculturalism, "The Real Thing?" in *20 Years of Multiculturalism: Successes and Failures,* ed. S. Hryniuk (Winnipeg, MB: St. John's College Press, 1992), pp.9–16.

48 John Berry, "Costs and Benefits of Multiculturalism: A Social-Psychological Analysis," in Hryniuk, *20 Years of Multiculturalism,* pp.83–199.

49 Stasiulis, "Symbolic Representation and the Numbers Game: Tory Policies on "Race" and Visible Minorities" in *How Ottawa Spends, 1991–1992,* ed. Frances Abele (Ottawa: Carleton University Press, 1991) pp.229–253.

50 Abu-Laban and Gabriel, *Selling Diversity.*

51 Bissoondath, *Selling Illusions.*

52 K. Mazurek, "Defusing A Radical Social Policy: The Undermining of Multiculturalism" in Hryniuk, *20 Years of Multiculturalism,* pp.17–28.

53 Bannerji, *The Dark Side of the Nation;* Rinaldo Walcott, "Critiquing Canadian Multiculturalism: Towards an Anti-racism Agenda" (M.A. Thesis, University of Toronto, 1994).

54 Bannerji, *The Dark Side of the Nation.*

55 Myer Siemiatycki and Engin Isin, "Immigration, Ethno-Racial Diversity and Urban Citizenship in Toronto," *Canadian Journal of Regional Sciences* Special Issue 20, 1–2 (1997), pp.73–102.

56 Colin Mooers, "Multiculturalism and Citizenship: Some Theoretical Reflections," CERIS Working Paper 37 (2005).

57 Étienne Balibar, "Is There a Neo-Racism?" in *Race, Nation, Class: Ambiguous Identities*, eds. Étienne Balibar and Immanuel Wallerstein (London: Verso, 1991).

58 Elliot Tepper, "Immigration Policy and Multiculturalism" in *Ethnicity and Culture in Canada*, eds. J.W. Berry and J. Laponce (Toronto: University of Toronto Press, 1994).

59 J. Stein et al., *Uneasy Partners: Multiculturalism and Rights in Canada* (Waterloo: Wilfrid Laurier University Press, 2007).

60 Sujit Choudry, "Protecting Equality in the Face of Terror: Ethnic and Racial Profiling and the s.15 of the Charter" in *The Security of Freedom: Essays on Canada's Anti-Terrorism Bill*, eds. Ronald Daniels and Patrick Kent Roach (Toronto: University of Toronto Press, 2001), pp.367–381; David Tanocich, "Rethinking the use of race in suspect descriptions" in *The Colour of Justice: Policing Race in Canada*, ed. D. Tanocich (Toronto: Irwin Law, 2006), pp.151–169.

61 Stein et al., *Uneasy Partners*; Bouchard and Taylor, *Building the Future*.

62 Edward Said, *Orientalism* (New York: Vintage Books, 1979).

63 Collacot, "Canada's Inadequate Response to Terrorism."

64 Kymlicka, *Multicultural Citizenship*.

65 Institute for Research in Public Policy, 2007.

66 Bouchard and Taylor, *Building the Future*.

67 Ibid., p.15.

68 Galabuzi, *Canada's Economic Apartheid*, p.181.

69 Jean Lock Kunz, A. Milan, and Sylvain Schetagne, *Unequal Access: A Canadian Profile of Racial Differences in Education, Employment and Income* (Toronto: Canadian Race Relations Foundation, 2000); Ruth Dibbs and Tracey Leesti, *Survey of Labour and Income Dynamics: Visible Minorities and Aboriginal Peoples* (Statistics Canada, 1995); Grace-Edward Galabuzi, *Canada's Creeping Economic Apartheid: The Economic Segregation and Social Marginalization of Racialized Groups* (Toronto: Centre for Social Justice, 2001); Andrew Jackson, "Poverty and Racism," *Perception* 24, 4 (2001); Armine Yalnyzian, *The Growing Gap: A Report on the Growing Income Inequality Between the Rich and Poor in Canada* (Toronto: Centre for Social Justice, 1998).

70 Feng Hou and Garnet Picot, "Visible Minority Neighbourhood Enclaves and Labour Market Outcomes of Immigrants," Research Paper Series Catalogue No. 11F0019M1E – no. 204 (Ottawa: Statistics Canada, 2003); Kevin Lee, *Urban Poverty in Canada: A Statistical Profile* (Ottawa: Canadian Council on Social Development, 2000); Michael Ornstein, *Ethno-Racial Inequality in the City of Toronto: An Analysis of the 1996 Census* (Toronto: City of Toronto, 2000); Abdolmohamed Kazemipur and Shiva Halli, *The New Poverty in Canada: Ethnic Groups and Ghetto Neighbourhoods* (Toronto: Thompson Educational Publishing, 2000).

71 Colin Linday, "Profiles of Ethnic Communities in Canada," Statistics Canada – Catalogue no. 89–621-XIE. Data is drawn from the 2001 Census and the 2002 Ethnic Diversity Survey.

72 B. Burnaby, C. James, and S. Regier, "The Role of Education in Integrating Diversity in the Greater Toronto Area," CERIS Working Paper 11 (2000).

73 The notion of a colour-coded vertical mosaic updates John Porter's concept of an

ethnically defined vertical mosaic based on the ethnic social stratification of Canadian society in the 1960s (Porter, *The Vertical Mosaic*). It suggests the emergence of a racially defined stratification of Canadian society, with a hierarchical social structure with racialized groups at the bottom and non-racialized groups at the top. See also, Peter Li, "The Market Value and Social Value of Race" and J. Lian and D. Matthews, "Does a Vertical Mosaic Really Exist? Ethnicity and Income in Canada, 1991," *Canadian Review of Sociology and Anthropology* 35, 4 (1998), pp.461–481.

Chapter 5: Canadian multiculturalism and its nationalisms

1 Oscar Handlin, *The Uprooted: The Epic Story of the Great Migrations That Made the American People* (Boston: Little Brown, 1951).

2 John F. Kennedy, *A Nation of Immigrants* (New York: Harper and Row, 1964); Charles W. Mills, *The Racial Contract* (Ithaca, NY, and London: Cornell University Press, 1997).

3 Walt Whitman, *Leaves of Grass (1855 first edition text)* (Radford, VA: Wilder Publishers, 2008).

4 Alexis Tocqueville, *Democracy in America* (New York: New American Library, 1964). Tocqueville did criticize U.S. policy towards Blacks and Natives, however, he never challenged the right of European (and later white) imperial ventures to impose their will upon subject people. Indeed, Tocqueville excused the practices of French imperialists against their colonized subjects. See Edward Said, *Culture and Imperialism* (New York: Vintage, 1993), p.241.

5 Ali Behdad, *A Forgetful Nation: On Immigration and Cultural Identity in the United States* (Durham, NC: Duke University Press, 2005).

6 Peter Linebaugh and Marcus Rediker, *The Many-Headed Hydra: Sailors, Slaves, Commoners, and the Hidden History of the Revolutionary Atlantic* (Boston: Beacon Press, 2000), especially pp.211–247; Behdad, *A Forgetful Nation*, p.84.

7 Behdad, *A Forgetful Nation*, p.97.

8 Michael Omi and Howard Winant, *Racial Formation in the United States: From the 1960s to the 1980s* (New York: Routledge & Kegan Paul, 1986).

9 Sylvia Wynter, "1492: A New World View" in *Race, Discourse, and the Origin of the Americas: A New World View*, ed. Vera Lawrence Hyatt and Rex Nettleford (Washington and London: Smithsonian Institution Press), pp.5–57.

10 Behdad, *A Forgetful Nation*, p.106.

11 I am indebted to Slavoj Žižek (1997) and the title he gave to his discussion of similar processes. However, while Žižek discusses "the cultural logic of multinational capitalism," my analysis is more attuned to the centuries-long historical process of "multinational capitalism" and I am, therefore, more interested in how neo-liberalism is a process that is profoundly reliant on shifting discourses of national state power within the context of an almost universal existence of capitalist social relations. See Slavoj Žižek, "Multiculturalism, or, the Cultural Logic of Multinational Capitalism," *New Left Review* 225 (1997) pp.28–51.

12 Ghassan Hage, *White Nation: Fantasies of White Supremacy in a Multicultural Society* (New York: Routledge, 2000).

13 In Hage's *White Nation*, he discusses this process in Australia, notably, another "White settler" society that has both mobilized a discourse of multiculturalism as well as institutionalized it in state policy.

14 Hage, *White Nation*.

15 Nandita Sharma, " 'Race,' Class and Gender and the Making of 'Difference': The

Social Organization of 'Migrant Workers' in Canada," *Atlantis: A Women's Studies Journal* 24, 2 (Winter 2000), pp.5–15; Nandita Sharma, *Home Economics: Nationalism and the Making of "Migrant Workers" in Canada* (Toronto: University of Toronto Press, 2006).

16 Sharma, *Home Economics*; Kerry Preibisch, "Gender Transformative Odysseys: Tracing the Experiences of Transnational Migrant Women in Rural Canada," *Canadian Woman Studies* 24, 4 (2005), pp.91–97.

17 Hiroshi Motomura, *Americans in Waiting: The Lost Story of Immigration and Citizenship in the United States* (Oxford: Oxford University Press, 2006), pp.15–37.

18 Radhika Mongia, "Race, Nationality, Mobility: A History of the Passport," *Public Culture* 11, 3 (1999), pp.527–556.

19 Sharma, " 'Race,' Class and Gender"; and Sharma, *Home Economics*.

20 Étienne Balibar, "The Nation Form: History and Ideology," in *Race, Nation, Class: Ambiguous Identities*, ed. E. Balibar and I. Wallerstein (London: Verso, 1991).

21 Paul Gilroy, *Against Race: Imagining Political Culture Beyond the Color Line* (Cambridge: Harvard University Press, 2002).

22 Étienne Balibar, "The Nation Form: History and Ideology."

23 See Makeda Silvera, *Silenced* (Toronto: Sister Vision Press, 1983); Sedef Arat-Koc, "In the Privacy of Our Own Home: Foreign Domestic Workers as Solutions to the Crisis in the Domestic Sphere in Canada," *Studies in Political Economy* 28, Spring (1989), pp.33–58.

24 In *Home Economics*, I discuss how the two policy initiatives (1967 and 1973) and also related through a moral panic against the extension of permanent residency (and its associated rights) to non-white immigrants, see especially Chapters 4 and 5.

25 See Bonita Lawrence and Enakshi Dua, "Decolonizing Antiracism." *Social Justice* 32, 4 (2005), pp.120–143.

26 Nandita Sharma and Cynthia Wright, "Decolonizing Resistance, Challenging Colonial States," *Social Justice* 35, 3 (2009), pp.120–138.

27 Gilles Deleuze and Félix Guattari, *A Thousand Plateaus: Capitalism and Schizophrenia*, trans. B. Massumi (Minneapolis: University of Minnesota Press, 1987).

28 See Michael Hardt and Antonio Negri, *Multitude: War and Democracy in the Age of Empire* (New York: Penguin Press, 2004); Linebaugh and Rediker, *The Many-Headed Hydra*.

29 Sergio Fiedler "The National or the Global: Between 'The People' and the Multitude," conference paper presentation, *Nationalism and Globalism*, University of Technology, Sydney, Australia, July 15 and 16, 2002.

30 Mohammed A. Bamyeh, "Fluid Solidarity," conference paper presentation, *Nationalism and Globalism*, University of Technology, Sydney, Australia, July 15 and 16, 2002.

31 Linebaugh and Rediker, *The Many-Headed Hydra*.

32 Chantal Mouffe, "Hope, Passion, Politics: A Conversation with Chantal Mouffe and Ernesto Laclau" in *Hope: New Philosophies for Change*, ed. Mary Zournazi (Routledge: New York, 2003), pp.144–45.

Chapter 6: Multiculturalism already unbound

An earlier version of this chapter was presented at the *From Multicultural Rhetoric to Anti-Racist Action* workshop held at the Munk Centre for International Studies, University of Toronto, October 2007. I would like to thank participants at the conference and the editors of this book for their helpful comments regarding the ideas expressed in this chapter. Research for this chapter was funded by the Shastri Indo-Canadian Institute.

1 Neil Bissoondath, *Selling Illusions: The Cult of Multiculturalism in Canada* (Toronto: Penguin Books, 1994); Jack Lawrence Granatstein, *Who Killed Canadian History?* (Toronto: Harper Collins, 1998); Kay J. Anderson, *Vancouver's Chinatown: Racial Discourse in Canada, 1875–1980* (Montréal and Kingston: McGill-Queen's University Press, 1991); Tania Das Gupta and Franca Iacovetta, Introduction to "Whose Canada Is It? Immigrant Women, Women of Colour and Feminist Critiques of Multiculturalism," *Atlantis* 24, 2 (2000).

2 D. Ley, "Multiculturalism: a Canadian defence" in *Reassessing Multiculturalism in Europe*, ed. S. Vertovec and S. Wessendorf (London: Routledge, 2008).

3 Janice Stein et al., *Uneasy Partners: Multiculturalism and Rights in Canada* (Waterloo: Wilfrid Laurier University Press, 2007).

4 John Ibbitson, "Let Sleeping Dogs Lie," in Stein et al., *Uneasy Partners*.

5 Stoffman, D., *Who Gets In: What's Wrong with Canada's Immigration Program – And How to Fix It* (Toronto: McClelland and Stewart Ltd., 2002).

6 Audrey Kobayashi, "Multiculturalism: Representing a Canadian Institution" in *Place/Culture/Representation*, ed. J. Duncan, and D. Ley (London and New York: Routledge, 1993), p.224.

7 Yasemin N. Soysal, *Limits of Citizenship: Migrants and Postnational Membership in Europe* (Chicago and London: University of Chicago, 1994); May Joseph, *Nomadic Identities: The Performance of Citizenship* (Minneapolis: University of Minnesota Press, 1999); Katharyne Mitchell, "Multiculturalism, or the United Colors of Capitalism?" *Antipode* 25, 4 (1993), pp.263–294.

8 Irene Bloemraad, "Citizenship and Immigration: A Current Review," *Journal of International Migration and Integration* 1, 1 (2000), pp.9–37.

9 Alejandro Portes and Josh DeWind, *Rethinking Migration: New Theoretical and Empirical Perspectives* (New York: Berghahn Books, 2007).

10 Saskia Sassen, *Losing Control? Sovereignty in the Age of Globalization* (New York: Columbia University Press, 1996).

11 Sassen, *Losing Control?*, p.xvi.

12 Stephen Vertovec, "Super-diversity and its Implications," *Ethnic and Racial Studies* 30 (2007), pp.1024–1054.

13 Ibid., p.28.

14 Ayelet Shachar, "The Race for Talent: Highly Skilled Migrants and Competitive Immigration Regimes," *New York University Law Review*, 8 (April 2006).

15 Sassen, *Losing Control?*, p.63.

16 Ninette Kelley and Michael Trebilcock, *The Making of the Mosaic: A History of Canadian Immigration Policy* (Toronto, Buffalo, and London: University of Toronto Press, 2000).

17 Valerie Knowles, *Strangers at Our Gates: Canadian Immigration and Immigration Policy, 1540–1997* (Toronto: Dundurn Press, 1997); R. Sampat-Mehta, "First Fifty Years of South Asian Immigration: A Historical Perspective," in *South Asians in the Canadian Mosaic*, ed. R. Kanungo (Montreal: Kala Bharati, 1984), p.12–31.

18 Citizenship and Immigration Canada (CIC) Facts and Figures 2010.

19 Joseph Schaafsma and Arthur Sweetman, "Immigrant Earnings: Age at Immigration Matters," *The Canadian Journal of Economics*, 34, 4 (2001); Jeffrey G. Reitz, "Immigrant Success in the Knowledge Economy: Institutional Change and the Immigrant

Experience in Canada, 1970–1995," *Journal of Social Issues* 57, 3 (2001), pp.579–613.

20 Yuri Ostrovsky, "Earnings Inequality and Earnings Instability of Immigrants in Canada," Analytical Studies Branch Research Paper Series, Statistics Canada (2008).

21 Will Kymlicka, "Disentangling the Debate," in Stein et al., *Uneasy Partners*.

22 Harald Bauder, " 'Brain Abuse,' or the Devaluation of Immigrant Labour in Canada," *Antipode* 35, 4 (2003), pp.699–717.

23 Jamie Peck and Adam Tickell, "Neoliberalizing Space," *Antipode* 34, 3 (2002), pp.380–404.

24 Ghassan Hage, " 'Asia' Hansonism and the Discourse of White Decline," *Inter-Asia Cultural Studies* 1, 1 (2000), pp.85–96.

25 David Theo Goldberg, "Neoliberalizing Race," presentation at Wilfrid Laurier University, February 29, 2008.

26 Andrew Herod, "Workers and Workplaces in a Neoliberal Global Economy," *Environment and Planning A* 32, 10 (2000), pp.1781–1790.

27 Goldberg, "Neoliberalizing Race."

28 Alexander Panetta, "Immigration Wait Times Growing," *The Globe and Mail* (Toronto), February 8, 2008.

29 Kareem D. Sadiq, "The Two-Tier Settlement System: A Review of Current Newcomer Settlement Services in Canada," CERIS Working Paper No. 34 (2004).

30 Goldberg, "Neoliberalizing Race."

31 Aihwa Ong, *Flexible Citizenship: The Cultural Logics of Transnationality* (Durham and London: Duke University Press, 1999); Katharyne Mitchell, "Transnationalism, Neoliberalism, and the Rise of the Shadow State," *Economy and Society* 30, 2 (2001).

32 Augie Fleras and Jean Leonard Elliott, *Engaging Diversity: Multiculturalism in Canada*, Second Edition (Toronto: Nelson Thomson Learning, 2002).

33 Ghassan Hage, *White Nation: Fantasies of White Supremacy in a Multicultural Society* (Sydney: Pluto Press, 1998), p.129; see also Bill Cope and Mary Kalantzis, "Speaking of Cultural Difference: The Rise and Uncertain Future of the Language of Multiculturalism," *Migration Action* 9 (1987).

34 Mitchell, *Transnationalism, Neoliberalism, and the Rise of the Shadow State*; Katharyne Mitchell, *Crossing the Neoliberal Line: Pacific Rim Migration and the Metropolis* (Philadelphia: Temple University Press, 2004).

35 Andrea Mandel-Campbell, *Why Mexicans Don't Drink Molson; Rescuing Canadian Business from the Suds of Global Obscurity* (Toronto, Douglas & McIntyre, 2007); Wendy Dobson, "The Indian Elephant Sheds its Past," C.D. Howe Institute, Commentary No. 235 (May 2006).

36 David Ley and Audrey Kobayashi, "Back to Hong Kong: Return Migration or Transnational Sojourn?" *Global Networks* 5, 2 (2005), pp.111–127; Don Devoretz and Kangqing Zhang, "Citizenship, Passports and the Brain Exchange Triangle," *Journal of Comparative Policy Analysis: Research and Practice* 6, 2 (2004), pp.199–212; Mandel-Campbell, *Why Mexicans Don't Drink Molson*, Conference Board of Canada, 2007; Sean W. Burges, "Canada's Postcolonial Problem: The United States and Canada's International Policy Review," *Canadian Foreign Policy* 13, 1 (2006).

37 Ayelet Shachar, "The Race for Talent."

38 Margaret Walton-Roberts, "Embodied Global Flows: Immigration and Transnational Networks between British Columbia, Canada, Punjab, India" (Unpublished PhD Thesis, University of British Columbia, 2001).

39 Radhika Mongia, "Race, Nationality, Mobility: A History of the Passport," *Public Culture* 11, 3 (1999), pp.527–556.

40 Ibid., p.552.
41 Ibid., p.554.
42 Citizenship and Immigration Canada news release, March 1, 2001. Minister Caplan led a Canadian delegation to New Delhi, Chandigarh, and Bangalore. She was accompanied by a number of MPs whose ridings are home to large Indo-Canadian communities.
43 Arthur G. Rubinoff, "Canada's re-engagement with India," *Asian Survey* 42, 6 (2002), p.854.
44 Arjun Appadurai, *Modernity at Large: Cultural Dimensions of Globalization* (Minneapolis: University of Minnesota Press, 1996), p.168.
45 GOPIO, accessed April 21, 2008, http://www.gopio.net/99_convention.htm.
46 GOPIO, 1989 Resolution 11; GOPIO, 2004 Resolution 1.
47 GOPIO, Summary of the GOPIO 2000 Convention, http://www.gopio.net/resolutions_2000.htm.
48 GOPIO, 2000 Resolution, 1: Point 11.
49 Personal interview with the CIC office manager, Canadian High Commission Delhi, December 17, 1999.
50 Margaret Walton-Roberts, "Transnational Geographies: Indian Immigration to Canada," *The Canadian Geographer* 47, 3 (2003), pp.235–250.
51 Peter O'Neil, "'Nannies' Exploit Visa Office to Enter Canada," *National Post*, October 18, 2007.
52 Ian Bailey and Unnati Gandhi, "Alleged Remark Stirs Ire of B.C. Delegation," *Globe and Mail* (Toronto), December 18, 2007.
53 Ibid.
54 David Theo Goldberg, "Racial Europeanization," *Ethnic and Racial Studies* 29, 2 (2006), pp.331–364; Susan Searls Giroux, "On the State of Race Theory: A Conversation with David Theo Goldberg," *Jac*, 26, 1–2 (2006), pp.11–66.
55 Alison Mountz, "Human Smuggling, the Transnational Imaginary, and Everyday Geographies of the Nation-State," *Antipode* 35, 3 (2003), pp.622–644.
56 Fourteen Lakh translates to about $50,000 Canadian dollars.
57 Margaret Walton-Roberts, "Globalization, National Autonomy and Non-Resident Indians," *Contemporary South Asia* 13, 1 (2004), pp.53–69.
58 Chandigarh is one of the main centres of overseas recruitment in India. See Rajan, Varghese, Jayakumar, "Overseas Recruitment In India: Structures, Practices and Remedies," CDS Working Paper 421 (2010), accessed January 3, 2011, http://cds.edu/download_files/wp421.pdf.
59 WWICS Brochure, Chandigarh Office, 1999.
60 Figures given are in 1999 prices.
61 WWICS Brochure, 1999.
62 Personal interview with the CIC office manager, Canadian High Commission Delhi, December 17, 1999.
63 Gupta, S., "Foreign direct investment in India: Policy reform and politics," *Canadian Foreign Policy* 13, 2 (2006), pp.19–36.
64 Kim Bolan, *Loss of Faith: How the Air India Bombers Got Away With Murder* (Toronto: McClelland and Stewart, 2005); Jennifer Hyndman, "Aid, Conflict and Migration: the Canada-Sri Lanka Connection," *Canadian Geographer* 47, 3 (2003), pp.251–268.
65 Walton-Roberts, "Transnational Geographies."
66 Information is drawn from an interview with the Deputy Secretary NRI Affairs, Delhi, February 22, 2000.

67 Darshan Singh Tatla, *The Sikh Diaspora: The Search for Statehood* (London: UCL Press, 1999).

68 Laurent Gayer, "The Globalization of Identity Politics: The Sikh Experience," *International Journal of Punjab Studies* 7 (2000), p.223–262; Verne A. Dusenbery, "A Sikh Diaspora? Contested Identities and Constructed Realities," in *Nation and Migration, the Politics of Space in South Asian Diaspora*, ed. Peter van der Verr (Philadelphia: University of Pennsylvania Press, 1995); Gayer, "The Globalization of Identity Politics," p.248.

69 Mark Juergensmeyer, "The Ghadar Syndrome: Nationalism in an Immigrant Community," *Punjab Journal of Politics* 14 (1979), p.14.

70 Benedict Anderson, *Imagined Communities: Reflections on the Origins and Spread of Nationalism*, Revised Edition (London and New York: Verso, 1991).

71 Gayer, "The Globalization of Identity Politics"; Appaduria, *Modernity at Large*.

72 Harry Gouldbourne, *Ethnicity and Nationalism in Post-Imperial Britain* (Cambridge: Cambridge University Press, 1991).

73 Tatla, *The Sikh Diaspora*.

74 Gayer, "The Globalization of Identity Politics," p.262.

75 Personal interview with the Under Secretary of the Ministry of External Affairs, Delhi, February 21, 2000.

76 Kim Bolan, "India to Review Visa Blacklist," *Vancouver Sun* (Vancouver), January 8, 2001.

77 In 1985, an Air India flight from Montreal to India via London exploded over Irish air space due to a terrorist bombing by Sikh separatists. See K. Bolan, *Loss of Faith*.

78 CBC News, "Tories regret participation in parade honouring alleged terrorist," accessed April 7, 2008, http://www.cbc.ca/canada/britishcolumbia/story/2007/04/19/parade-politicians.html; Kim Bolan, "Mounties Claim Veto Power over Sikh Parade," *Times Colonist* (Victoria), March 28, 2008.

79 Harjot Oberoi, "Imaging Indian Diasporas in Canada: An Epic Without a Text?" in *Culture and Economy in the Indian Diaspora*, ed. Bhiku Parekh, Gurharpal Singh, and Steven Vertovec, (London and New York: Routledge, 2003) p.183–196.

80 Appadurai, *Modernity at Large*, p.171.

Chapter 7: Recognition politics and reconciliation fantasies: Liberal multiculturalism and the "Indian land question"

1 Throughout the paper I use the term "ethnic communities" to refer to people whose cultural identities lie outside what is seen as the core Canadian cultural identity (white Anglophone and, sometimes, white Francophone) and who are also not of Indigenous descent. I recognize that this is a problematic term, not least in that it suggests that this core cultural identity is itself not "ethnic."

2 Noel Dyck, *What is the Indian "Problem"? Tutelage and Resistance in Canadian Indian Administration* (St. John's: Memorial University of Newfoundland, 1991).

3 I use the terms "Indigenous" and "Aboriginal" interchangeably to refer to those who occupied the place we now call Canada prior to European colonization. I use the term "First Nation" in reference to peoples recognized as "Indians" under the federal *Indian Act*.

4 Himani Bannerji, *The Dark Side of the Nation: Essays on Multiculturalism, Nationalism, and Gender* (Toronto: Canadian Scholars Press, 2000), p.5.

5 Richard Day, *Multiculturalism and the History of Canadian Diversity* (Toronto: University of Toronto Press, 2000), p.4.

6 Richard Day and Tonio Sadik, "The B.C. Land Question, Liberal Multiculturalism, and the Spectre of Aboriginal Nationhood," *B.C. Studies* 234 (Summer 2002): pp.5–34. Quote is from pages 7–8. Following Day and Sadik, in this chapter I use the term "liberal multiculturalism" to refer to both multiculturalism as state policy and practice (official multiculturalism) and the body of intellectual work (liberal multicultural theory) that supports it.

7 Day, *Multiculturalism*.

8 Ibid.

9 Ibid., p.9.

10 Charles Taylor, *Reconciling the Solitudes: Essays on Canadian Federalism and Nationalism* (Montreal and Kingston: McGill-Queen's University Press, 1993), p.190.

11 Canada, *Multiculturalism Act*, S.C. 1988, c. 31.

12 The *Calder* decision represented a key advance in the Nisga'a peoples' century-long land struggle. By undermining the Crown's long-held assertion that Aboriginal title had either never existed or had long ago been extinguished, the case also advanced the land claims of other First Nations. For a general overview of the case, see Christina Godlewska and Jeremy Weber, "The *Calder* Decision, Aboriginal Title, Treaties, and the Nisga'a," in *Let Right Be Done: Aboriginal Title, the Calder Case, and the Future of Indigenous Rights*, ed. Hamar Foster, Heather Raven, and Jeremy Weber (Vancouver: UBC Press, 2007), pp.1–33.

13 *Delgamuukw v. British Columbia* [1997], 3 SCR 1010.

14 DIAND, *Highlights from the Report of the Royal Commission on Aboriginal Peoples: People to People, Nation to Nation* (Ottawa: Department of Indian Affairs and Northern Development), http://www.ainc-inac.gc.ca/ap/pubs/rpt/rpt-eng.asp.

15 Ibid.

16 Ibid.

17 Paul Tennant, *Aboriginal Peoples and Politics: The Indian Land Question in British Columbia, 1849–1989* (Vancouver: UBC Press, 1990), pp.17–25.

18 R. Cole Harris, *Making Native Space: Colonialism, Resistance, and Reserves in British Columbia* (Vancouver: UBC Press, 2002), p.xviii.

19 Nicholas Blomley, "'Shut the Province Down': First Nations Blockades in British Columbia, 1984–1995," *B.C. Studies* 111 (Autumn 1996): pp.5–35. For an overview of the role of court decisions during this period see Tennant, *Aboriginal Peoples and Politics*, chapter 16.

20 Christopher McKee, *Treaty Talks in British Columbia: Negotiating a Mutually Beneficial Future* (Vancouver: UBC Press, 2000), p.34.

21 *The Report of the British Columbia Claims Task Force* (Vancouver: British Columbia Claims Task Force, 1991), p.7.

22 British Columbia, *Treaty Negotiations in British Columbia: An Assessment of the Effectiveness of British Columbia's Management and Administrative Processes* (Victoria: Office of the Auditor General, 2006).

23 British Columbia Treaty Commission, *Common Table Report: August 1, 2008*, http://www.bctreaty.net.

24 B.C. Treaty Commission, *British Columbia Treaty Commission: Annual Report for 2000* (Vancouver: British Columbia Treaty Commission, 2000). For a fuller discussion of these fundamental differences, see James Tully, "Reconsidering the B.C. Treaty Process," in *Speaking Truth to Power: A Treaty Forum* (Vancouver: British Columbia Treaty Commission, 2001).

25 In its 2009 annual report, the B.C. Treaty Commission reported that there were 60

First Nations participating in the process, representing 111 of the approximately 200 *Indian Act* bands in British Columbia.

26 British Columbia, *The New Relationship*, copy available on the Government of British Columbia website, http://www.gov.bc.ca.

27 Ibid.

28 Justine Hunter, "How Campbell Changed His View," *Globe and Mail* (Toronto), October 13, 2007.

29 *Discussion Paper on Instructions for Implementing the New Relationship*, available on the Government of British Columbia website http://www.gov.bc.ca/, February 19, 2009.

30 Judith Lavoie, "New Bill to Recognize Aboriginal Rights, Title," *CanWest News Service*, March 6, 2009, available at http://www.vancouversun.com.

31 *Discussion Paper on Instructions for Implementing the New Relationship*.

32 Lavoie, "New Bill to Recognize Aboriginal Rights."

33 Vaughn Palmer, " 'Recognition Act' Runs into a Legal Opinion that Worries Some Liberals," *Vancouver Sun*, March 13, 2009.

34 Allan Donovan et al., "Recognition Act Commentary: A Submission to the Recognition Working Group (RWG) by First Nations Lawyers," Unpublished paper, no date, 22 pages.

35 See, in particular, *Delgamuukw v. British Columbia*.

36 Arthur Manuel, "Beware of B.C.'s Proposed Recognition and Reconciliation Act," *Georgia Straight,* July 23, 2009, http://www.straight.com/.

37 Originally published as: Glen Coulthard, "Subjects of Empire: Indigenous Peoples and the 'Politics of Recognition' in Canada," *Contemporary Political Theory* 6 (2007), pp.437–60.

38 Charles Taylor, "The Politics of Recognition," in ed. A. Guttman, *Re-Examining the Politics of Recognition* (Princeton: Princeton University Press, 1994), pp.25–73.

39 Coulthard, "Subjects of Empire," p.438.

40 Ibid., pp.438–39.

41 Day, *Multiculturalism*, p.217.

42 Bannerji, *The Dark Side of the Nation*, p.90.

43 Richard Day, "Who is this We that Gives the Gift? Native American Political Theory and the Western Tradition," *Critical Horizons* 2 (2001), pp.173–201. Cited in Coulthard, "Subjects of Empire," p.446.

44 Day, *Multiculturalism*, p.3.

45 Ibid., p.35.

46 The statement is posted on the Indian and Northern Affairs Canada web site, http://www.ainc-inac.gc.ca/gs/rec_e.html.

47 Catherine Rolfsen, "Reconciling the Truth," *Edmonton Journal*, June 3, 2007.

48 Carole Blackburn, "Producing Legitimacy: Reconciliation and the Negotiation of Aboriginal Rights in Canada," *Journal of the Royal Anthropological Institute* 13 (2007), pp.621–638.

49 Ibid., pp.625–626.

50 Day and Sadik, "The B.C. Land Question," p.14.

51 B.C. Treaty Commission, *Looking Forward, Looking Back: A Review of the B.C. Treaty Process* (Vancouver: B.C. Treaty Commission, 2001).

52 Andrew Woolford, *Between Justice and Certainty: Treaty Making in British Columbia* (Vancouver: UBC Press, 2005), p.174.

53 Tully, "Reconsidering the B.C. Treaty Process."

54 Blackburn, "Producing Legitimacy," pp.625–26.
55 Bannerji, *The Dark Side of the Nation*, p.119.
56 Anderson, "Thinking 'Postnationally,'" p.381.
57 Bannerji, *The Dark Side of the Nation*, p.81.
58 Day, *Multiculturalism*, pp.222–27.

Chapter 8: Reconciliation with Indigenous ghosts: On the politics of postcolonial ghost stories

A version of this chapter was published in *Cultural Geographies* in 2008 (Emilie Cameron, "Indigenous Spectrality and the Politics of Postcolonial Ghost Stories," *Cultural Geographies* 15 [2008], pp.383–393). Thank you to David Lambert, Philip Crang, Laura Cameron, Audrey Kobayashi, Bruce Braun, and Lisa Helps for their comments and suggestions on various versions. Thank you also to the people who have shared their stories of the Stein Valley with me, and particularly to Wendy Wickwire for sharing her extensive knowledge of the park's history.

Epigraph: Gayatri Chakravorty Spivak, *A Critique of Postcolonial Reason: Toward a History of the Vanishing Present* (Cambridge, Mass.: Harvard University Press, 1999), p.173.

1 Eva Mackey, *The House of Difference: Cultural Politics and National Identity in Canada* (Toronto: University of Toronto Press, 1999); Will Kymlicka, "American Multiculturalism and the 'Nations Within,'" in *Political Theory and the Rights of Indigenous Peoples*, eds. Duncan Ivison, Paul Patton, and Will Sanders (Cambridge: Cambridge University Press, 2000); Sneja Gunew, "Postcolonialism and Multiculturalism: Between Race and Ethnicity," *Yearbook of English Studies* 27 (1997), pp.22–39.
2 Mackey, *The House of Difference*, p.50.
3 Himani Bannerji, *The Dark Side of the Nation: Essays on Multiculturalism, Nationalism and Gender* (Toronto: Canadian Scholars' Press and Women's Press, 2000), Mackey, *The House of Difference*.
4 Sneja Gunew, *Haunted Nations: The Colonial Dimensions of Multiculturalisms* (London: Routledge, 2004); Gunew, "Postcolonialism and Multiculturalism"; Bannerji, *The Dark Side of the Nation;* Yvonne Brown, "Ghosts in the Canadian Multicultural Machine: A Tale of the Absent Presence of Black People," *Journal of Black Studies* 38 (2008), pp.374–387.
5 Kymlicka, "American Multiculturalism and the 'Nations Within,'" p.219.
6 See Audrey Kobayashi and Sarah de Leeuw, "Tensioned Landscapes and Contested Identities: The Social Geographies of Difference and Sameness within Indigenous and Non-Indigenous Relationships," in *Handbook of Social Geography*, eds. Susan Smith, Rachel Pain, Sallie Marston, and J.P. Jones III (London: Sage, 2009), pp.118–138.
7 Gunew, *Haunted Nations*, p.9.
8 Avery Gordon, *Ghostly Matters: Haunting and the Sociological Imagination* (Minneapolis: University of Minnesota Press, 1997), pp.205–206.
9 Derek Gregory, *The Colonial Present: Afghanistan, Palestine, Iraq* (Oxford: Blackwell, 2004).
10 Daniel Clayton, "Absence, Memory, and Geography," *BC Studies* 132 (2001/2002), pp.65–79; Ian Baucom, "Specters of the Atlantic," *South Atlantic Quarterly* 100 (2001), pp.61–82.
11 Akhil Gupta in Gregory, *Colonial Present;* Donald Moore, *Suffering for Territory: Race, Place, and Power in Zimbabwe* (Durham, NC: Duke University Press, 2005).
12 Jacques Derrida, *Spectres of Marx*, trans. P. Kamuf (London: Routledge, 1994).

13 For example, Warren Cariou, "Haunted Prairie: Aboriginal 'Ghosts' and the Spectres of Settlement," *University of Toronto Quarterly* 75 (2006), pp.727–734; Joshua Comaroff, "Ghostly Topographies: Landscape and Biopower in Modern Singapore," *Cultural Geographies* 14 (2007), pp.56–73; Dydia DeLyser, "Authenticity on the Ground: Engaging the Past in a California Ghost Town," *Annals of the Association of American Geographers*, 89 (1999), pp.602–632; Derrida, *Spectres of Marx*; Timothy Edensor, "The ghosts of industrial ruins: ordering and disordering memory in excessive space," *Environment and Planning D: Society and Space* 23 (2005), pp.829–849; Ken Gelder and Jane Jacobs, *Uncanny Australia: Sacredness and Identity in a Postcolonial Nation* (Melbourne: University of Melbourne Press, 1998); Marlene Goldman and Joanne Saul, "Talking with Ghosts: Haunting in Canadian Cultural Production," *University of Toronto Quarterly* 75 (2006), pp.645–655; Gordon, *Ghostly Matters*; Steve Pile, *Real Cities: Modernity, Space, and the Phantasmagorias of City Life* (London: Sage, 2005); Leslie Robertson, *Imagining Difference: Legend, Curse, and Spectacle in a Canadian Mining Town* (Vancouver: UBC Press, 2005); Ann Laura Stoler, *Haunted by Empire: Geographies of Intimacy in North American History* (Durham: Duke University Press, 2006); Karen Till, *The New Berlin: Memory, Politics, Place* (Minneapolis: University of Minnesota Press, 2005); Jon Wylie, "The Spectral Geographies of W.G. Sebald," *Cultural Geographies* 14 (2007), pp.171–188.
14 Cheryl McEwan makes a similar observation in her recent piece on postcolonialism and the politics of enchantment. See Cheryl McEwan, "A very modern ghost: postcolonialism and the politics of enchantment," *Environment and Planning D: Society and Space* 26 (2008), pp.29.
15 Catharine Parr Traill in Goldman and Saul, "Talking With Ghosts," p.645.
16 Earle Birney in ibid.
17 Margot Northey, *The Haunted Wilderness: The Gothic and Grotesque in Canadian Fiction* (Toronto: University of Toronto Press, 1976).
18 D.M.R. Bentley, "Shadows in the Soul: Racial Haunting in the Poetry of Duncan Campbell Scott," *University of Toronto Quarterly* 75 (2006), pp.752–770.
19 D.M.R. Bentley, *The Confederation Group of Canadian Poets* (Toronto: University of Toronto Press, 2004).
20 Duncan Campbell Scott, *New World Lyrics and Ballads* (Toronto: Morang and Co., 1905).
21 Stan Dragland, *Floating Voice: Duncan Campbell Scott and the Literature of Treaty 9* (Concord, ON: Anansi, 1994); Laura Smyth Groening, *Listening to Old Woman Speak: Natives and alterNatives in Canadian Literature* (Montreal and Kingston: McGill-Queen's University Press, 2004).
22 Duncan Campbell Scott, *The Administration of Indian Affairs in Canada* (Toronto: Canadian Institute of International Affairs, 1931), p.27.
23 Cariou, "Haunted Prairie," p.727.
24 Margaret Atwood, *Strange Things: The Malevolent North in Canadian Literature* (London: Virago, 2004); Goldman and Saul, "Talking with Ghosts."
25 Gelder and Jacobs, *Uncanny Australia*; David Crouch, "National Hauntings: The Architecture of Australian Ghost Stories," *Journal of the Association for the Study of Australian Literature* (2007), pp.94–105; Peter Read, *Haunted Earth* (Sydney: University of New South Wales Press, 2003). See also Gunew, *Haunted Nations,* for a consideration of haunting in both Canadian and Australian contexts.
26 Renée Bergland, *The National Uncanny: Indian Ghosts and American Subjects* (Hanover: University Press of New England, 2000), p.1.

27 Government of Canada, *Highlights from the Report of the Royal Commission on Aborigi-nal Peoples: People to People, Nation to Nation* (Royal Commission on Aboriginal Peoples, 1996), http://www.ainc-inac.gc.ca/ch/rcap/rpt/lk_e.html.
28 Ibid.
29 Ibid.
30 See the Spring 2006 issue of the journal, 75 (2).
31 Michael M'Gonigle and Wendy Wickwire, *Stein: The Way of the River* (Vancouver: Talon Books, 1989), p.16.
32 Annie York, Richard Daly, and Chris Arnett, *They Write Their Dream on the Rocks Forever: Rock Writings in the Stein River Valley of British Columbia* (Vancouver: Talon Books, 1993).
33 Wendy Wickwire, Personal Communication (Lytton, BC, June 24, 2006).
34 These efforts were facilitated by a longer history of imagining the Stein in spiritual terms. The spiritual significance of the valley was noted by anthropologists as early as 1900 (see James Teit, "The Thompson Indians of British Columbia" in *American Museum of Natural History, Volume II, Anthropology I, The Jesup North Pacific Expedition,* ed. Franz Boas (New York: The Knickerbocker Press, 1900)) and has more recently been featured in various "New Age" publications (e.g., *Power Trips: The Travel Guides to Mother Earths' Sacred Spaces,* 9 (1998)).
35 M'Gonigle and Wickwire, *Stein.*
36 "Voices for the Wilderness, August 1–3, 1987. Stein Valley Festival," University of British Columbia Archives, spam 22025.
37 Bruce Braun, *The Intemperate Rainforest: Nature, Culture, and Power on Canada's West Coast* (Minneapolis: University of Minnesota Press, 2002).
38 Napoleon Kruger in M'Gonigle and Wickwire, *Stein,* p.147.
39 David Suzuki in ibid., p.11.
40 Ruby Dunstan and Leonard Andrew, *Lytton and Mount Currie Bands Stein Declaration* (Lytton and Mount Currie BC, 1987); Institute for New Economics, *Stein Valley: An Economic Report for the People of Thompson Lillooet Region* (Vancouver: Institute for New Economics, 1985); M'Gonigle and Wickwire, *Stein;* Western Canada Wilderness Committee, *Stein Valley: The Choice is Ours, Where Do You Stand?* (Vancouver: Western Canada Wilderness Committee, 1987).
41 Napoleon Kruger in M'Gonigle and Wickwire, *Stein:* p.147.
42 The Nlaka'pamux launched a comprehensive land claim with the federal government in the late 1980's. According to the Provincial Government's Ministry of Aboriginal Relations and Reconciliation, the Lytton First Nation is currently engaged in treaty talks through the BC Treaty Commission, but the Nlaka'pamux Nation Tribal Council (comprised of a number of other Nlaka'pamux Nations, excepting the Lytton Nation) continues to refuse to recognize the province as negotiator and is pursuing its members' claims through other channels.
43 David Rossiter and Patricia Wood, "Fantastic Topographies: Neo-Liberal Responses to Aboriginal Land Claims in British Columbia," *Canadian Geographer* 49 (2005), pp.352–367; Daniel Clayton, "Absence, Memory, and Geography."
44 Quinn Jordan-Knox, Personal Communication (Vancouver, BC, March 22, 2004).
45 I have conducted only six in-depth interviews with visitors to the Stein Valley, all of whom are Canadian citizens, residents of British Columbia, identify as white, and are aged between 27 and 63. This is certainly not a sufficient sample of interviews to make claims about the prevalence of stories about the Stein's haunting, but five of the six interviewees were familiar with stories of the Stein's haunting before under-

taking a trip to the park. These stories are thus suggestive rather than conclusive evidence of the Stein's haunting, but I would argue they are useful on these terms.

46 Maureen Roger, Personal Communication (White Rock, BC, March 14, 2004).

47 George Tracey, Personal Communication (Surrey, BC, March 14, 2004).

48 Cariou, "Haunted Prairie," p.727.

49 B.C. Parks, *Stein Valley Nlaka'pamux Heritage Park* (Victoria: Government of British Columbia), accessed March 12, 2004, http://www.env.gov.bc.ca/bcparks/explore/parkpgs/stein_val/stein_brochure.pdf.

50 Gelder and Jacobs, *Uncanny Australia.*

51 Cariou, "Haunted Prairie," p.728.

52 Lytton Indian Band and Mount Currie Indian Band, "Stein Perspective: the Lytton and Mt. Currie Indian Peoples" in *Stein Valley Educational Report* 6 (1987), p.8.

53 Spivak, *A Critique of Postcolonial Reason.*

54 Baucom, "Specters of the Atlantic," p.75.

55 R. Cole Harris, *Making Native Space: Colonialism, Resistance, and Reserves in British Columbia* (Vancouver: UBC Press, 2002), p.151.

56 Baucom, "Specters of the Atlantic," p.64.

57 Government of Canada, *Highlights from the Report of the Royal Commission,* n.p.

58 Sarah Ahmed, *The Cultural Politics of Emotion* (Edinburgh: Edinburgh University Press, 2004).

59 Daniel David Moses and Terry Goldie, eds., *An Anthology of Canadian Native Literature in English* (Toronto: Oxford University Press, 1992), p.xvii.

60 Donna Haraway, "A Game of Cat's Cradle: Science Studies, Feminist Theory, Cultural Studies," *Configurations* 2 (1994), p.71.

61 Dunstan and Andrew, *Lytton and Mount Currie Bands Stein Declaration.*

62 Cariou, "Haunted Prairie," p.730. See also James (Sa'kei'j) Youngblood Henderson, "Postcolonial Ghost Dancing: Diagnosing European Colonialism" in *Reclaiming Indigenous Voice and Vision,* ed. Marie Battiste (Vancouver: UBC Press, 2000), pp.57–76, for a consideration of how non-Aboriginal peoples have misunderstood ghost dancing and an interpretation of its contemporary importance.

63 For more on the relationship between multiculturalism and the politics of Indigenous recognition, see Brian Egan's chapter in this volume.

64 Jo Frances Maddern and Peter Adey, "Editorial: spectro-geographies," *Cultural Geographies* 15 (2008), p.292.

Chapter 9: Resurfacing landscapes of trauma: Multiculturalism, cemeteries, and the migrant body, 1875 onwards

First epigraph: Karen Selick, "One Little, Two Little, Three Little Land Claims," *Canadian Lawyer* June (1997), p.46. Second epigraph: Judith Butler, *Precarious Life: The Powers of Mourning and Violence* (New York: Verso, 2004), p.34.

1 Letter from Dr. J.S. Lynch to J.A.N. Provencher, 12 April 1877, as reprinted in Nelson Gerrard, *Icelandic River Saga* (Winnipeg: Saga Publications, 1985), p.38.

2 It is difficult to identify the exact number of graves at Nes. Nelson Gerrard writes that records from Thorgrímur Jónsson, a local carpenter who made coffins during the epidemic, names nineteen Icelandic smallpox victims buried there, but numerous other burials also took place on the site. Gerrard, *Icelandic River Saga,* p.37.

3 Gerrard, *Icelandic River Saga,* p.315; *The Poetic Edda,* trans. Carolyn Larrington (New York: Oxford University Press, 1999), p.9.

4 Gerrard, *Icelandic River Saga*, p.iv.

5 Achille Mbembe, "Necropolitics," *Public Culture* 15, 1 (2003), pp.11–40, and p.35.

6 Libraries and Archives Canada, "Contact: Making the West Canadian" (Virtual Exhibit), accessed July 7, 2009, http://www.collectionscanada.gc.ca/05/0529/052902/05290299_e.html.

7 See also, Donovan Giesbrecht, "Métis, Mennonites and the 'Unsettled Prairie,' 1874–1896," *Journal of Mennonite Studies* 19 (2001), pp.103–111.

8 See for example J.S. Woodsworth's later comments on the industry, faith, and "clean blood" of Icelanders. J.S. Woodsworth, *Strangers Within our Gates, or Our Coming Canadians* (Toronto: Frederick Clarke Stephenson / Missionary Society of the Methodist Church, 1909), p.92.

9 For a more detailed discussion of the Icelandic land grant and the rejection of Ramsay's land claim see Anne Brydon, "Dreams and Claims: Icelandic-Aboriginal Interactions in the Manitoba Interlake," *Journal of Canadian Studies* 36, 2 (Summer 2001), pp.164–190, and Ryan Eyford, "Quarantined Within a New Colonial Order: The 1876–1877 Lake Winnipeg Smallpox Epidemic," *Journal of the Canadian Historical Association* 17, 1 (2006), pp.55–78.

10 See Giorgio Agamben, *Homo Sacer: Sovereign Power and Bare Life* (Chicago: Stanford University Press, 1998).

11 Olive Dickason as quoted in Brydon, "Dreams and Claims," p.175.

12 Mary Ellen Kelm, *Colonizing Bodies: Aboriginal Health and Healing in British Columbia, 1900–50* (Vancouver: UBC Press, 1998), p.xix.

13 Brydon, "Dreams and Claims," p.171.

14 Thorleifur Jóakimsson, *Brot af Landnámssögu Nýja Íslands*, Winnipeg, 1919, as translated in Gerrard, *Icelandic River Saga*, p.27.

15 Thorstína Walters, *Modern Sagas: The Story of the Icelanders in North America* (Fargo: North Dakota Institute for Regional Studies, 1953), p.63.

16 See for example, Letter dated August 3 1875, Morris Papers, Provincial Archives of Manitoba, MG12 BI 1066, as quoted in Brydon, "Dreams and Claims," p.171.

17 Walters, *Modern Sagas,* p.63.

18 Eyal Weizman, *The Politics of Verticality: West Bank Settlements* (London: Open Democracy, 2002), http://www.opendemocracy.net/conflict-politicsverticality/article_801.jsp.

19 See for example, Laura Goodman Salverson, *The Viking Heart* (Toronto: McClelland and Stewart, 1929), pp.128–9; Laura Ingalls Wilder, "Indians in the House," *Little House on the Prairie* (New York: Harper & Row, 1971); Thomas King also satirizes this narrative in a short story describing the use of a "coveted" white baby as a Bingo prize. Thomas King, "The Baby in the Airmail Box," *Short History of Indians in Canada* (Toronto: HarperCollins, 2005), pp.34–49.

20 Guttormur J. Guttormsson's, "John Ramsay the native Indian," *Andvari, Nýr flokkur* (1975), pp.75–83, http://servefir.ruv.is/vesturfarar/e/SamIndianar.html.

21 See also Ann Laura Stoler discussion of children and "alien cultural longings and affective estrangements." Ann Laura Stoler, *Carnal Knowledge and Imperial Power: Race and the Intimate in Colonial Rule* (Berkeley: University of California Press, 2002), p.156.

22 Stefanía Magnússon, "Indians Greet Birth of First Icelandic Child," in *Icelandic-Canadian Oral Narratives*, ed. Magnus Einarsson (Ottawa: Canadian Museum of Civilization, 1990), p.373.

23 Historica, "Settling Canada" (seven-part mini-drama/advertisement series) 1994–

2004, http://www.histori.ca/minutes/settlingcanada; Library and Archives Canada, "Making the West Canadian" (Virtual History Exhibit) 2005, http://www .collectionscanada.gc.ca/05/0529/052902/05290203_e.html.

24 Matthew Frye Jacobson, *Roots Too: White Ethnic Revival in Post-Civil Rights America* (Cambridge: Harvard University Press, 2006), p.7.

25 Jacobson, *Roots Too*, p.195.

26 Manitoba Museum, "Mass Migration to Manitoba After 1870 (Museum Exhibit), Winnipeg, Manitoba, 1970-present.

27 William Thorsell, "Stop 114: The Migration, Norval Morriseau, First Peoples," *Audio Tour: Director's Choice* (Museum Audio Tour Recording) (Toronto: Royal Ontario Museum, 2007), http://www.rom.on.ca/media/audio/flash.php?stop=114.

28 Charles E. Israel, *The Newcomers: Inhabiting a New Land* (Toronto: McLelland and Stewart, 1979), p.6.

29 Historica, "History by the Minute," Toronto, 2005, http://www.histori.ca/default .do?page=.index.

30 Historica, "Underground Railroad" (mini-drama/advertisement), Toronto, 1995, http://www.histori.ca/minutes/section.do?className=ca.histori.minutes.entity .ClassicMinute.

31 Historica, "Soddie" (mini-drama/advertisement) Toronto, 1995, http://www .histori.ca/minutes/section.do?classname=ca.histori.minutes.entity.classicminute.

32 Historica, "Orphans" (mini-drama/advertisement), Toronto, 1995, http://www .histori.ca/minutes/section.do?className=ca.histori.minutes.entity.ClassicMinute.

33 Historica, "Sitting Bull," "Louis Riel," "Tommy Prince" (mini-drama/advertisement), http://www.histori.ca/minutes/theme.do?id=10010&className=ca.histori .minutes.entity.ClassicMinute.

34 Kirby Miller, *Emigrants and Exiles: Ireland and Irish Exodus to North America* (Toronto: Oxford University Press, 1985,) pp.123,130.

35 Ruth Leys, *Trauma: A Genealogy* (Chicago: University of Chicago Press, 2000), p.7.

36 Wulf Kansteiner, "Finding Meaning in Memory: A Methodological Critique of Collective Memory Studies," *History and Theory* 41, 2 (2002), p.191.

37 Brian Osborne, "Landscapes, Memory, Monuments, and Commemoration: Putting Identity in its Place," *Canadian Ethnic Studies* 33, 3 (2001), p.47.

38 Terry Goldie, *Fear and Temptation: The Image of the Indigene in Canadian, Australian, and New Zealand Literatures* (Montreal: McGill-Queen's University Press, 1989), p.113.

39 S.J. Björnsson "*Skýrsla yfir dána árið 1876,*" (Report of Deaths before 1876) Skipalækur, Manitoba, Feb. 1, 1877. Translation and citation courtesy of Nelson Gerrard, Eyrarbakki Icelandic Heritage Centre, Arborg, Manitoba.

40 Maureen Katherine Lux, *Medicine that Walks: Disease, Medicine, and Canadian Plains Native People, 1880–1940* (Toronto: University of Toronto Press, 2001), p.126.

41 Len Kruzenga, "Lost Spirits: cemeteries, graves at former Residential Schools forgotten and neglected," *Grassroots News*, Winnipeg, February 20, 2007, p.20.

42 See, for example, interviews with residential school survivors regarding the deaths of childhood friends and siblings, CBC Television, "Hidden Graves, Stolen Children" (Special News Feature), *The National*, first aired June 1, 2008, http://www .cbc.ca/national/blog/special_feature/stolen_children/hidden_graves.html.

43 Butler, *Precarious Life*, p.67.

44 Kansteiner, "Finding Meaning in Memory," p.184.

45 Paul Gilroy, *Postcolonial Melancholia,* (New York: Columbia University Press, 2005), p.114.

46 Frantz Fanon as quoted in Goldie, *Fear and Temptation*, p.151.
47 Ibid.
48 Anders Swanson, *The Three Sisters* (Mural) Acrylic on Vinyl, Winnipeg, 2007.

Chapter 10: Mere "song and dance": Complicating the multicultural imperative in the arts

1 *Canadian Charter of Rights and Freedoms*, in *Canada Act 1982*, 1982, c. 11 (UK).
2 *Canadian Multiculturalism Act*, RSC 1985, c. 24 (4th Supp.).
3 Denise Helly, "Le financement des associations ethniques par le programme du multiculturalisme canadien" (paper presented to the Institut national de recherche scientifique, Centre d'urbanisation, culture et société, March 2004). Others have also criticized the policy of multiculturalism: George Elliott Clarke has noted that the program/policy of multiculturalism "avoids and occludes the discussion of racism." Himani Bannerji critiques the absence of any analysis of relations of power and argues that politics, identity, and history lead to the development and deployment of multiculturalism as a technique of governance of the state apparatus. See George Elliott Clarke, "Multiculturalism and Its (Usual) Discontents," *Canada Watch* (Fall 2009), p.3, http://www.yorku.ca/robarts/projects/canada-watch/multicult/pdfs/Clarke.pdf; and Himani Bannerji, *The Dark Side of the Nation: Essays on Multiculturalism, Nationalism and Gender* (Toronto: Canadian Scholars' Press, 2000).
4 Philip has argued that while the concept of multiculturalism might have some validity, it is her view "that its original intent was to diffuse potential racial and ethnic problems." See M. NourbeSe Philip, *Frontiers: Essays and Writings on Racism and Culture* (Stratford: The Mercury Press, 1992), p.117. See also Carol Tator, Frances Henry, and Winston Mattis, *Challenging Racism in the Arts: Case Studies of Controversy and Conflict* (Toronto: University of Toronto Press, 1998), p.6, who discuss the construction of a new, transforming multiculturalism.
5 *Canadian Charter of Rights and Freedoms*, s. 27.
6 For an analysis that attempts to reinvigorate Section 27 by advocating an interpretive approach to the provision that emphasizes the multiple dimensions of other Charter rights, see Natasha Bakht, "Reinvigorating Section 27: An Intersectional Approach," *Journal of Law & Equality* 6, 2 (2009), pp.135–161.
7 In several recent controversies in Canada, the claims by minority groups for recognition of their diverse and deep commitments to their cultural/religious specificity have produced the reaction that multiculturalism has gone too far, indeed, that it threatens the core values of Canadian society. My own view of this reaction is that it sets up a false dichotomy where minority rights are pitted against Canadian values. Thus, a minority group typically seeking equality is demonized, while law and policies that continue to perpetuate inequality for many groups in Canadian society are simultaneously and uncritically put on a pedestal. The consequence of ridding ourselves of multiculturalism may mean to be left with the opposite, monoculturalism. This is not an approach that I would favour. A more satisfactory move forward is to engage with multiculturalism critically, that is, to be conscious of its flaws and to infuse within it an analysis that reveals its limits. This paper is an attempt to reveal some of these defects in the hopes of moving toward a truly critical multicultural dialogue. See for example, Vrinda Narain, "Critical Multiculturalism, Equal Citizenship and the Accommodation of Difference," in *Feminist Constitutionalism*, eds. Beverley Baines, Daphne Barak-Erez, and Tsvi Kahana (Cambridge: Cam-

bridge University Press, forthcoming). On multiculturalism going too far see, Bakht "Reinvigorating Section 27: An Intersectional Approach."

8 Clarke notes that some multicultural dollars, even if only a pittance, went to fund literary anthologies by ethnocultural minorities. These canon-building initiatives established the Canadianness of a minority group while also permitting the authors to align themselves with the experiences of other minority intellectuals. Clarke, "Multiculturalism and Its (Usual) Discontents," p.4.

9 Dr. Rasesh Thakkar has described bharata natyam training in Canada as a "transfer of culture from generation to another generation, from one region to another region as to another country, and from another time to this modern day." See Rasesh Thakkar, "Transfer of Culture through Arts – the South Asian Experience in North America," in *Ethnicity, Identity, Migration – The South Asian Context*, eds. M. Israel and N. Wagle (Toronto: University of Toronto Press, 1993), p.223.

10 Philip, *Frontiers*, pp.116–117.

11 This perhaps also explains the persistent misuse of the word "traditional" in describing bharata natyam. Bharata natyam is actually a classical technique, much like ballet. Yet it is often referred to in the west as traditional dance, likely because some people have trouble envisioning it as a modern-day dance form complete with interpretive and choreographic potential.

12 Himani Bannerji et al.,"A Conversation with Himani Bannerji: Multiculturalism is . . . anti-racism," *Kinesis* 8 (February 1997).

13 In 1963, when the Ontario Arts Council (OAC) was created, it primarily funded ballet companies. In 1986, a Multicultural/Folk Arts Dance Grant was created, followed by a Culture Specific Dance Grant in 1990. After a consultation with artists on the topic of cultural diversity, Lina Fattah, the OAC's Multicultural Coordinator, made recommendations to the OAC. In particular, artists "felt that labels such as 'multicultural' or 'ethnic' stereotyped them and excluded them from participation in the general stream of Canadian art. They believed that definitions of what was artistic needed to be broadened greatly. In general, participating artists wanted to access regular OAC programmes and not be slotted in 'multicultural' slots." Katherine Cornell, "Defining Dance: Canadian Cultural Policy on Multicultural Dance," in *Proceedings of the Meeting of Cultures in Dance History Conference*, ed. Daniel Tercio (Lisbon: Technical University of Lisbon, 1999).

14 Tator, Henry, and Mattis have stated, "We believe one measure of racism in a society is the extent to which cultural and racial differences mark one's position and status as 'other' within the processes of cultural production" (*Challenging Racism in the Arts*, p.5).

15 Philip has argued that Arts Councils have nurtured and fostered "big C" culture, which many interpret to mean "art." In Ontario, this has meant that activities of the "Big Five" (the Canadian Opera Company, National Ballet, Stratford Festival, Shaw Festival, and Toronto Symphony) are assured arts funding. See Philip, *Frontiers*, pp.114–115.

16 Ibid., p.116.

17 There is always confusion, both officially and popularly, as to whether Indigenous peoples fall within the multicultural paradigm. Aboriginal scholars have made compelling arguments for why they ought not to be lumped into a multiculturalism framework. See for example, Robert Paine, "Aboriginality, Multiculturalism, and Liberal Rights Philosophy," *Ethnos* 64, 3 (1999): 325.

18 Philip, *Frontiers*, p.112.

19 The Canada Council for the Arts, for example, now accepts applications from
    dance professionals working in all dance world cultures and in a wide range of
    dance genres and specializations. Such genres include but are not limited to Abo-
    riginal (Powwow forms, Contemporary, Traditional/Regional, Métis, Inuit);
    African (Afro-Caribbean, Contemporary, Traditional); East Asian (Peking Opera,
    Traditional Chinese, Korean); South Asian (Bharata Natyam, Kathak, Odissi,
    Kathakali, Contemporary); Urban (Hip hop/Breakdance, Contemporary); Ballet
    (Classical, Contemporary, Neo-classical); and Contemporary (Aerial, Improvisa-
    tion, Modern, Jazz, Other). An early instance of when arts funding was provided by
    a government agency on a basis other than its value as multicultural had the follow-
    ing effect: "For that glorious moment, Bharatanatyam of India had ceased to be
    'exotic' or 'ethnic'; it had become Canadian – a thing of Canadian pride and cele-
    bration." See Thakkar, "Transfer of Culture through Arts," p.227. On the different
    dance genres funded by the Canada Council, see Canada Council for the Arts,
    "Grants to Dance Professionals," http://www.canadacouncil.ca/grants/dance/
    nc127245475245156250.htm.
20 The more pernicious way in which funding organizations perpetuate the status quo
    is in their failure to represent the ethnic composition of the population on their
    staff, boards, committees, panels, and juries. "I am . . . suggesting that there is a
    causal relationship between the composition of the various boards and committees
    of these funding agencies and the underfunding of Black artists and groups." See
    Philip, *Frontiers*, pp.120–121.
21 Toronto's International Caravan was one of the most successful multicultural festi-
    vals in the country. Leon Kossar was described as a pioneer in celebrating Canadian
    cultural diversity, and co-founded the festival in 1968, which ran till 2004. See
    "Caravan founder changed the city," *The Toronto Star*, 8 August 2001, http://www
    .thestar.com/obituary/atog/article/108439.
22 Carabram is Brampton's annual multicultural festival. The Carabram 2009 website
    states that "Carabram provides an opportunity for families to experience the rich
    culture, food, crafts, drink and entertainment of different ethnic groups in Bramp-
    ton and the surrounding community attracting thousands to this event. . . . Come
    on out to Carabram, Brampton's Multicultural premiere Festival and enjoy the rich
    diversity of our great City, Brampton!" "Carabram.org: Brampton's Multicultural
    Festival" (2009), http://www.carabram.org.
23 A Google search of the term "bharata natyam" on October 1, 2008, returned
    394,000 hits.
24 Alistair Macaulay,. "A Spirit of South Asia is Moving in Manhattan," *New York
    Times*, August 21, 2008 (emphasis added).
25 Sanjoy Roy, "Dirt, Noise, Traffic: Contemporary Indian Dance in the Western
    City; Modernity, Ethnicity and Hybridity," in *Dance in the City*, ed. Helen Thomas
    (London: Macmillan Press Ltd., 1997).
26 See "Shobana Jeyasingh Dance Company" (2009), http://www.shobanajeyasingh
    .co.uk.
27 Founded in 1982, The Joyce Theater is considered one of the premiere perfor-
    mance venues for dance in the United States. The venue attracts an annual audi-
    ence of more than 140,000. Since its inception, The Joyce has welcomed over 270
    leading New York City-based, national, and international dance companies to its
    stage. See "Joyce Theater: Mission & History," http://www.joyce.org/about/
    mission.php.

28 "The hegemonic mapping of a (white) cultural identity on to a (British) national one thus produces a more complex experience for those non-whites than the simple idea of cultural difference suggests." Some have described this as a feeling of double consciousness or inexclusion, being inside and outside at the same time. Roy, "Dirt, Noise, Traffic," p.72. See also Salman Rushdie, "Imaginary Homelands," in *Imaginary Homelands: Essays and Criticism 1981–1991* (London: Granta Books, 1991), pp.15–16.

29 Shobana Jeyasingh Dance Company, *1996–1997 Tour*, Marketing Brochure (1996).

30 Jennifer Dunning, "When Folkways Point the Way to Innovation," *New York Times*, June 1, 1997. I do not raise the success of the Shobana Jeyasingh Dance Company in Britain or the misapprehension of its work in North America to suggest that Britain has solved all issues as they relate to arts funding and representation of dance from racialized groups and non-dominant artistic practices. On the contrary, anecdotal evidence from Indian dance artists in Britain suggests that they have ongoing concerns with arts presenters and the various funding agencies in the U.K. The scope of this paper however, does not permit a comparative analysis of the contextual differences between official and unofficial multiculturalism and its impact on the arts in these two countries.

31 Shobana Jeyasingh recounts an astonishing story of being interviewed on the radio in Britain about her choreography and then quite casually and seriously being asked for a recipe for chicken tikka.

32 Tator, Henry, and Mattis, *Challenging Racism in the Arts*, p.6.

33 The definition of "obiter dictum" provided in *Black's Law Dictionary* is: "Words of an opinion entirely unnecessary for the decision of the case.... A remark made, or opinion expressed, by a judge, in his decision upon a cause, 'by the way,' that is, incidentally, or collaterally, and not directly upon the question before him, or upon a point not necessarily involved in the determination of the cause, or introduced by way of illustration, or analogy or argument. Such are not binding as precedent." *Black's Law Dictionary*, 6th ed. (St. Paul, Minn: Thompson West, 2004), "obiter dictum."

34 Paula Citron, "Indian Dance with a Modern Touch," *Globe and Mail* (Toronto), December 14, 2002.

35 Homi Bhabha, "The Third Space," in *Identity: Community, Culture, Difference*, ed. J. Rutherford (London: Routledge, 1994), p.208.

36 Philip has stated "there are very clear guidelines as to what 'multiculturalism' ought to mean in this society. If that aspect or interpretation is missing from the work in question, the artist will not be funded – even under a multicultural mandate." Philip, *Frontiers*, p.127.

37 Roy, "Dirt, Noise, Traffic," p.71.

38 Shobana Jeyasingh "Getting Off the Orient Express," *Dance Theatre Journal* 8, 2 (1990), pp.34–37.

39 Roy, "Dirt, Noise, Traffic," p.82.

40 Philip, *Frontiers*, pp.115–116.

41 "Earnings by most Canadian artists are hovering at poverty levels and the situation is likely to worsen as the worldwide recession deepens, according to a statistical profile of the country's artists ... Aboriginal artists are especially poor earners ... on average, 30-per-cent lower than the average for all artists." James Adams, "Starving artists? That's not far from the mark," *Globe and Mail*, December 4, 2009. See also Hill Strategies Research Inc., Arts Research Monitor 9.6 – December 2010, http://www.hillstrategies.com/docs/ARM_vol9_no6.pdf.

42 Hill Strategies Research Inc., Arts Research Monitor, p.2.
43 Eva Mackey, *The House of Difference: Cultural Politics and National Identity in Canada* (Toronto: University of Toronto Press, 2002), p.22.

Chapter 11: The colour of poverty

Based on a talk presented at the conference *From Multicultural Rhetoric to Anti-Racist Action.*

Contributors

Natasha Bakht is an assistant professor at the University of Ottawa's Faculty of Law. Natasha's research interests are in the intersecting areas of religious freedom and women's equality. Natasha is also an Indian contemporary dancer and choreographer.

Laurie K. Bertram received her PhD in the Department of History at the University of Toronto in 2010 and is a postdoctoral fellow in the Department of History at the University of Alberta. Her research interests include material and visual culture, memory and trauma, and the history of food and fashion in North American immigrant communities.

Emilie Cameron is an assistant professor in the Department of Geography and Environmental Studies at Carleton University. She is interested in Indigenous/non-Indigenous relations in Canada and the ways in which stories structure colonial and decolonizing geographies.

George Elliott Clarke hails from Windsor, Nova Scotia, and is the inaugural E.J. Pratt Professor of Canadian Literature at the University of Toronto. A prizewinning poet and novelist, Clarke is also revered for his plays, opera libretti, and literary scholarship.

Glen Coulthard is an assistant professor in the First Nations Studies Program and the Department of Political Science at the University of British Columbia. He has published numerous articles on contemporary political theory, indigenous thought and politics, and radical social and political thought. He is Yellowknives Dene.

Brian Egan is an adjunct assistant professor in the School of Environmental Studies at the University of Victoria. His research focuses on historical and contemporary Indigenous struggles over land and natural resources in British Columbia.

Grace-Edward Galabuzi is an associate professor in the Politics and Public Administration Department at Ryerson University and a research associate at the Centre for Social Justice in Toronto. His research interests include the experiences of racialized groups in the Canadian labour market.

Uzma Shakir is a community-based researcher, advocate, and activist. She has been the Executive Director of Council of Agencies Serving South Asians (CASSA) for approximately eight years and is past Executive Director of the South Asian Legal Clinic of Ontario (SALCO).

Nandita Sharma is an associate professor of Ethnic Studies and Sociology at the University of Hawai'i at Manoa. Her activist scholarship deals with migrant labour, national state power, ideologies of racism and nationalism, processes of identification and self-understanding, and social movements for justice.

Rinaldo Walcott is an associate professor of sociology at OISE University of Toronto. His teaching and research are in the areas of Black diaspora theory, postcolonial studies, and contemporary debates on identity, racism, nation, and migration.

Margaret Walton-Roberts is an associate professor in the Geography and Environmental Studies Department at Wilfrid Laurier University and the director of the International Migration Research Centre. Her research addresses gender, immigrant settlement in mid-sized Canadian cities, and the impact of transnational networks in both source and destination locales.

Index